FORD MADOX FORD

AND THE VOICE OF UNCERTAINTY

«ANN BARR SNITOW»

FORD MADOX FORD

and the Voice of Uncertainty

Louisiana State University Press

Baton Rouge and London

The author is grateful for permission to reprint excerpts from the following works:

Ford Madox Ford, *Parade's End* (New York: Alfred A. Knopf, 1961), copyright © 1950 by Alfred A. Knopf, Inc.

Ford Madox Ford, *The Good Soldier*, vol. I of *The Bodley Head Ford Madox Ford* (1915; rpr. London: Bodley Head, 1962).

Brita Lindberg-Seyersted, *Pound/Ford: The Story of a Literary Friendship* (New York: New Directions, 1982), copyright © 1982 by the Trustees of the Ezra Pound Literary Property Trust. Reprinted by permission of New Directions Publishing Corporation and Faber and Faber Ltd.

David Dow Harvey, *Ford Madox Ford, 1873–1939: A Bibliography of Works and Criticism.* Copyright © 1962 by Princeton University Press. List pp. xi–xiii, reprinted by permission of Princeton University Press.

Two undated letters from Conrad to Ford (one in the Henry W. and Albert A. Berg Collection, New York Public Library, Astor, Lenox and Tilden Foundations; the other a copy in the Violet Hunt Papers, Olin Library, Cornell University, Ithaca, N.Y.). Excerpts reprinted by permission of Cambridge University Press, publishers of the forthcoming complete edition of Conrad's letters, edited by F. R. Karl.

Ford Madox Ford, *Mr. Apollo: A Just Possible Story* (London: Methuen, 1908).

Library of Congress Cataloging in Publication Data

Snitow, Ann Barr, 1943–
    Ford Madox Ford and the voice of uncertainty.

    Bibliography: p.
    Includes index.
        1. Ford, Ford Madox, 1873–1939—Criticism and interpretation.   2. Uncertainty in literature.   I. Title.
PR6011.O53Z87   1984   823'.912   83-11987
ISBN 0-8071-1113-9

THIS BOOK IS DEDICATED TO
Neil James Alexander Sloane

CONTENTS

ACKNOWLEDGMENTS

Just as this project has been long, so, happily, is the list of helpful colleagues and strong friends who have assisted me in various ways over the years. I am grateful above all for the elegant and firm judgment, the wisdom and the kindness of my tutor, Joan Grundy, at the University of London where this research was begun. I have felt very fortunate to have the help of this dedicated scholar. I also thank at the University of London, Barbara Hardy, whose seminar on the novel was invaluable to me, and the late Geoffrey Tillotson, who told the graduate students in his seminar to stick to their own methods (however unfashionable or indirect) and to read other critics "only for amusement and preferably at bedtime."

In the United States, Ford's biographer, Arthur Mizener, was kind enough to discuss the details of Ford's life with me for many hours. His thoroughness has put all Ford scholars in his debt. Edward Naumburg generously allowed me to browse in his private library which contains many unique Ford treasures. My other rich manuscript resource has been Olin Library at Cornell University and I thank the staff of the Rare Book Room there for their kind assistance.

Gail Kuenstler and the late Lydia Ressner were instrumental in my finding my way back into this project after a hiatus of several years. Ms. Kuenstler also worked on the finishing stages when her help with footnotes and editing was invaluable. She was thus a sort of guardian angel presiding over start and finish. Henry Shapiro played a similarly crucial role, discussing the work with me at intervals since its inception and helping me to see afresh the unity of its underlying themes. I am also grateful to Kurt Oppens for sharing his subtle readings of Ford's favorite Henry James tales.

Other old friends have encouraged me and helped at various stages of the work. I wish to mention particularly Evelyn Frankford, Linda Metcalf, Nanette Rainone, Reynold Ruffins and Simms Taback. Noelle Sterne has typed and retyped each chapter and no scholar can have been more fortunate than I in having such a painstaking typist who so well understood and sympathized with the work.

At Louisiana State University Press I thank Beverly Jarrett and my always willing and helpful editor, Judith Bailey. Thanks, also, to the invaluable workers of the eleventh hour, Julie Abraham, John Easterly, Dena Leiter, and Bob Schaffer.

I also want to acknowledge the intellectual leadership of four scholars whose work—each one's so different—on the Edwardian period has been deeply suggestive to me: Samuel Hynes, V. S. Pritchett, Hugh Kenner, and Paul Fussell. During the final editing stages of this book a fifth has been added: in 1980 Thomas Moser's *The Life in the Work of Ford Madox Ford* appeared. This sensitive biography has the subtlety to know Ford, the generosity to fully appreciate him.

Finally, this book is dedicated to Neil James Alexander Sloane who knew me and supported me in my intellectual projects before I had ever heard of Ford Madox Ford. I owe to him the very idea that I might study in England and he knows how much more.

CHRONOLOGICAL LIST OF FORD'S BOOKS
INCLUDING COLLABORATIONS AND
FORD'S OWN TRANSLATIONS

Date given is actual year of publication, not necessarily year on title-page.

1891. *The Brown Owl*. Children's fairy-tale.
1892. *The Feather*. Children's fairy-tale.
1892. *The Shifting of the Fire*. Novel.
1893. *The Questions at the Well* [pseud. "Fenil Haig"]. Poems.
1894. *The Queen Who Flew*. Children's fairy-tale.
1896. *Ford Madox Brown*. Biography.
1900. *Poems for Pictures*. Poems.
1900. *The Cinque Ports*. "A Historical and Descriptive Record" (half-title) of Kent and Sussex port towns.
1901. *The Inheritors*. Novel, written in collaboration with Joseph Conrad.
1902. *Rossetti*. Art criticism and biography.
1903. *Romance*. Novel (historical adventure story), written in collaboration with Joseph Conrad.
1904. *The Face of the Night*. Poems.
1905. *The Soul of London*. Sociological impressions.
1905. *The Benefactor*. Novel.
1905. *Hans Holbein*. Art criticism.
1906. *The Fifth Queen*. Novel (historical romance; first of the "Katharine Howard" trilogy).
1906. *The Heart of the Country*. Sociological impressionism.
1906. *Christina's Fairy Book*. Children's fairy-tales.
1907. *Privy Seal*. Novel (historical romance; second of the "Katharine Howard" trilogy).
1907. *England and the English*. Sociological impressionism; published only in America; composed of the previously published *The Soul of London* and *The Heart of the Country* plus *The Spirit of the People*.
1907. *From Inland*. Poems.

This list, compiled by David Dow Harvey, appeared in his *Ford Madox Ford, 1873–1939: A Bibliography of Works and Criticism* (Princeton: Princeton University Press, 1962).

CHRONOLOGICAL LIST OF FORD'S BOOKS

1924. *Some Do Not.* Novel (first of the "Tietjens" tetralogy).

1924. *The Nature of a Crime.* Novella, written in collaboration with Joseph Conrad; previously published in 1909 in *English Review.*

1924. *Joseph Conrad: A Personal Remembrance.* Biography, reminiscence, and criticism.

1925. *No More Parades.* Novel (second of the "Tietjens" tetralogy).

1926. *A Mirror to France.* Sociological impressionism.

1926. *A Man Could Stand Up.* Novel (third of the "Tietjens" tetralogy).

1927. *New Poems.*

1927. *New York Is Not America.* Essays in sociological atmospheres.

1927. *New York Essays.*

1928. *The Last Post.* Novel (last novel of the "Tietjens" tetralogy; titled *Last Post* in England).

1928. *A Little Less Than Gods.* Novel (historical romance).

[1928. *Perversity.* Translation of a novel by Francis Carco; possibly not by Ford.]

1929. *The English Novel.* Essay in literary criticism and history.

1929. *No Enemy.* Disguised autobiography (concerning the war years; written shortly after the war).

1931. *Return to Yesterday.* Reminiscences (up to 1914).

1931. *When the Wicked Man.* Novel.

1933. *The Rash Act.* Novel.

1933. *It Was the Nightingale.* Autobiography and reminiscences (from 1918).

1934. *Henry for Hugh.* Novel.

1935. *Provence.* Impressions from France and England.

1936. *Vive le Roy.* "Mystery" novel.

1936. *Collected Poems.*

1937. *Great Trade Route.* Impressions of France, the United States and England.

1937. *Portraits from Life.* Essays in personal reminiscence and literary criticism about ten *prosateurs* and one poet; published in England in 1938 as *Mightier than the Sword.*

1938. *The March of Literature.* Survey of literature "From Confucius to Modern Times."

《 》

1950. *Parade's End.* Posthumous publication in America of the "Tietjens" tetralogy in one volume.

1962. *The Bodley Head Ford Madox Ford.* Two volume republication of *The Good Soldier,* selected reminiscences and poems, and the *Fifth Queen* trilogy.

FORD MADOX FORD
AND THE VOICE OF UNCERTAINTY

> Ford had all the virtues but on any given occasion he would manage to use the wrong one.
>
> EZRA POUND

INTRODUCTION: EDWARDIAN AND MODERN

FORD MADOX FORD was among the first English writers to develop a style, and more particularly a tone of voice, that has become the common property of all writers in the twentieth century. This voice is subjective, ironic, indirect, often ludicrous or comic.

Ford himself would, I think, have recognized the eclecticism I employ here to get at the many sources of this complex tone. As an impressionist he always tried to give the feeling of the always elusive whole through the most fragmentary and varied of means. To describe tone, one must make a leap of empathy, must try to know everything, the personal life and the larger culture, the private intention and the literary ambience in which it grows. These elements, public and private, coalesce in a voice, and in that voice we hear the many sorts of truth about experience we crave to know and can know in no other way.

In discussing Ford's tone, I have wanted above all to say something about his experience of and impact on culture. Tone is a delicate marker not only of Ford's sensibility and thematic intent but also of his particular literary and social moment. And Ford meets halfway those who read his work as cultural history. He was always interested to name his place in a culturally complex society. He also moved consciously in a world of other artists and was sensitive to every trend and countertrend, himself often a point of connection among the literary experiments of his time. To study Ford is to study the history of consciousness between 1898 and, say, 1928 (the year his postwar masterpiece *Parade's End* was completed), thirty years that encompass the growth of early modernism.

Close readings of Ford's novels are particularly interesting for the way they can reveal, in the shifting textures of his prose, the great upheaval that took place in all the arts just before the First World War. He was a novelist, a sort of Pre-Raphaelite, interested in the realism of Flaubert, who yet managed to influence the radical new poets. His realism, though historically related to late Victorian movements, took the peculiarly modern form of subjective impressionism. He was both an innovator and a transitional figure. As so often happens, having initiated changes, he could not always have the ease of an inheritor in exploiting them. He was often lost, pained, confused, but at his best, his difficulties became his themes. He was a social novelist who felt himself lost in a compartmentalized and fragmented world where the role of social novelist was a peculiar one to play, requiring desperate acts of reclamation.

Ford raised his condition of not knowing to an art. He found ways to express the most subtle of the humiliations of the modern mind. Though he had no way to get beyond his enforced subjectivity or to see around it, he nevertheless found a voice that well described this now most familiar condition.

Quite naturally, this voice was almost always double, ambivalent, self-questioning—in short, ironic. Ford was not alone in grasping this tone and mining it for all its possibilities both for concealment and for revelation. And like so many other twentieth-century writers, he often put a comic spin on his irony, undercutting his meanings still further, until his ironies became a bottomless succession of unresolved attitudes towards the experiences they described.

While all writers bridge the gap between contradictions of one kind or another in themselves or in their situation, Ford felt himself to be particularly pressured to mediate between extremes. His beautiful, elliptical impressionism, laced with its unpredictable ironies, carried him from a collaboration with Joseph Conrad to a passionate meeting of the minds with Ezra Pound. By nature a struggler and an innovator at that point where social changes and literary ones meet, he was born at a moment when these changes were rapid and often excruciating to the sensitive mind.

Take, for example, that all important year, 1914: Ford was forty; he only partly understood what the new poets, his friends the vorticists and imagists, were doing, but he clearly recognized that their world was supplanting that described in his new novel of that year, *The Good Soldier*. But the new men recognized that in the voice of *The Good Soldier*, if not in its world view, there was something important for them. Wyndham Lewis published a piece of the novel in the first issue of his revolutionary little magazine *Blast* where it rubs shoulders with the work of Pound and Eliot.[1]

What did this Pre-Raphaelite realist-romantic friend to Conrad know that was so helpful to the young of 1914? D. H. Lawrence, whom Ford was the first to publish in his *English Review* in 1908 (as he was the first to publish so many) and who was definitely one of the revolution's new, young men, described in 1920 what he called the poetry of the past, "the poetry of the beginning and the poetry of the end" which has an "exquisite finality." In contrast he saw the new poetry as "the poetry of that which is at hand: The immediate present. In the immediate present there is no perfection, no consummation, nothing finished. The strands are all flying, quivering, intermingling into the web, the waters are shaking the moon. There is no round, consummate moon on the face of running water."[2] Though Lawrence is talking about his own poetry here, he perfectly describes the impressionistic technique Ford was evolving with Conrad in prose twenty years before.

From the first, Ford's perception of things was fragmented and subjective. He called modern life a "gnat dance" that could only be rendered from within on a small scale.[3] In all his novels there is not a moment when one can see the "round, consummate moon." If Ford's characters notice the moon at all, it is as a flickering, shaking reflection, "on the face of running water."

In this style, comic-ironic doubt undercuts all meaning in what was, before the war, an entirely new mode. Ford was one of those who prepared the ground for younger writers by rejecting the booming public voice of Victorian poetry. "You see I was born, suckled, weaned, and cradled amongst poets—poets who made great noises. And they terrified my young years and made adolescence a weariness to me. I had to listen to numbers of people like the Rossettis and Browning and Tennyson reading verse aloud." Ford rejected this voice. "I was trying to attain to quietude,"

1. *Blast* (June 20, 1914).

2. D. H. Lawrence, "Preface to the American Edition of *New Poems*," in Edward D. Mc-Donald (ed.), *The Posthumous Papers of D. H. Lawrence* (New York, 1936), 218–19.

3. Ford Madox Ford, Preface, *Collected Poems* (London, 1914), 14. The name Ford, rather than Hueffer, will be used in footnotes throughout, though it was only in 1919 that Ford made the change by deed poll. He also used pseudonyms. These are to be found in the bibliography.

he wrote. "I should like to write a poem—I should like to write all my poems—so that they would be like the quiet talking of someone walking along a path behind someone he loved very much—quiet, rather desultory talking, going on, stopping, with long pauses, as the quiet mind works. . . ."[4] Though Ford felt passé in 1914 and could not see what his place might be in that extraordinary creative burst that preceded the war, he nonetheless belonged in *Blast*, side by side with that other quiet, rather desultory talker, T. S. Eliot. The voice of

> Let us go then, you and I
> When the evening is spread out against the sky
> Like a patient etherized upon a table

is the voice Ford was seeking for, too.

This new, quieter voice was to be one of the cultural by-products of the war. In the light of that disaster, public declarations about the fine and the glorious were revealed in all their gross dishonesty. Global statements crumbled before the terrifying mystery: how did we get *here* from *there*? So much of what was written in the trenches was not about the war at all or was about the war as seen through a reversed telescope. Because the scope of the war could not be grasped, writers tried to find what bits of experience remained for people caught in a holocaust. David Jones's *In Parenthesis* showed the fighting men as connected somehow to their Welsh past, which seemed so remote from trench life. Ford's hero Tietjens in *Parade's End* makes a similar attempt to connect the unbelievable present with the recognizable past. No one who was honest wrote sweepingly, yet everyone tried to construct out of the ruins of history and of private experience a small place to stand. As E. M. Forster wrote of T. S. Eliot's early poems:

> They were innocent of public-spiritedness: they sang of private disgust and diffidence, and of people who seemed genuine because they were unattractive or weak. The author was irritated by tea-parties, and not afraid to say so, with the result that his occasional 'might-have-beens' rang out with the precision of a gong.
>
> > I should have been a pair of ragged claws,
> > Scuttling across the floors of silent seas.

4. Ford, "Notes for a Lecture on Vers Libre," in Frank MacShane (ed.), *Critical Writings of Ford Madox Ford* (Lincoln, 1964), 155–56.

Here was a protest, and a feeble one, and the more congenial for being feeble. For what, in that world of gigantic horror, was tolerable except the slighter gestures of dissent? He who measured himself against the war, who drew himself to his full height, as it were, and said to Armadillo-Armageddon "Avaunt!" collapsed at once into a pinch of dust. But he who could turn aside to complain of ladies and drawing-rooms preserved a tiny drop of our self-respect, he carried on the human heritage.[5]

The war was the last phase in the revolutionary break with nineteenth-century art. Memory, tradition, and war became blended into a subjective vision that was both the end of nineteenth-century forms of literature and the beginning of new romantic forms. By the twenties, artists had ceased to apologize for being newfangled. Unlike novelists, poets fought the change out noisily among themselves. By 1913, there had already been so much public argument about the upheavals in poetry that Ezra Pound could adopt the tone of historian and define some of the new trends:

> There has been so much scribbling about a new fashion in poetry, that I may perhaps be pardoned this brief recapitulation and retrospect.
>
> In the spring or early summer of 1912, 'H. D.,' Richard Aldington and myself decided that we were agreed upon the three principles following:
>
> 1. Direct treatment of the 'thing' whether subjective or objective.
>
> 2. To use absolutely no word that does not contribute to the presentation.
>
> 3. As regarding rhythm: to compose in the sequence of the musical phrase, not in sequence of a metronome.[6]

These principles were Ford's in both poetry and prose. The connection is not oblique. It was Ford who in 1911 suggested a more modern voice to Pound, a "living tongue," a less stilted poetic diction. Unlike so many young writers whom Ford helped, Pound always acknowledged this debt. In his obituary of Ford in 1939 he called him the first English writer "who

---

5. E. M. Forster, *Abinger Harvest* (1936; rpr. London, 1965), 106–107.
6. Ezra Pound, "A Retrospect," in T. S. Eliot (ed.), *The Literary Essays of Ezra Pound* (Norfolk, Conn., 1954), 3.

held that French clarity and simplicity in the writing of English verse and prose were of immense importance as in contrast to the use of a stilted traditional dialect, a 'language of verse' unused in the actual talk of the people, even of 'the best people,' for the expression of reality and emotion."[7]

Ford could suggest to the younger writers a quiet voice, subtly shot through with comic ironies; he was less helpful to them in formulating a conscious definition of their changing situation. To his cost, he only partly understood how swiftly his subject matter, his dream of a sort of socialist feudalism, was being undermined in the world of the new social bureaucracy, of the new physics, of Bergson, and of Freud. Like so many other Edwardians rudderless in the political vacuum before 1914, Ford felt vaguely that things were not what they had been. His gift was in finding a voice for rendering this feeling which he was unable to explain. Again, like so many of his contemporaries, he valiantly tried to stretch the novel to include both his feelings of confusion and his giddy dream of resolution.

While the ironic voice in Ford's fiction was precocious, its subject matter looked backwards: he wrote swan songs for prewar culture. Though this combination of conservatism and innovation allies him with both Edwardians and modernists, in understanding Ford's cultural dilemma no date is important after 1914. For all that he bloomed again and again into the many literary movements of his time (Edwardian London, Paris in the twenties, America in the thirties), and for all that he influenced and predated some of their experiments, in some essentials Ford was not modern as those slightly younger men, Pound, Eliot, and Joyce, were modern. The more one studies him among his Edwardian contemporaries, the more one recognizes his affinity with their particular conflicts; he was quintessentially Edwardian, and this book is, above all, about Ford as an Edwardian writer.

Paradoxically, though, to place Ford firmly as an Edwardian is not at all to exclude the importance of modernist elements in his work. In the odd Sargasso Sea that was English cultural life, prewar, nineteenth-century, and modernist modes collided. While modernists went striding forward technically, many, like Ford, cast their eyes longingly back to where they

7. Pound, "Ford Madox (Hueffer) Ford; Obit," in Brita Lindberg-Seyersted (ed.), *Pound/Ford: The Story of a Literary Friendship* (New York, 1982), 171.

came from. Rejected by and therefore rejecting the ever growing and, in their view, the ever more philistine audience, the early modernists were usually mandarin, isolated, nostalgic. As Pound wrote to Ford to cheer him up after the war when no one remembered him:

> Il y avait un jeune type sur l'isle
> Who had not the universal appeal.
> There Bennet and Wells
> Is the bookies that sells
> Inspite of our stylistic squeal.[8]

Sure that only a few shared their sensibility, the innovators had to find some other anchor. Each writer dealt with this essentially political difficulty in his own way. Yeats invented his own theory of history. Pound and Eliot tried to incorporate all the riches of culture into their vision of the wasteland of the present.

Ford, too, evolved for himself an elaborate relationship with the past. Looking over the heads of what he considered to be his philistine Edwardian audience and over the heads of the Victorian great who had overwhelmed him as a child, he picked sometimes on the seventeenth-century man, sometimes on the medieval man as his ideal, always men living in an ordered society. In Ford's case, these myths of the past had too many elements of self-delusion and indulgence to be persuasive. They are often fatuous mazes: in parabolic passages of great formal invention, he can be saying something as comically nostalgic as "Return to the land and eat garlic" (one of the messages of his philosophical travel book *Provence*). More usually, the many-faceted style forbids this kind of distillation, but the reader senses, beneath the complexity, ideas that are similarly oblique, whether charming or absurd. He is at his best only when irony undercuts and complicates his tragicomic dream of feudal society.

Sometimes as historical novelist, sometimes as nostalgic sociologist, Ford tried to give the past a philosophical unity as a kind of shield against modern society's incoherence. He groped for the true subjects of modern

8. Ezra Pound to Ford Madox Ford, May 26 [1921], in Lindberg-Seyersted (ed.), *Pound/ Ford*, 59–60. See also Ford, "On Impressionism" (1913), in MacShane (ed.), *Critical Writings*, 50–55 *passim*. Here Ford flirts with the idea that Yeats later made famous that art can be addressed only to the peasant or "to those who are not preoccupied." His ideal reader is a close relative of Yeats's ideal in "The Fisherman" (1919).

life as well as for appropriate forms. If the former were more difficult to discover than the latter, there is good reason for this to be so. It is harder to make intellectual sense of Lawrence's strands "all flying, quivering, intermingling into the web" than to weave together the strands well laid out by one's predecessors. And yet Ford sensed that new, vibrating web and at his best moments knew it to be his true theme. He wrote in 1913:

> Modern life is so extraordinary, so hazy, so tenuous with, still, such definite and concrete spots in it that I am forever on the look out for some poet who shall render it with all its values. I do not think that there was ever, as the saying is, such a chance for a poet; I am breathless, I am agitated at the thought of having it to begin upon. . . . I should say . . . that the very strongest emotion . . . that I have ever had was when I first went to the Shepherd's Bush Exhibition and came out on a great square of white buildings all outlined with lights. There was such a lot of light—and I think that what I hope for in Heaven is an infinite clear radiance of pure light! There were crowds and crowds of people—or no, there was, spread out beneath, the lights, an infinite moving mass of black, with white faces turned up to the light, moving slowly, quickly, not moving at all, being obscured, reappearing.
>
> I know that the immediate reflection will come to almost any reader that this is nonsense or affectation. "How," he will say, "is any emotion to be roused by the mere first night of a Shepherd's Bush exhibition? Poetry is written about love, about country lanes, about the singing of birds." I think it is not—not nowadays. We are too far from these things. What we are in, that which is all around us, is the Crowd—the Crowd blindly looking for joy or for that most pathetic of all things, the good time. I think that that is why I felt so profound an emotion on that occasion. It must have been the feeling—not the thought—of all these good, kind, nice people, this immense Crowd suddenly let loose upon a sort of Tom Tiddler's ground to pick up the glittering splinters of glass that are Romance, hesitant but certain of vistas of adventure, if no more than the adventures of their own souls—like cattle in a herd suddenly let into a very rich field and hesitant before the enamel of daisies, the long herbage, the rushes fringing the stream at the end.

I think pathos and poetry are to be found beneath those lights and in those sounds—in the larking of the anaemic girls, in the shoulders of the women in evening dress.[9]

This is both a very romantic vision of the new subject matter and a serious quest for something new. Ford had discovered "the feeling" if "not the thought."

And yet, for all his perceptions and innovations, the nature of Ford's seriousness is elusive. One often has to postulate it, take his word for it, agree to gloss over absurdities of all kinds in the style, method, and meaning of his novels and essays. His particular mixture of atavism and invention gives rise to peculiar moments in both his story and style. Confusion, forced hilarity, depression, what E. M. Forster called Eliot's "feeble protest" mixed with voices that protest too much—all these tonal elements cut too many ways, diffusing Ford's effects and exhausting his reader. Sometimes one rebels against this undermined seriousness and becomes irritated or bored. Perhaps this is one reason why Ford was so much maligned by critics and friends. They were not sure how to take him. He was so serious about art, so often a good artist and sensitive critic, and yet he was ridiculous, writing books that were usually either absurdly elaborate or alarmingly hollow.

It is my purpose here to examine this unstable mix of tones and intentions in Ford's novels, and more cursorily in his other writing, and to make some generalizations about what part this seriocomic confusion plays in his art. This mixture of tones is characteristic of some of Ford's contemporaries as well and is a symptom not only of complexities in Ford's work but of complexities facing most artists and particularly novelists at the beginning of this century. They all felt the shaking of the walls of the city; a tension in their tone, expressing an uneasy mixture of feelings, became one of the new modes heralding a changed way of life.

A BRIEF OVERVIEW

The method here has been to retrace Ford's moves toward finding a voice. This was a journey he made carrying complicated baggage, and it was in

9. Ford, Preface, Collected Poems, 15–16. Cf. Ezra Pound, "In a Station of the Metro," Lustra (1916): "The apparition of these faces in the crowd; / Petals on a wet, black bough."

his nature to take backward as well as forward steps on any trip. I have tried to stay close to him, to observe him as he made detours, experimented, or was decoyed by mentors whose help was a mixed blessing.

First came Pre-Raphaelitism, a movement whose strengths and internal contradictions had a major influence on Ford's way of thinking and writing. But Ford's Pre-Raphaelitism belongs above all to his childhood, informing the depth structures of his themes and style. His more conscious process of growth as an artist dates from 1898 when, as a young man of twenty-four, he began his collaboration with Conrad.

Conrad was not so much a teacher as a catalyst, forcing Ford to confront the need for new ways to present material. When they first began working together, most of their friends were sceptical and some, like Henry James, prophesied doom. "To me this is like a bad dream which one relates at breakfast. . . . Their traditions and their gifts are so dissimilar. Collaboration between them is to me inconceivable."[10] What is interesting about this is that James was entirely right; Ford and Conrad *were* very different, both in subject matter and in the dramatic effect of their styles. But neither lost touch with his own natural manner or intentions during their association, and each gained immeasurably from the partnership. If either lost anything, and this is impossible to measure, it was probably Ford. Conrad was already formed when they met, and what was morose in him may have encouraged a certain pretentious heaviness in Ford, who by nature had a much more volatile relationship to both gloom and laughter. But this is a byway of speculation. In general, the collaboration was a creative explosion for Ford.

It was followed by a period in which he had to pick up the pieces and examine them further. These Edwardian years (roughly 1903 to 1914) were for Ford a period of intense experimentation. The romances, fantasies, satires, social comedies, and farces he wrote during this time are seriously flawed books. They show how little he could exploit his strengths or suppress his weaknesses. Yet, all the elements of Ford's greatest fiction are there, albeit in an extraordinarily maladjusted relationship to each other.

Ford's wandering tone in these experimental books is always a subtle indicator of how much he is in control of style or meaning. When he un-

10. David Garnett describes this conversation between Violet Hunt and James in *The Golden Echo* (London, 1953), 64.

dercuts his own seriousness with comic irony, as he so often does, one is experiencing in a rough and self-defeating form the ambivalence Ford was later to express so powerfully. Three chapters describe the novels of these years: first treated are those novels of this period he called romances, then those that employ the techniques and materials of fantasy, and finally, those that are primarily satirical.

For the critic who would be above all a historian, the dangers of this division by genre are considerable. The emphasis on genre always posits some kind of universal institutions of form or, at the very least, an intense, ahistorical continuity within the precincts of art relatively unaffected by changes in social life. Thus V. S. Pritchett, using this metaphor of generic continuity in the history of the English comic novel, can divide the tradition up into a masculine and a feminine strain, two sets of characteristics which he can then claim to follow as a connective thread from the eighteenth century to the twentieth. The method provides its own species of useful insights. For example, in describing Sterne as typical of the feminine strain of English comedy, Pritchett provides a description of a mode that does recur throughout the history of comedy, one that is particularly marked in the temperament of Ford Madox Ford:

> Sterne follows consciousness from sentence to sentence, image to image, wilfully, even in an exhibitionist manner. He is receptive to sensation and believes in the mingling of meanings and in the oblique. . . . He is a talker and very much a soliloquist. The characters in his novels do occasionally talk to each other, but they are always thinking of something else. They are self-obsessed. They live a good deal in the imagination. The speech they are interested in is the broken syntax of speech-in-the-mind and while that rambles on—not pointlessly, for Sterne is constructing a mosaic—Society, the great gregarious English burden with its call to presentable moral duty, melts away. It is replaced by an immense detail, seen as it might be under a magnifying glass that enlarges and makes everything seem to stand still. This is precisely the effect of trauma or fantasy upon us, for the magnifying glass has shown us at once a real object which is made dream-like by enlargement.[11]

11. V. S. Pritchett, *George Meredith and English Comedy* (New York, 1969), 17–18. Ford did not care for Sterne, who, he said, "wilfully and even cynically sentimentalised over human vicissitudes." He preferred Smollett, "a remorseless novelist." See Ford, *The Critical At-*

Insofar as this is indeed a description of a universal comic type, it is related to elements of Jonson's style in *Volpone* and to Ionesco's in *The Chairs*. It is certainly an excellent description of Ford's comedy. However, the continuity Pritchett sees as the "feminine mode" in comedy may not be solely a generic one, a literary strain of comic method that survives more or less intact. Another hypothesis is equally useful. The "trauma or fantasy" Pritchett sees as giving the feminine strain in English comedy its particular form may be a historical trauma, a fantasy shared as a myth by a large group of people in one time or place. In other words, the continuity between Sterne and Ford may be related to historical continuity in general and, more specifically, to similar "traumas or fantasies" the two periods share.

Though in the discussions that follow the generic approach honors the inherent qualities of the romance, the fantasy, and the satire, distinct forms with their own histories, the main focus is elsewhere. These three are selected from all the possible subgenres of the novel because they represent the imaginative loci of the Edwardian age. It is common to find in novels written between 1900 and 1914 a generic subtitle that involves one or several of these types. (Chesterton's *The Man Who Was Thursday* is subtitled *A Nightmare*. Bennett's *The Grand Babylon Hotel* is *A Fantasia on Modern Themes*. Wells's "The War of the Worlds" was known as one of his "Scientific Romances." In *Henry James*, Ford gives us the following comic divertissement on the subject of James's romantic themes: James "gave us *The Spoils of Poynton*, a romance of English grab; *What Maisie Knew*, a romance of the English habit of trying to shift responsibility; *The Turn of the Screw*, a romance of the English habit of leaving young children to the care of improper maids and salacious ostlers."[12] Taken together, these forms provided an expressive medium for the mixture of unease, excitement and nostalgia which is distinctly Edwardian. Identifying and discussing genre does not so much provide an answer to the question of what Ford and his contemporaries were feeling and doing as it provides a form in which to ask that all-important historical question: What were the "traumas or fantasies" that informed Ford's novels and the age? The task here is

---

titude (London, 1911), 15. Certainly Smollett's authorial restraint was closer to Ford's *ideal* of narrative method, but the actuality of Ford's practice has many affinities with the sentimental Sterne.

12. Ford, *Henry James* (1913; rpr. New York, 1969), 147.

to examine the way in which Ford transformed the literary models typical and expressive of his time into his own unmistakable blend of irony, absurdity, and deep feeling.

In Ford's case, the study of these three generic kinds lends itself to an order without placing much strain on historical chronology. After Conrad, his next mentor was James, whom he saw through a Conradian lens, as a romancer. He then came briefly under Wells's influence and dashed off some typically Edwardian fantasies. Finally, in the years 1910–1914 he responded to the intense, early wave of modernism of those years by writing satirically about the immediate Edwardian past.

The Good Soldier represents the culmination of this period of experimentation. It raises questions familiar to readers of the earlier novels but, for the first time, Ford controlled these elements in their relation to one another. *The Good Soldier* is a masterpiece of the Edwardian era, an evocation of the period's particular tragicomic self-delusions. Here, for the first time Ford showed how much he consciously knew about the vertiginous contradictions of that time and how clearly he could make his own summing up.

At the same time *The Good Soldier* is also a masterpiece of modernism. It raises questions that were main issues to the next generation of artists. Its despair over cultural collapse, its enforced subjectivity, its comic ironies tempered by an ultimate, desperate romanticism are all familiar qualities of early twentieth-century art.

Then came the war. Despair like that to be seen in *The Good Soldier* was one of its by-products, but another and more central feeling to emerge after 1918 was a spirit of what Ford called "reconstruction." After such knowledge, what forgiveness? The postwar generation began again. Ford joined them in part, in part held back, still and always an old Janus head, always inventive, always atavistic. The war was a strong current that precipitated writers out of the Edwardian eddy and scattered them in all directions. Ford rode this current, leaving the London of his youth behind to go to the Paris of the twenties, the America of the thirties. In the novels of this postwar period, and most successfully in his great tetralogy *Parade's End*, Ford looked back and tried to reconstruct. Unable to resolve conflict, he lived it out and wrote it out; this enactment is what kept the novels of *Parade's End* alive.

This study ends with Ford's completion of *Parade's End* in 1928, though he continued writing novels until his death in 1939. Alas, these last books—subtle in structure and voice—are arid in content; they are frozen exercises in Edwardian sensibility. Like dead hands, his old obsessions, his old paralysis of subjectivity and confusion, reached out and claimed him once more, an old man still mad about writing, the complete writer to the end.

Plato once remarked that when the modes of music change, the walls of the city are shaken. Perhaps one should slightly modify this—suggesting as it does that a change in modes is the cause of the shaking walls, that is to give art a greater importance than it deserves. Let us say, rather, that a change in the modes is the first symptom of an instability that will presently manifest itself in more material and political ways.

W. H. AUDEN

Part I

THE SHAKING OF THE WALLS
OF THE CITY

Late, late one eventide
Saw we o'er still waters
Turrets rise and roof frets
Golden in glory,
Heard for a heart-beat
Women choirs and harpings
Waft down the wave-ways.

FORD MADOX FORD
Poems for Pictures (1900)

« 1 »

FORD AND THE PRE-RAPHAELITES

BY FAR the largest influence on Ford Madox Ford as he began to write in the 1890s was that of the Pre-Raphaelites. In 1889 when Ford was sixteen, his father died, and he moved with his mother and brother into the house of his grandfather, the Pre-Raphaelite painter Ford Madox Brown. Juliet, Ford's sister, went to live with their cousins, the William Rossettis, who lived two doors away. This was the beginning of Ford's close contact with the Pre-Raphaelites.

The first of Ford's many mentors was undoubtedly his beloved grandfather, whose detailed biography he wrote painstakingly when he was only twenty-three.[1] The Pre-Raphaelite great, "morally and physically twenty-five feet high," flowed in and out of his childhood making him nervous and giving him ideas.[2] The nerves caused him to experience a revulsion against these men, drawn on a grand scale, who pontificated about art in his grandfather's studio. But the ideas of the Pre-Raphaelites or, perhaps more accurately, their preoccupations stayed with him.

The term *Pre-Raphaelite* meant many different things over the fifty years or so that it was current, and Ford made use at one time or another

1. *Ford Madox Brown: A Record of His Life and Work* (1896). In addition to his ubiquitous Pre-Raphaelite echoes, Ford wrote three books about the movement: *Rossetti* (1902), *The Pre-Raphaelite Brotherhood* (1907), and *Memories and Impressions* (1911).
2. Ford, *Memories and Impressions* (New York, 1911), x.

and in one way or another, of most of the elements variously attributed to the movement. Sometimes tracing Pre-Raphaelitism as an element in his work is like trying to find in dreams the scraps of reality left over from the day before. In one book, a streak of medievalism recalls his Pre-Raphaelite origins. In another, a cadence suddenly calls up Rossetti. In one novel, *The Simple Life Limited*, the Pre-Raphaelite social reformer's dream of a return to nature is lovingly satirized. A man with a beard like "a dirty waterfall" suspiciously reminiscent of William Morris presides over a community of Simple Lifers who wear uncomfortable homemade clothes. In this particular manifestation, Pre-Raphaelitism appears like a rather charming, rather ridiculous remnant of the past. But the very same Pre-Raphaelite ideals of a more simple, agrarian life, of moral rectitude, and of individual fineness in the face of growing commercialism lie behind the most serious elements of Ford's greatest novel, *Parade's End*.

The original group of painters who made up the Pre-Raphaelite Brotherhood in 1849 were so different from each other that their association was inevitably brief, but they shared a militancy that reached back to the early romantics. Like Wordsworth, they wanted to describe nature freshly and to strip art of convention. Eventually, Ford came to see their effort to revivify art and reencounter the real as stilted and confused. He wrote lovingly, but jeeringly, of how Holman Hunt, Dante Gabriel Rossetti, or John Millais would tirelessly assemble archaic objects, then paint them as if they were nature, ending up with a carefully posed, didactic scene. The result was odd: as Ford described Holman Hunt's *Rienzi Vowing to Obtain Justice for the Death of His Brother*, there is as much intensity in "the very wrinklings of the hosiery of [a] dying child" as in the picture's elaborate narrative.[3]

The English had Pre-Raphaelitism; the French, impressionism. As he matured as an artist, Ford was gradually to shift his aesthetic allegiance from the former to the latter. Nonetheless, the roots of his impressionism are set deep in the static pictorial intensity of the Pre-Raphaelites. Indeed, Ezra Pound once called him an *halluciné*: as an impressionist, he selected detail where the Pre-Raphaelites had faithfully reproduced all, but the quality of those pictorial effects he did choose to render are often Pre-Raphaelite in their visual acuity.

3. Ford, *The Pre-Raphaelite Brotherhood* (London [1907]), 90.

Rossetti's "The Woodspurge," written in 1856, approaches what was to become Ford's kind of impressionism:

> The wind flapped loose, the wind was still,
> Shaken out dead from tree and hill:
> I had walked on at the wind's will,—
> I sat now, for the wind was still.
>
> Between my knees my forehead was,—
> My lips, drawn in, said not alas!
> My hair was over in the grass,
> My naked ears heard the day pass.
>
> My eyes, wide open, had the run
> of some ten weeds to fix upon;
> Among those few, out of the sun,
> The woodspurge flowered, three cups in one.
>
> From perfect grief there need not be
> Wisdom or even memory:
> One thing then learnt remains to me,—
> The woodspurge has a cup of three.

The only lines in this poem that differ in technique from Ford's way of depicting emotion and of rendering the subjective experience of physical reality—"From perfect grief there need not be / Wisdom or even memory"—are too didactic for the subjective writer Ford was to become. Otherwise, the fusion in the poem of the emotion of grief with the arbitrary reality of the wood spurge flower is analogous to the effect of some of Ford's best writing. Strong emotion often hides behind the small details. Seeing and feeling are often at odds in Ford's work while at the same time there is a suggestive tension between them. He broadened the Pre-Raphaelite picture out beyond the literal frame by letting his characters free associate with the world before them. A fixed gaze leaves the mind free to wander. Increasingly in Ford's writing, the use of this kind of Pre-Raphaelite fixation on detail came to represent not the objective exactitude the brotherhood had had in mind, but instead an almost opposite feeling of being lost in a world that contains only objects and no reliable overall pattern.

Nevertheless, Ford was worried about some of the same things the Pre-Raphaelites worried about. Though he was able to see and describe a world more fragmented than they dared to confront, like them he distrusted that shifting world. One reason the Pre-Raphaelites seized the moment they had chosen to depict in such a harsh grasp was because they feared the changes they saw all around them. In France the impressionists fell in love with change and tried to paint it. The Pre-Raphaelites fought it. And their world fought it. Pater recommended the fleeting moment as worthy of an artist's attention, but he wanted it to be enshrined in adamant. Rossetti began his sonnet sequence *The House of Life* with the line, "A Sonnet is a moment's monument." They seized the moment indeed, and though Ford knew their tenacity could not succeed, like them he romantically regretted the small, passing moments. With them he cried, "O temps, suspends ton vol!"

Perhaps because the Pre-Raphaelites were Victorians their hearts were set on finding no essential conflict between scientific realism and moral didacticism. A painter like Holman Hunt managed to seem revolutionary to his contemporaries by a trick of history that links his scientific rigor in copying nature to that of a passionately observant Darwin. They both struck blows against unexamined and therefore deadened religiosity. The realism of Hunt when he painted Christ as a poor carpenter's son shares the spirit that was to lie behind all the waves of realism that would sweep English literature from George Moore to Arnold Bennett and H. G. Wells. They all tried to incorporate the new into a vision that still maintained faith in an objectively true overview of things. But as they worked, science was changing. Psychology and the theory of relativity offered subjective or otherwise disturbing definitions of the real. If there was to be a contradiction between direct observations and absolute values, the Pre-Raphaelites had their clear preference. As Ford put it in his elegiac study, *The Pre-Raphaelite Brotherhood*, they lost sight of the ideal of truth to nature almost as soon as they had codified it:

> For already they had pronounced the doctrine that a picture must enshrine some worthy idea. It was not sufficient that it should be well painted. Thus quickly had they reverted to one at least of the doctrines of the Grand Style, and set themselves back, as it were, to the days before Gainsborough existed. They had, in fact, missed

thus early the road along which modern art was travelling. It was, I
think, Monet who said: "The principal person in a picture is the
light." The Pre-Raphaelites had by 1849 arrived at the conclusion
that the principal person in a picture was the Incident pointing a
moral.[4]

The question of how best to rejuvenate art, the issue that interested
both the Pre-Raphaelites and the French impressionists, was central in the
England of the nineties when Ford began writing. The naturalists were
being taken seriously. Moore, George Gissing, and a number of their fol-
lowers were claiming one sort of inspiration from France, while the decadents of the Yellow Book and the Savoy were claiming another. The naturalists imported the democratic, scientific spirit that made realism a matter
of depicting the everyday life of ordinary people. The decadents, who
were seen in some respects as the legatees of Pre-Raphaelitism, imported a
love of the exquisite, the archaic, and the aristocratic. They loved form
and emotion for their own sake.

The Pre-Raphaelites had cared for what both of these groups valued:
the realism of everyday and the distilled, idealized memory of former
times. It was during Ford's formative years as a writer that English artists
were confronting these two views of art. Ford stands as a transitional figure
between the Pre-Raphaelite view of moral rectitude (which for them was
a compound of faithful realism and backward-looking idealism) and the
newer idea from France that an artist's moral duty was, as Ford himself
always put it, "to register [his] own times in terms of [his] own time."[5] He
became an impressionist both in his technique and in his interest in cap-
turing the ebb and flow of modern life. At the same time, he shared the
Pre-Raphaelites' view that modern life had lost moral solidity and that its
amoral, subjective drift—so well captured by impressionist style—was a
tragedy.

《 》

The Pre-Raphaelite influence is everywhere to be seen in the first things
Ford wrote, fairy tales. The Brown Owl was published when he was eighteen years old, inspired by Madox Brown, who did illustrations for the first

4. Ibid., 114.
5. Ford, Preface, Collected Poems, 13.

edition of 1891; others followed.[6] It is fitting that Ford began his writing life with fantasy—a taste he shared with so many writers of his generation and which he was to indulge in many forms in later years. The Pre-Raphaelites were great *phantastes*, particularly in their romantic medievalism. In Ford's tales the settings are like drawings by Arthur Rackham, though darkened by some of Swinburne's more frightening visions of nature. There are Vikings and castles and people set adrift in boats—motifs beloved of George Macdonald, William Morris, and Edward Burne-Jones. The plots are all romantic and fantastic, but mixed in with the highly colored scenes and the golden-haired maidens are a number of other elements foreign to the tone of most Pre-Raphaelite writing. The princesses in these stories use real voices and experience real discomforts in the midst of imaginary situations. This slightly startling mixture gives these children's books their charm and often makes them funny. "Oh, most adorable maiden, be mine," says a demon suitor to the Queen who Flew; "marry me, and I will reform; I'll give up smoking; I'll never swear; I'll—I'll go to church—only marry me. . . . But if you won't marry me, madam, perhaps we can do a little business in my line. I pride myself that my system is the very best—the seven years' purchase system, you know."[7] Talk like this is certainly derivative. The mixture of urbanity and innocence of the heroines in these stories could have come from a caption to a George du Maurier cartoon in *Punch*. Prince Treblo in *The Feather* is surely borrowed from Thackeray's *The Rose and the Ring*. The princesses in *The Brown Owl* and *The Queen Who Flew* deflate threats with precisely Alice in Wonderland's down-to-earth child's sense of justice. Ford imitated the best examples of the genre, and with great success. Later this tone changed hands and more serious writers could use it in realistic social comedies about the middle classes. H. G. Wells used it in *Mr. Polly*. Shaw put this kind of chatty voice into some of his characters' mouths. And Ford was himself to use it in his satires.

However, at the same time that he was writing his charming fairy tales Ford was also churning out poems, many of them with pure Pre-Raphaelite

6. *The Feather* (1892), *The Queen Who Flew* (1894) and the ambitious, unpublished "The Land of Song: A Phantasy" (MS, ca. 1894–96, Olin Library, Cornell University, Ithaca, N.Y.).

7. Ford, *The Queen Who Flew* (1894; rpr. New York, 1965), 47.

pedigrees.[8] There was no levity in the dark longings of Rossetti and Swinburne, and the Pre-Raphaelite painters, disgusted with the popular Victorian taste for the anecdotal, also strove to be solemn. Thus, the Pre-Raphaelites could be heavy fathers for a young man like Ford.

But in his children's stories Ford found a wonderful solution for this difficulty. He put real princes in real armor as he saw his grandfather Madox Brown doing when painting Tristan, then laughed when they moved awkwardly. Thus comedy bridged the gap between realism and archaism. This mixture of the romantic and the real, which was often to cause dissonance and unclarity in Ford's books, works well in fairy tales: it suggests the sort of confusion of elements we encounter in dreams; its incongruity gives the story one more dimension of surprise; and finally, it appeals to children who demand a certain everyday logic behind the wildest magic.

The tone of these fairy tales—lyrical descriptions interrupted by charming, colloquial banter—would seem to connect Ford with such humorists of the nineties as Oscar Wilde, Max Beerbohm, and the Aubrey Beardsley of *Venus and Tannhäuser* more closely than with their precursors the Pre-Raphaelites. But even as he moved away from his childhood mentors Ford never allied himself with the urbane and cynical modern wits of the nineties. His comedy was destined to be of another kind. If anything, in reaction, he sided more with men like W. E. Henley and Kipling, heeding their masculine, anti-aesthetic rallying cries. But what he gained from them all in the cultural melange of the nineties was a vision of the very possibility of irreverence. To be young in London in 1890 was to breathe new air. As Ford remembered it in 1911: ". . . that was the day of discoveries. It was an exciting, a wonderful time. . . . The tone of all [the] new literature was, of course, very different from that of Pre-Raphelism. It was in many ways more vivid, more actual, and more of every day, just as it was certainly less refined and less precious. And I must confess that I at least revelled in this new note."[9]

If the Pre-Raphaelites had had more contradictions than solutions to offer the young Ford in the areas of style, subject matter, and above all,

8. Ford's early poems were collected into two volumes, *The Questions at the Well* (1893), under the pseudonym Fenil Haig) and *Poems for Pictures* (1900).

9. Ford, *Memories and Impressions*, 251–52.

tone, they did bequeath him a love of fantasy. Their attention to detail, coupled with their romantic longing, left Ford with a clear picture of what a better world would look like that remained with him as myth. When the Pre-Raphaelites tried to imagine an improved public and private life, what first came to mind was a magical undoing of the last several hundred years. The nostalgia they felt about the past threw a net of romance over everything.

In later years, the most persistent overt examples of Pre-Raphaelite influence on Ford are his historical novels. Almost one-third of Ford's books elaborately reconstruct some historical period in which a form of moral certainty is being undermined by a more modern pluralism. As late as 1935, Ford was writing books like *Provence*, in which he lovingly described the medieval culture of southern France and seriously recommended that culture's solutions to a troubled modern world. And this was not the sentimental regression of an old man. At the height of his powers in 1913, just before he wrote that most despairing of modern novels, *The Good Soldier*, he produced a painstaking reconstruction of the fall of the medieval ideal, *The Young Lovell*.

But there is a basic difference: in spite of the intricacy and serious purpose of these historical novels, Ford, like the Pre-Raphaelites, failed when he tried to bring the past alive. He used highly selected impressions much as the Pre-Raphaelites had used photographic detail as a way to build a bridge to carry him back in time, but there were enormous cultural obstacles to this journey. His historical novels have much of the lifeless fixity of Pre-Raphaelite realism. When Ford followed the Pre-Raphaelites most closely, most literally, then he ensnared himself in their worst weaknesses. They gave him most when he let their nostalgia, their highly colored sense of romance, and their passion for craft inform the general spirit of his essentially different work.

« »

In 1894 Ford married a childhood sweetheart, Elsie Martindale, and moved to the country. Years later he was to say of this excursion into the Pre-Raphaelite style of cottage gardening that it was a wrong turning prompted by the false doctrines of William Morris. "I went . . . for thirteen years into the country. I lived entirely, or almost entirely, among peasants. This was, of course, due to that idealizing of the country life which was so extraordinarily prevalent in the earlier nineties among the disciples of William Morris and other Cockneys. It was a singularly unhealthy frame of mind."[10] But the ten years that Ford lived in various cottages in Kent and environs had their restorative function, too. Being "trained for a genius" had made Ford's adolescence a forcing house of talent.[11] His first novel, a volume of poems, and several fairy tales were all behind him at the age of twenty, but any sure sense of his own beliefs and desires had been obscured by this frenzy of activity and by outside pressures and influences.

His marriage and move to the country represented a retrenchment, away from the pressures of London. Misguided as the original impulse may have been, Ford came to love the coastal country where he settled, and although he did indeed lose hay crops and see his chickens die, he never lived "almost entirely among peasants." Ford's biographers have assembled a list of the people he visited or who visited him at his various country cottages between 1894 and 1898 that includes many of the best writers of the period from both England and America: Edward and Constance Garnett, H. G. Wells, Stephen Crane, John Galsworthy, Henry James, and W. H. Hudson.[12]

The year 1898 was a watershed in a number of ways. Ford and Elsie moved to Limpsfield, Surrey, which was within easy reach of London. Limpsfield was a center for the Fabians, so that Ford was once again plunged into the intellectual life that surrounded his adolescence, though this time the central figures were Sidney and Beatrice Webb, Bernard Shaw, and H. G. Wells.

But Fabian ferment was not of central importance to Ford. He was always to be vague in matters of politics, precise only in matters of art. It was the proximity in Limpsfield of the Garnett household that made the greatest difference to him. There he met all the young writers whose manuscripts Edward Garnett was reading for Fisher Unwin. And, most important of all, through Garnett, in the fall of 1898 he met Joseph Conrad.

Also in that year the new yellow press announced to a long-peaceful

10. *Ibid.*, 254.
11. *Ibid.*, 216.
12. The fullest and most useful accounts of these years are in Frank MacShane's *Ford Madox Ford* (New York, 1965), Arthur Mizener's *The Saddest Story: A Biography of Ford Madox Ford* (New York, 1971), and Thomas Moser's *The Life in the Fiction of Ford Madox Ford* (Princeton: Princeton University Press, 1980).

England that the old conflict was heating up in South Africa between English and Boers. The Boer War was a crisis of England's faith in her own rectitude. Ford and his friends were shocked by it and disillusioned by what it revealed about English public life. Ford thought of the war as "a chasm separating the new world from the old," words that are an intimation of what he was to feel so deeply in 1914.[13] But of course, he had had from the first, as part of his Pre-Raphaelite inheritance, a sense of the passing away of a happier time, a sense which was hourly being confirmed by a hundred changes great and small. In all, his was a singularly appropriate preparation for collaborating with that cynical exile and weary traveler, Joseph Conrad.

13. Ford, *Memories and Impressions*, 171.

We wanted the Reader to forget the Writer—to forget that he was reading. We wished him to be hypnotized into thinking that he was living what he read—or, at least, into the conviction that he was listening to a simple and in no way brilliant narrator who was telling—not writing—a true story. Mind you, that was not easy: it was perhaps easier for me than for Mr. Conrad; or perhaps it would be more just to say that I desired it more than Mr. Conrad did.

FORD, *Thus to Revisit*, 1921

Part II

COLLABORATING WITH CONRAD

And it is to be remembered that during all those years the writer wrote every word that he wrote with the idea of reading aloud to Conrad, and that during all those years Conrad wrote what he wrote with the idea of reading it aloud to this writer.

FORD, *Joseph Conrad*, 1924

« 2 »

COMEDY AND IRONY: COMPARING THE VOICES OF CONRAD AND FORD

BEFORE CONRAD

FORD'S first novel, *The Shifting of the Fire*, was published in 1892 when he was nineteen. It is a melodramatic Victorian romance interesting, at first glance, only because it is the one published novel we have by Ford before he was touched by Conrad's influence. But though *The Shifting of the Fire* seems familiar enough, a sentimental, rather flavorless romance, the closer one looks the more odd it becomes and the more prophetic of Ford's later work.

The novel tells the story of thwarted marriages and mistimed longings that Ford was always to tell: Edith and Clem wish to marry but Clem loses all his money. To regain Clem, Edith marries a rich old man for his fortune. After melodramatic reversals and misunderstandings, the old man dies, Edith regrets her immature rashness, and Clem (who had feared Edith was her husband's murderer) comes to trust her once more.

Ford has placed his characters in positions that are incongruous. Beneath the glib flow of borrowed and tired conventions, the plot is surprisingly unsavory and lacks the genre's unity, its consistent willingness to please. Important scenes, absurdly unlikely scenes, and mundane conversations are all at the same pitch of intensity so that there is no building of suspense.

In *The Shifting of the Fire*, Ford already shows signs of being closer in temperament to the Joyce of *Ulysses* than he is to any Victorian novelistic tradition. Even in a novel as self-consciously overplotted as this, Ford is interested not in linear movement but in revealing experience in layers, horizontally. He shares Joyce's longing to place the whole situation before the reader at once and to spend his time thereafter ringing changes upon it.

There are other presentiments in this first novel of the writer Ford was to be. When the heroine Edith's cruel husband dies, she faints over his corpse; her lover witnesses the scene, but not as a romantic hero whose beloved has fallen in a picturesque, seemly swoon. "He remained in a paralysed amazement surveying the living and the dead, lying together on the floor. In his strained state of mind he had hard work to keep from laughing at the grotesque figure of the corpse as it lay, stiff and unnatural like an artist's lay figure, across Edith; but a sudden sense of the incongruous horror of it came into his mind, and, running forward, he lifted the heavy body up as well as he could."[1] In popular romances, difficulties lead to pathos and to sentiment. Ford's hero, on the other hand, placed under strain, wants to laugh. Much as he loves Edith, her faint reveals to him a side of her sufferings that is grotesque and incongruous. In the romance, human suffering does not rob the characters of their grace or dignity; Ouida's heroes are never humiliated and Elinor Glyn's heroines faint into chairs or their lovers' arms. But Edith's suffering is of another kind. Ford's characters have lost the control that lends dignity to pain. In the course of his writing life, Ford increasingly wished to transform bewilderment, embarrassment, and grief into feelings that *could* be subsumed inside romance. While he could not leave human helplessness and absurdity out as the romance genre traditionally requires, he gradually found ways to link the ideal and the fallible views of human experience which were both so necessary to him.

In *The Shifting of the Fire* this momentary glimpse of the absurd is quickly swallowed up by the more banal sentiments of melodrama. Nevertheless, the passage above has great descendants in Ford's work. Compare it, for example, with Maisie Maidan's death scene in *The Good Soldier*: "Leonora had not cared to look round Maisie's rooms at first. Now, as soon as she came in, she perceived, sticking out beyond the bed, a small pair of feet in high-heeled shoes. Maisie had died in the effort to strap up a great

1. Ford, *The Shifting of the Fire* (London, 1892), 289.

portmanteau. She had died so grotesquely that her little body had fallen forward into the trunk, and it had closed upon her, like the jaws of a gigantic alligator."[2]

In *The Good Soldier* this kind of minute, grinning horror works. In *The Shifting of the Fire*, the same kind of thing gets buried under the conventions of gothic romance. Suffering ladies drive their fingernails "into the soft white palms of [their] hands" and when "the end comes" to someone they love they abandon themselves "so entirely to [their] anguish" that one is at last obliged "almost to use force to drag [them] from the room."[3] Ford tosses this nonsense off with the ease that was always his. He never had any difficulty in adapting himself to the superficial attributes of any number of genres and styles. But there is always that other Ford beneath the imitated manner who destroys the popular success of the book by surfacing at odd moments to reveal elements in the story that pull it out of shape.

The clearest index to the presence and activities of this Ford underneath is always tone. In *The Shifting of the Fire* the friendly speaker is the author being chummy with his readers; the intimate voice he uses is distracting since it is hardly in keeping with the strenuous story itself. Nonetheless, this chatty voice, so often artificial and inappropriate here, is a near relative of the tone Ford developed in his best novels.

Two things had to change before Ford's natural tone could become an instrument of rather than a distraction from his meaning. First, he needed to place the intimate voice inside the story rather than use it as a distant comment from without. Second, he had to find materials more suited to the kind of subjective, impressionistic view of the universe that was naturally his. His early books can all be seen as experiments in trying to adjust these natural elements of his style to each other.

The authorial point of view necessary to write a romantic melodrama is very different from what Ford later described as his own way of recording reality. In 1905, in *The Soul of London*, he says that it is not London as a whole that he will show but "some minute detail of the whole" since we tend to see things "with the eye of a bird that is close to the ground."[4] If we do not usually think of a bird's-eye view as one "close to the ground," this

2. Ford, *The Good Soldier*, Vol. I of *The Bodley Head Ford Madox Ford* (1915; rpr. London, 1962), 73.
3. Ford, *The Shifting of the Fire*, 239, 233.
4. Ford, *The Soul of London* (London, 1905), 18.

distortion is entirely typical of the impressionistic Ford, not primarily interested in outline, plot, or character, but always looking at reality as a series of fragments seen through some subjective, often unenlightened eye, an eye that never has a clear view of the meaning of the whole.

Ford's "eye of a bird" makes a literal and rather jarring appearance near the end of *The Shifting of the Fire*. Through most of the book he managed to maintain, however unevenly, the omniscient author's point of view. Then without warning, during yet another crisis in the plot, we find ourselves suddenly inside the mind of a raven, which comments on events from a tree branch. For Ford the impressionist such antic plays on point of view were to become central. The very image of "the shifting of the fire" itself illustrates the point: as the novel opens Edith and Clem meet in a firelit room in which each subtle play of light, each shift of the embers, changes their view of each other and their situation. Once Ford began to work with Conrad, this distinct but unformed preoccupation with point of view was, of course, to be passed through the crucible of Conrad's intense fascination with narrative voice. *The Shifting of the Fire*, though, reveals an essential Ford, a bedrock of temperament, tone, and world view never seriously modified by what was in so many other respects transforming—the immense power of Conrad's technical influence.

Conrad's hold on Ford's imagination was to last a lifetime, but *The Shifting of the Fire* reminds us of all the other streams of feeling and literary experiment that always informed his work. Most of the subgenres of the novel in which Ford and all the Edwardians were interested make some kind of an appearance here: the romance, the adventure mystery, the satire, even, for those few moments with the raven, the fantasy. In the next years, in his search for a subject matter and a tone, Ford made a tour of these forms available to the Edwardian novelist. Though this journey neither began nor ended with Conrad, it was he who tried to make the always skittish Ford settle down to the long task of being a self-conscious artist.

AN OVERVIEW OF THE COLLABORATION

When Ford and Conrad met in 1898, Ford was twenty-five and still writing juvenilia while Conrad, who had spent his apprenticeship in a harder school than writing, was forty-one and had skipped producing any juvenilia at all. Certainly Conrad began with a high seriousness and a sense of the difficulty of his task that was foreign to the facile writer of *The Shifting of the Fire* and the fairy tales.[5] Ford was not to produce a major work until long after the collaboration was over, but he made a crucial contribution to Conrad's growing success, while Conrad's influence was decisive in his own development.

Now that the acrimony of Ford's enemies has faded to a memory, and the facts of the collaboration have emerged, we know how essential Ford was to Conrad as both catalyst and support. However one assesses the shape of Conrad's career, the years of the collaboration are among his greatest, when his creative powers were at their height. Indeed, Bernard C. Meyer argues persuasively that Conrad's years with Ford were his most productive and that the end of their friendship was a loss from which Conrad never fully recovered as man or artist.[6] Critical distance reveals to us an intense partnership, even a symbiosis, since there was not only mutual benefit but also a special interlocking of needs between two very dissimilar creatures. Such collaborations are rare in the history of literature.

As anyone knows who has tried to write with another, the process is painful, surprisingly slow, and finally, revelatory. There is no better way to learn of one's own proclivities, of the unique shape of one's own sensibility. There are moments—and such moments Conrad and Ford had the grace to share—when there seems to be a third person writing. The élan

5. Conrad had already published "The Black Mate," *Almayer's Folly, An Outcast of the Islands*, "The Idiots," "An Outpost of Progress," "The Lagoon," *The Nigger of the "Narcissus,"* "Karain," "The Return," "Youth," and he had worked during the years 1895–1898 on *The Rescue*, which was not finished and published until 1918. Ford had published *The Brown Owl, The Feather, The Shifting of the Fire, The Questions at the Well* (poems), *The Queen Who Flew*, and *Ford Madox Brown* (biography), and he had worked on the unpublished manuscripts, "The Land of Song: A Phantasy" (a fairy tale, *ca.* 1894–96), "A Romance of the Times Before Us" (a German invasion story, two versions, *ca.* 1896–98), "Seraphina" (Later the collaborative novel *Romance, ca.* 1896–98), and part of a life of Henry VIII, never completed. Some fragments in the Olin Library at Cornell indicate that there were also other projects, but no other unfinished manuscript survives.

6. Bernard C. Meyer, *Joseph Conrad: A Psychoanalytic Biography* (Princeton: Princeton University Press, 1967). See also Mizener's *The Saddest Story*, his Afterword to Ford and Conrad, *Romance* (1903; rpr. New York, 1968), and Moser's *The Life in the Fiction of Ford Madox Ford*. In describing Ford's collaboration with Conrad, I am forced to speak of Conrad's writing life monolithically, ignoring of necessity the small changes, the shape and motion of his career. I have had to generalize about his qualities while trying to be as specific as possible about Ford's. Nevertheless, while speaking generally about Conrad's narrative techniques, his themes and his tone of voice, I have tried to keep very clearly before me the specific works of those years when Conrad and Ford collaborated most closely.

generated by such moments is itself a force, refueling the energy of both artists. The collaboration was crucial in Ford's writing career because it was a period of prodigious growth and occasionally of intense, creative joy. It was also the time in which his themes, his style, and in general his methods of working, were all formed.

« »

The influence of Joseph Conrad on Ford's writing represented less of a departure from what the Pre-Raphaelites had taught him than has commonly been supposed. Of course Conrad and the Pre-Raphaelites arrived at what they were doing through entirely different routes. Ford's imagination is perhaps the only ground on which Conrad and these older artists can be said to have ever met, yet the instant ease with which Ford and Conrad began to work together may be traceable in part to the underlying similarities between Conrad and the Pre-Raphaelite great Ford had known so well. The Pre-Raphaelites stressed the primacy of the faithfully observed object; they wished, as Conrad said he wished, "to render the highest kind of justice to the visible universe."[7] Behind this obvious similarity in their interest in being true to nature lies another, deeper similarity in the very way in which they both formulated this idea. At the same moment that they insisted that they were merely faithful recorders of the visible, they introduced transcendent ideas like "justice" and "truth." For Conrad these big moral categories were more ambiguous—he insisted that the ultimate goal of art, and of life, is "obscured by mists"[8]—but he nevertheless formulated his rejection of the transcendent idea in art in terms not unfamiliar to the nineteenth-century moralist.

The Pre-Raphaelites relied on history and religion for their images of the exotic and the eternal. Conrad achieved an analogous, romantic distance by describing faraway places. They were both realists of the exotic, rendering with painstaking detail scenes distanced by time or by place or, in a picture like Ford Madox Brown's *Work*, by the ritualized, symbolic content that lies beneath the ostensibly mundane subject matter. Conrad's idea of accuracy included the same painstaking attention to the static detail to be seen in so many Pre-Raphaelite pictures. Rich, beautifully real-

7. Conrad, Preface to *The Nigger of the "Narcissus"* (written in the year Conrad met Ford), in Walter Wright (ed.), *Joseph Conrad on Fiction* (Lincoln, 1964), 160.
8. *Ibid.*, 164.

ized, static images are what linger in the mind long after one has put down one of Conrad's novels. They are often constructed of a series of tableaux, like the historical paintings of Millais or Madox Brown. An impressionist in his technique, Conrad nonetheless looked for permanence, though, unlike the Pre-Raphaelites, he rarely found it. In Conrad's books there is always a quality of horrified *surprise* at the soullessness of modern institutions. For him, the danger was still exotic and mystifying. It was not what it was so quickly to become, a part of the very air we breathe.

« »

For a number of reasons, among them the contradictory motives behind the writing of the collaborative novels, *The Inheritors: An Extravagant Story* (1901) and *Romance* (1903) and the novella *The Nature of a Crime* (1909), the intense and suggestive working relationship between Ford and Conrad did not lead to their writing any noteworthy books together. The importance of the months of detailed technical discussion that went into *Romance* in particular became significant not in *Romance* itself but elsewhere in the work of both writers.

Each of the technical devices Ford learned from Conrad underwent the same kind of sea change as Ford gradually assimilated it into his own work. For example, Conrad taught Ford to reorder events so that the story would move "forward faster and faster and with more intensity;" Ford, however, was not primarily interested in speed and he shrank from the moment of crisis. Or again, Conrad used "justification," the technique of supplying elaborate details, to give his stories realism, weight, and an inexorable quality of inevitability; Ford, however, had a more antic use for justification. His concentration on details often has a random quality. The narrator's eye tends to fix on some irrelevancy while the real action is dimly glimpsed going on in another room. In general Ford tended more to glance aside than to drive ahead. Though Conrad's enormous gift for structural invention made a great impact on him, forcing him to look critically at his too diffuse work, he was eventually to use some of Conrad's structural refinement for the expression of precisely that diffuse image of the world that characterized his earliest fictions.

Of all the technical lessons Conrad taught Ford, perhaps the most suggestive was the idea that there must be a controlled distance between the narrative surface and the feelings and meanings it describes. Before learning this control, Ford would often flee from the potential thematic tension in his work into superficiality or garrulity. Conrad's way of limiting point of view and placing things at a distance offered an alternative to Ford's tendency to slacken off and retreat from his difficulties.

In Conrad's hands, a large arsenal of distancing devices kept a militant control over every aspect of the work. But in Ford the limited point of view, the most central of Conrad's distancing devices, had an entirely different effect. Elegant formal control remains, but emotional control and distance are swept away on the tide of confusion and pain the narrator feels at not knowing enough. In Ford, the limited narrator, the Marlow figure, or the limited author himself, suffers from his limitations and we suffer with him.

Conrad taught Ford a good deal about the way the world worked and made him more sensitive to the baroque possibilities concealed behind the simple law of cause and effect. However, ultimately, Conrad saw all the social complications he was able to generate in his books as aspects of the same universal human condition. Ford, in contrast, was a nominalist at heart.

Conrad and Ford were among the first writers to sense the general failure of faith in the nineteenth-century bourgeois ideal of the uniqueness and power of the individual. Attention to the development of individual characters was increasingly taking second place in the public imagination to an interest in the accelerating rate of social and political change that was such a dramatic aspect of the Edwardian years. Novelists like Wells and Bennett embraced this shift in interest by expanding the novel's subject matter into a sort of catalogue of social and material detail. In a novel like The Old Wives' Tale personal agency gives way to a concept of forces quite unrelated to will or personality. Conrad and, more particularly, Ford included this kind of itemization of impersonal social forces and impedimenta, but they did more. In their novels, the elaboration of the narrative surface itself began to replace the elaboration of character. Subjectivity blurred the outline of a character's uniqueness. Indeed, narrative tone became the new focus of interest, one might even say the new subject matter. They tried to render the subjective perception of what it feels like to be alive, while the individualized qualities of character, the highly differentiated selves of nineteenth-century fiction receded, sometimes into caricature. Ford's novels are a moving expression of this shift in energy and attention, with all its losses, new insights, and contradictions.

As narrative surface and tone became more self-consciously central to the meaning and effect of modern novels, irony became more important as a way of giving material the depth formerly to be found in the examination of character. Irony for Conrad was saying one thing while meaning another or several others. Irony for Ford was saying one thing and not being finally sure of what that other meaning was lurking beneath. The subtext of irony, the intended impression beneath the surface assertion, keeps shifting in a Ford novel. This is not to accuse Ford of imprecision, or at least not always. At his best, Ford took the potential Conradian irony had for the expression of complex attitudes and multiplied it many times until irony, in his hands, became the successful statement of a bottomless ambivalence.

Conrad was a comedian in the very limited sense that he used many of the technical resources of comedy to delineate his darker themes. This use in Conrad of the devices of comedy for the expression of such things as loss, human limitation, and confusion was a suggestive mixture for Ford, one that corresponded to the natural bent of his imagination. Nevertheless, in spite of their shared interest in the serious use of the materials of comedy, the distinction made earlier between Conrad and Ford's use of irony holds for their use of comic elements as well. For Conrad comic elements were part of the machinery by which he made moral judgments. In Ford this grand summing up was replaced by an absurdly limited vision that imposed a grotesquerie on his characters and situations. His comic voices were more various than Conrad's and their meanings more ambiguous and suggestive. Comedy proliferated into every area of his work; it was a note struck somewhere, however faintly, in every chord of his rich tonal mixture.

THE SOUNDING PHRASE

"The differences in our temperaments," Ford wrote, "were sufficiently well marked. Conrad was brave: he was for inclusion and hang the consequences. The writer, more circumspect, was for ever on the watch to suppress the melodramatic incident and the sounding phrase."[9] Ford always emphasized this difference between his and Conrad's central preoccupations: Conrad was more interested in outline while Ford was more con-

9. Ford, *Joseph Conrad: A Personal Remembrance* (1924; rpr. New York, 1965), 43.

cerned about voice, or rhetorical level. As he put it: "Mr. Conrad's un-
ceasing search was for a New Form for the novel, mine for a non-literary
vocabulary."[10]

In the thirties, looking back on the changes in literary language that
had taken place during his lifetime, Ford wrote: "By the nineties . . . not
only had the literary language become unusable by the common man the
world over; it had become nauseous when it was not merely grotesque.
. . . In my battalion after mess, when they wanted to feel good they would
say to me: 'Speak like a book, H. . . . Do speak like a book for a minute or
two.' And I would begin bravely: 'After mature consideration I have arrived at the conclusion . . .' There would be already titters . . . 'that his
Majesty's Officers of this Unit of the Five. . . .'"[11] This anecdote perfectly
captures Ford's particular relationship to the general and far-reaching shift
in the tone of literary language to which he alludes. He grew up knowing
how to talk like a book. In his critical pronouncements he could easily
assume a pontificating tone all his life, and his criticism and memoirs,
wonderful as they can be, suffer sometimes from a sort of professorial
grandness.[12] He was collaborating with a man who had no English small
talk and who was incapable of any sort of casualness. Conrad learned English from books and all accounts of his attempts at colloquial conversation are comical. Nor was he ever the man to keep his verbal effects small,
though in his creation of Marlow, he began experimenting with a tone of
voice—casual, colloquial, quiet—which Ford and many of his generation
were to develop further. For them, there was a certain bad faith in "talking
like a book."

It is only by an elaborate act of creative imagination that one can reconstruct today how ubiquitous was "the sounding phrase" in the life of
the Englishman of, say, 1898 to 1903, the most intense years of the collaboration. There was a sort of verbal inflation. The nationalistic rhetoric of
imperialism and the Boer War swelled the tide, and when Alfred Harms-
worth began publishing the first half-penny paper in 1896, he banned
what he saw as the aristocratic habit of irony from his editorials so that the

10. Ford, *Thus to Revisit: Some Reminiscences* (1921; rpr. New York, 1966), 40.
11. Ford, *Portraits from Life* (Chicago, 1936), 278.
12. Ford himself helped kill the style in which he wrote these and because of their rigor
mortis, the tone of these subtle and complex essays is only tangentially explored in the course
of this book.

sounding phrase joined popular culture without the healthy leavening of wit.

Ford was not above the temptation of the sounding phrase. Indeed, both the magisterial and the sentimental voices came all too easily to him, and if he had allowed Conrad's similar verbal expressiveness to further puff him up, we would not remember him as a writer today. But Ford had a saving instinct that told him a new voice was needed, and he had the subtlety of ear and mind to begin to invent it. This saving instinct was perhaps little more than doubts and fears transformed into delicacy and empathic power. Ford was on the border where an old tone began to sound outworn, a new one to be developed. He wobbled back and forth insecurely among the new voices he and others were trying out. One might say that in the end he came to talk small by tumbling down absurdly from inappropriate and hollow big talk.

Conrad's tone of voice was, as Ford knew, as much the result of difficulties as of willed or controlled choices. He left the heavy mark of his struggles with language on his work. In contrast, Ford's struggles with language were more diffuse. After paying his generous respects to what he called Conrad's "gorgeous cadences," Ford went on to evolve his own, entirely different narrative voice.[13]

CULTURAL IDENTITY AND TONE

For different reasons, and to different degrees, the literary tone of both Ford and Conrad is informed by a feeling of precariousness in cultural identity. Conrad made his paradoxical love for and estrangement from England clear in a moving letter of 1905 to Edmund Gosse, written from Capri, where he had hoped in vain to get some work done:

> I am more anxious than ever to get back to Pent Farm [Conrad's house in Kent], under whose lowly (and imperfectly watertight) roof five volumes have had the audacity to get themselves written. I've done very badly here. It's all very well for Englishmen born to their inheritance to fling verse and prose from Italy back on their native shores. I, in my state of honourable adoption, find that I

---

13. Ford, *Portraits from Life*, 286.

need the moral support, the sustaining influence of English atmosphere even from day to day.[14]

Conrad always wrote about the experience of exile; surprisingly, Ford did
too, even before meeting Conrad. Indeed, he was not really one of the
"Englishmen born to their inheritance"; his father, scholar, music critic of
the Times and German expatriate, espoused the alien and then unpopular
cause of Wagner, while his mother grew up among artists, always a suspect
and alien breed within English culture. This background made Ford self-
conscious. The daily gestures of his countrymen were always visible to him
as national traits, a point of view usually reserved for the outsider. He
loved the mores of English life, from the doings of Meary Walker, the poor
woman of Kent he described in The Cinque Ports, to the lazy authority of
the upper-class club men about whom he wrote condescending anecdotes.
Nevertheless, in these latter stories particularly, he always gives himself
away: "During the Boer War I lunched at Rye with a provincial Lord
Mayor and a London Alderman who had passed the chair—who had, that
is to say, been Lord Mayor of London."[15] There is the insider's phrase, "had
passed the chair," and there the outsider's translation. Like Conrad, Ford
could take nothing for granted.

Part of Ford's pervasive sense of oddness and isolation stemmed from
his ambiguous class position. He grew up among people who had confronted the national preoccupation with class by rejecting the values of a
hierarchy based on birth and money. But the Pre-Raphaelites had a snobbery of their own. They looked down on both the bourgeoisie and the aris-
tocracy since neither were presumed to know much about art. This elevated isolation was coupled, however, with a galling financial insecurity
and a lack of social status in the world at large. Each bore this contradiction with his own degree of fortitude. Many were firm in rejecting the lux-
uries of upper-class life. In general, though, the Pre-Raphaelites revered
tradition in a way consonant with English class values, only for them, as
the name of their movement shows, the actual content of this tradition
was far to seek.

Literary history has named Ford a liar, and one of the lies that most
infuriated his contemporaries was his claim to have been at a public

14. G. Jean-Aubry, Joseph Conrad: Life and Letters (Garden City, N.Y., 1927), II, 15.
15. Ford, It Was The Nightingale (Philadelphia, 1933), 76.

school. With distance perhaps we can more sympathetically understand
this as the lie not only of a snob but also of an uneasy, bohemian outsider.
Child of the Pre-Raphaelites, he assumed the existence of an elite and felt
the need to be a part of any that offered itself. In fact, Ford was sent to a
school with advanced ideas, but even there the ambivalence persisted: the
educational methods were liberal, imported from Germany, but on the
playing fields, public school ideas about games were sacred.[16]

Like Conrad, however, Ford had been enough excluded from the confident stolidity of the middle classes to have a certain yearning for the ordinary. His relatives had always encouraged him to join their vanguard:
"Whether it was the Rossettis or the Garnetts of the Left or straight Labour, Fabian, or Morris Socialist agitators, I was seldom, between the ages
of twenty or thirty, without someone putting Left pressure upon me."[17]
Conrad, too, had been a child brought up among the embroilments of the
Left. His rejection of his father's kind of political life was profound. He
chose to view politics as from a great height, and this detachment must
have been soothing to the anxious and embattled young man Ford was
when they met. Ford embraced Conrad's world view in a romantic way. He
admired Conrad's characters, "men slightly obtuse, men extremely well
able to look after their investments, their tomorrow's food, their purchases
of real estate or of commercial vessels"—all types ordinary in themselves
but exotic enough for a young man who had grown up among unrepentant
and often penurious bohemians.[18]

Ford had mixed feelings all his life about whether or not to be ashamed
of knowing nothing about business, whether or not to be ashamed of having no money, whether or not to be ashamed of being an artist. He was
confused enough to mar a number of his books by never clarifying his
point of view and by vacillating in his attitude towards his characters'
struggles. Sometimes his heroes, eager to be aristocratic in a continuously
wobbling sense of that word, are a bit too good, a bit too fine. Ford is so
concentrated on cutting them out from the herd that they barely come in
contact with the coarse, pulsating vigor of the action that goes on around
them. They miss it, and in the weaker novels, the reader is often forced to
miss it too. The contradictions Ford felt are everywhere in the novels: an

16. See Mizener, The Saddest Story, Chap. 1 passim.
17. Ford, Return to Yesterday (New York, 1932), 82.
18. Ford, Thus to Revisit, 96.

artist or an aristocrat must know nothing about business, but the Puritan ideology of the street says that a man who knows nothing about business is a fool. An artist is the world's most developed type, but the Puritan ideology of the street is suspicious of artists. Not having money may indeed mean that you don't care about money, but without money you are liable to every indignity. You may even be considered dishonorable since middle-class values have eroded an earlier aristocratic insouciance about paying one's bills.

Of course, Ford's anxiety about class hardly disqualifies him as a bona fide Englishman. The pain of having an ambiguous class position has always been a major theme of the English novel. Sometimes Ford saw the complex moral and social issues novelists like George Eliot had been talking about in novels like *Daniel Deronda*, but more often he drifted among contradictory class concepts feeling a confusion he could describe but not dispel, a confusion reflected in his using an ambiguous tone to describe the identities of his characters. Though both Ford and the Pre-Raphaelites often appropriated the issue of class as a symbol, their mixture of idealism and romance cast an obscuring shadow over the complicated reality of class, leaving them, and so many of the modernists to follow, to mourn over an abstract loss.

Ford's most effective and authentic presentations of the theme of debased cultural values were always written from an outsider's point of view. The narrator of *The Good Soldier* is an American who is both attracted and repelled by the mores of English life, which never cease to surprise him. Even Tietjens is an alien since, in the world Ford is describing in *Parade's End*, the kind of aristocrat Tietjens wished to be is already long extinct. Both Dowell and Tietjens feel lost in the world as it is. They are, for different reasons, déclassé.

Over the years Ford's complex feelings about his own Englishness hardened into a dissatisfaction with what Conrad wittily called the "milor anglais" he had formerly wished to be.[19] But this estrangement from what had always seemed to him the best in the English tradition happened very gradually. It was only after the First World War that his old desire to be truly English seems to have left him once and for all. After 1919 he never

19. Ford, *Joseph Conrad: A Personal Remembrance* (1924; rpr. New York, 1965), 128.

lived permanently in England again. In 1924, however, he could still romanticize his relationship with Conrad, that other expatriate, by writing "we met at first as two English gentlemen do in a club."[20] For, in spite of all that can be said about Ford as an outsider, in some respects he was not one. Even when he is being his hardest on England, a trace of his love, his desire to identify, creeps in, if only in the form of a mythological school tie. He was always abstractly obsessed with traditional English values. In all he writes, he is ambivalent about the culture he describes, ambivalent about whether or not he is, or wants to be, thought of as English, but in this he is like the black who can pass as white, the Jew who changes his name. In one context he plays the part of the bohemian artist, friend to anarchists, owner of an outré cloak that once belonged to Rossetti, citizen of the world. In other circles, he drops this part, has an English tailor, talks of his club. These identities are all real. They are nothing so simple as lies. At his best Ford was able to analyze his feelings of uncertainty about class and nationality; at his worst, they overwhelmed him and his material.

Conrad, in contrast, could never afford the luxury of Ford's species of ambivalence. He was the most obviously foreign of creatures, a man who could never for a moment pass as the product of an English public school or write the sort of urbane essays that place Ford in the chatty Edwardian mainstream. Instead, Conrad wrote to his dearest friend, that other exile, R. B. Cunninghame Graham, "Most of my life has been spent between sky and water and I live so alone that often I fancy myself clinging stupidly to a derelict planet abandoned by its previous crew."[21] After such a declaration, the need to find a spiritual home is, understandably, desperate. Conrad saw outlines because he was looking from a distance. Collaborating with him forced Ford to give his vague dissatisfactions more shape. Conrad always had to pause for the right word, and this pause was one of the great lessons Ford learned from him. Conrad's need to start from scratch helped the younger man reject the easy identification with his culture's idées reçues, which came so naturally to him. Conrad, in turn, needed Ford's subtle knowledge of the English language, his sensitivity to every shading of tone.

20. *Ibid.*, 128.
21. Jean-Aubry, *Joseph Conrad*, I, 208.

VOICE: THE COMIC IRONISTS

Though every novel has its own particular mixture of narrative tones, a mixture which is an expression of its specific themes, all authors have a certain voice that underlies the different tonal effects of each of their works, a general and involuntary quality in their writing. The primitive first impressions of a cursory reader of Conrad's voice are of grandeur, moroseness, and irony. His voice is sceptical, and irony is one of the central technical means by which he communicates his doubts.

A reader's general impression of the voice in a Ford novel is somewhat different. When he achieves distance, it is only after a considerable struggle against garrulity and sentimentality. He uses irony in the service of a more direct feeling of sympathy for his characters. Conrad, the antisentimentalist, would never have allowed himself Ford's plaintiveness, his occasional journeys into romantic emotionality, a bit querulous, a bit depressed. But in Ford's best books and even, for moments, in his very worst ones, this voice is also the bearer of a true pathos, a genuine and moving sadness.

Irony is central to the voice of both writers but with this difference: for Conrad, irony was a literary device he could choose to use or not to use; for Ford, it was an inescapable habit of mind, an expression of irresolvable ambivalence. In his introduction to *The Secret Agent*, Conrad spoke of consciously deciding to use the "ironic treatment" of his subject as the only way to express all that he had to say "in scorn as well as in pity."[22] In Ford the pity is always there but the scorn in Conrad's irony has been modified. Ford's heroes rarely sin as absolutely as, say, Nostromo. They are already in a position of reduced power and importance in the world. But even when they do find themselves, often inadvertently, in a position of crucial leverage, they do not fail with Nostromo's kind of magnificent moral collapse. The issues are always more subjective, less clear. Irony is not the product of a clash between human desires and human capabilities but is instead a sort of dissonance that spins off the top of bewilderment, misunderstanding and anxiety. Even when the standard by which a Ford character lives is fairly clear, Ford's judgment of failure is entirely different from Conrad's. In *The Good Soldier*, for example, Edward Ashburnham is a

22. Conrad, Preface (1920) to *The Secret Agent* (1907), in Wright (ed.), *Joseph Conrad on Fiction*.

libertine. His sexual exploits are revealed gradually with all the dramatic effects that conventionally accompany scandal. But the moral ground of judgment for these acts keeps shifting. Dowell is shocked by Edward's liaisons, but he is also empathetic. He sinks further and further into the experience of his friend Edward until the objective idea of scandal or moral failure is completely dissolved into the subjective fact of Edward's suffering and his longing. By the end of the novel, all standards of judgment have been reversed or, rather, rendered irrelevant. Dowell decides Edward, not Leonora, is decent and moral or, once again, that decency and morality have ceased to be the issue. He decides that of the two he can only love Edward, not Leonora. This judgment is only final in the field of Dowell's personality, which makes up the whole field of consciousness of the novel. Irony comes from the shifting of Dowell's judgments away from moral conventions and more and more towards some kind of personal feeling for Edward. Pity takes over; scorn disappears. In Ford, irony is the product of the clash between rival versions of reality, each of which undercuts the other in a series of reversals that never ends.

In spite of these differences between Conrad and Ford in the use of irony, they are both not only profoundly ironic writers but also, specifically, comic ironists, though their comedy is not the kind that brings a smile to the lips. Indeed, they are not happy to be comedians, but they employ certain techniques and share certain sensibilities traditionally associated with comedy. With no intention to make us laugh, both of them are interested in the grotesque, the farcical, and the absurd. Or rather, Conrad finds the universe absurd, while Ford finds there is no universe beyond the psyche, a condition of limitation that often renders his heroes ridiculous and comically humiliated.

Ford was born at a moment when confidence in a continuity of values was increasingly difficult. (Quite literally: 1873, the year of Ford's birth, was the beginning of a depression which, it can be argued, was the beginning of the end of English economic health and security. Subsequent recoveries were based on imperialist spending that postponed but also contributed to the eventual collapse of English economic and social hegemony.) Conrad was a man stretched out on this particular rack of social change and cultural diminution, and Ford began to find his own themes as he empathized with Conrad's predicament and saw its similarity to his own. But when Conrad's grand vision, Destiny, led the way, Ford could not successfully follow. In Destiny, Conrad, like the Pre-Raphaelites, had something Ford and his contemporaries lacked, a noble adversary. Even in the midst of his cold, secular nightmares, Conrad saw a large universe as the stage for all man's acts. He hoped, both for himself and for his characters, for a kind of dignity that Ford and his generation were beginning to give up for lost. Constructing his materials out of an enormous sense of pain, Conrad managed to dramatize in fiction what it was like to be a nineteenth-century moralist suffering from a twentieth-century doubt. But in spite of this pain, for him there was always Destiny. What Joyce called those "big words that make us so unhappy" were still able to function for him as genuine sources of meaning and strength.

The English have often looked with a certain jesting suspicion at such words. In *Experiment in Autobiography*, H. G. Wells remembered, "One could always baffle Conrad by saying 'humour.' It was one of our damned English tricks he had never learnt to tackle."[23] What was this "humour" he could never understand? It certainly could include a playfulness, a sentimentality, even a fatuity he could not tolerate, traits he must often have criticized in Ford's writing. It included the vague, the dreamy, the chatty, so different from the continental exactitude of Flaubert for which he struggled. Conrad wanted precision while Ford thrived on muddle. Indeed, one of their perennial arguments was about the difference between French and English, between precision and "blur":

> Conrad's indictment of the English language was this, that no English word is a word; that all English words are instruments for exciting blurred emotions. 'Oaken' in French means 'made of oak wood'—nothing more. 'Oaken' in English connotes innumerable moral attributes: it will connote stolidity, resolution, honesty, blond features, relative unbreakableness, absolute unbendableness—also, made of oak. . . . The consequence is that no English word has clean edges: a reader is always, for a fraction of a second, uncertain as to which meaning of the word the writer intends. Thus, all English prose is blurred.[24]

Though this passage is about language generally, it suggests some of the differences between Conrad's and Ford's use of comic voice in particular. Ambiguity, aimlessness, self-pity, cozy charm, whimsical absurdity, and

23. H. G. Wells, *Experiment in Autobiography* (1934; rpr. London, 1969), 621–22.
24. Ford, *Joseph Conrad*, 229.

real sentiment—all rush into Ford's writing where Conrad's more pointed ironies would fear to tread. Of course, there are moments in Conrad's comedy that are farcical or absurd, moments of profound tonal complexity. But these moments are relatively rare; they are almost always related to the problems encountered in the creative process itself. It is in trying to tell his story that Marlow experiences the most unendurable and mysterious kind of frustration and the most irreducible sense of absurdity: "Do you see the story? Do you see anything? It seems to me I am trying to tell you a dream—making a vain attempt, because no relation of a dream can convey the dream-sensation, that commingling of absurdity, surprise, and bewilderment in a tremor of struggling revolt, that notion of being captured by the incredible which is of the very essence of dreams."[25] Only a few years later, in 1905, Freud was to describe the serious and functional tie between jokes and the unconscious. Conrad, furious at man's lack of control over irrationality, could never have accepted in Freud's spirit the absurd anarchy of dreams. He was in constant revolt against disorder, appalled at finding it so hard to tell even the simplest truth, and horrified by the way in which absurdities and surprises kept slithering out of some dark place in the self. But he knew about "the dream-sensation, that commingling of absurdity, surprise, and bewilderment," and he shared this knowledge with his young collaborator, who was to write a kind of comedy almost entirely made up of that dream-sensation, of loss of control, of confusion and absurdity.

Ford's absurdities are connected to some of the oldest kinds of English comedy; he is an English humorist as Conrad never is. But even as Ford explored kinds of humor absent in Conrad, he was also incorporating elements from the European tradition Conrad taught him. Ford reduced the scale of his characters' universe and imprisoned them in their own subjectivity in a way that makes him a grandfather to that most French of creations, the theater of the absurd. Using both Conrad's coldly ludicrous style and the warmer mockery of English comedy, Ford came up with a melancholy absurdity entirely his own. As a practitioner of the art of English comedy, Ford was a cuckoo in the nest. He ate up the best that England had to offer, but nourished on this food, he developed into an even stranger and more unfamiliar bird than Conrad.

25. Conrad, *Heart of Darkness* (1899; rpr. New York, 1910), 95.

It is a curious characteristic of the work of Conrad that, not only can you not recognisably imitate it, you hardly ever feel even the impulse to do so, and the one writer who really sedulously be-aped the more exotic romances of the author of "An Outpost of Progress" achieved performances so lugubrious that he seems to have warned off any other imitators of his example.

FORD, *Joseph Conrad*, 1924

«3»

TWO VOICES IN STRANGE DUET
LEARNING TECHNIQUES THAT SHAPE TONE

COMPARING "SERAPHINA" AND *ROMANCE*

PERHAPS the best way to see how collaborating with Conrad contributed to the development of Ford's characteristic tonal mixtures is to look closely at their most intensely shared effort, the transforming of Ford's weak manuscript "Seraphina" into the dense adventure story *Romance*. *Romance* is the story of John Kemp, who runs away to sea for adventure and is from the first moment embroiled in the intrigues of scoundrels, falsely blamed for crimes he cannot even imagine committing, and finally, in the West Indies affianced to the beautiful, romantic Seraphina, whose affairs are equally embattled and who requires repeated rescue. Kemp's story was distantly based on the last trial for piracy at the Old Bailey, and the novel ends in court, where the abused and confused Kemp is miraculously acquitted and reunited with his Seraphina. The original plan was that Conrad was to add "a few touches of description, sea atmosphere, mists, riggings and the like," and then, "in a fortnight," Ford and Conrad had hoped to have a painless best seller.[1] In fact the book took more than two years of fairly constant labor on Ford's part and violent if

1. Ford, *Joseph Conrad*, 22.

intermittent bouts on Conrad's, and it was published in 1903, five years after they first agreed to knock this quick adventure story into salable shape.

Anyone who wants to recapture the excitement, desperation and confusion of those days has only to read Ford's evocative memoir *Joseph Conrad*. They lived in each other's hair, corrected each other's proofs, worked all night. For Ford, these two years were magnificent, a period of passionate apprenticeship. He did not mind nursing Conrad's spirits, taking dictation from him, staying up all night to help him rewrite the two installments of "The End of the Tether" that got burned by an exploding oil lamp. Ford's *Joseph Conrad* has a particular sweetness of tone that recalls the unique dedication of youth.

From the time Ford met Conrad onwards, there is always in his novels a figure of fixed principle (sometimes sympathetic, sometimes corrupt) and another figure who finds it very hard to understand what side to take. The description of this pair undergoes many permutations but the essential relationship that must have existed between Ford and Conrad is there beneath. Conrad's doubts were on such a grand scale that to Ford, a younger, less clearheaded and disciplined man, they looked like certainties.

Mixed Motives: Hitting the Taste of the Street

Conrad wrote to Galsworthy in March of 1902: "Seraphina is finished and gone from the house she has haunted for this year past. I do really hope it will hit the taste of the street."[2] Such was the first motive for writing *Romance*. Ford and Conrad both needed money and Conrad needed it desperately. As their early reviews came in mixed, they were both disappointed. Conrad's friend Walszenski wrote to say he understood the impulse behind all Conrad's works except *Romance*; he begged for an explanation. Conrad wrote to Ford:

> What is one to say? Mind—he does not judge, criticize, or disapprove—he simply wants to know. . . . One would not be far wrong if one wrote—"Ne voyez vous pas que c'est une bonne farce!!!" But that would not do perhaps. Also one could write: "Le besoin de manger, de fumer, de boire, de porter une culotte comme tout le monde." But he is not the sort of person to believe in the Obvious-

2. Mizener, *The Saddest Story*, 73.

ness of the Incredible. I suppose the estetic [sic] racket is the prac-
ticable answer, satisfying if incomplete. I should think that with the
other two we cover the whole ground of our motives.[3]

Conrad offers three motives for writing Romance: the need to eat and drink
like everybody else, an antic spirit of irreverence at odds with their usual
artistic seriousness, and finally, "the estetic racket." This list of motives
reveals the paradoxical nature the whole project had from the first. The
self-conscious division they made between an interest in writing well and
an interest in getting an exciting tale told was bound to undermine a genre
as dependent on illusion as is romantic adventure. Aware of their own lack
of conviction, Ford and Conrad poured on aesthetic clout to compensate.
But the gap between subject and method remained. At moments the atmosphere of Romance is so weighed down with the too skillful evocation of
beautiful palaces or dangerous dungheaps that one begins to suspect that
this is indeed "une bonne farce," a parody of every whiffy romance of the
hundreds becoming so popular in the 1890s.[4]

The complicated mixture of feelings that informed the writing of Romance can be seen in the letter Conrad finally wrote to his puzzled friend
Walszenski to explain "que vient faire Romance dans [son] oeuvre":

> There are certain things that are difficult to explain, especially after
> they have happened. I consider Romance as something of no impor-
> tance; I collaborated on it at a time when it was impossible for me to
> do anything else. It was easy to relate a few events without being
> otherwise involved in the subject. The idea we had was purely aes-
> thetic: to depict in an appropriate way certain scenes and certain

3. Conrad to Ford, n.d. [1903], typed copy in Violet Hunt Papers, Olin Library, Cornell
University, Ithaca, N.Y.

4. Ford and Conrad looked on writers like Stevenson, Anthony Hope, John Meade
Falkner and Rider Haggard as writers of no lasting artistic importance, but in a related tradition were writers like W. H. Hudson and Robert Cunninghame Graham, who were their
friends and even, in some respects, their mentors. Both popular adventure stories like Treasure Island (1883), She (1887) and The Prisoner of Zenda (1894) and well-told exotic tales like
Hudson's The Purple Land (1885), Graham's The Ipane (1899), and Kipling's Jungle Books
(1894 and 1895) were an expression of a developed national taste for the exotic adventure
story. Lafcadio Hearn's stories and essays, Out of the East (1895) and Exotics and Retrospectives
(1898) were popular, and the enormous sales of Treasure Island led to all kinds of books in the
vein, from Arthur Machen's Three Imposters (1895) to Romance itself. A number of these
stories of adventure were workmanlike in a way Ford and Conrad could admire.

situations. Also it did not displease us to be able to show that we could do something which was very much en vogue with the public at the moment. The heroic gospel of St Henry [James], dear Sir, rules the entire world and, as you know, there is more than one way of laughing at it. There were moments when both Hueffer and I were very gay while working on this construction. Nevertheless we took pains with the technical side of the work. You will admit that it is well written. Flaubert (he was a real saint) applied himself well to achieve a spectacular success.[5]

Here then was the task—to construct a novel as rich in evocative atmosphere as Flaubert's *Salammbô* while laughing at the adventure genre all the way to the bank. Nothing is impossible, but one suspects that there was enough bad faith in this conception of the project to affect the outcome even after five years of struggle to make everything fit. Ford and Conrad kept pulling the novel apart; they were perfectionists, temperamentally unsuited to the writing of potboilers. Each incident went through many versions, many tonal permutations. There is nothing harder than doing something well with the left hand.

When the proofs came back, things still seemed somehow wrong. As Conrad wrote to Blackwood's, apologizing for once again holding up publication by more revisions, "Some passages struck me as lacking vigour—others as wrong in tone—too much *written* in fact; and therefore I want to write them once more."[6] From this painfully worked-over book the gaiety at St. Henry's expense has long since evaporated. But the earnestness of the effort to write breathtaking adventure with aesthetic elegance remains, and at moments, the tremendous will of these collaborators to make *Romance* work still has the power to impress.

Mixed Genres: Realism and Romance

In the voice of the narrator, John Kemp, Ford and Conrad solved at the level of technique some of their ambivalence about writing an adventure story. *Romance* was unreal, but there was a good reason for that. The book

5. Zdzasław Najder (ed.), *Conrad's Polish Background: Letters to and from Polish Friends*, trans. Halina Carroll (London, 1964), 236.

6. William Blackburn (ed.), *Joseph Conrad Letters to William Blackwood and David S. Meldrum* (Durham, N.C., 1958), 219.

was going to be a perfectly painstaking, realistic picture of the effect of memory on reality. This kind of technical feint to resolve basic difficulties is typical of both writers, at both their best and their worst.

In "Seraphina" Ford had had the idea of making romance a subjective quality found only in the mind of the beholder, but he did not bother to suffuse this subjective view throughout the narrative. The novel begins in a simple past tense similar to the one used in *Treasure Island*. It is not until the story is well advanced that Ford elaborates on the importance of point of view by casually dropping the subtle narrative idea that Conrad was to help him make central in *Romance*. The passage is a description of the very English John Kemp at the Cuban dance where he meets the exotic Spanish heroine, Seraphina:

> I was in a position of some distinction. The ladies, who were, no doubt, tired of the men of their small town—just as might be the case at home in a country village—were all anxious to secure me as a partner. For them even I was something rich and strange—a fierce wicked heretic, much as a Spaniard would seem at home. But there was one among them who by right of station and superior merits of face and figure outweighed all the rest and to her I was accorded as partner. She was the daughter of the chief magistrate of the place and her name was Seraphina Riego.[7]

No wonder Conrad was aghast when he first saw Ford's "Seraphina." Here is the heroine introduced in an offhanded way almost halfway through the book and all the excitement of the event being passed off as no great matter. This, in contrast, is what the collaborators squeezed onto page one of *Romance*:

> To yesterday and to today I say my polite "Vaya usted con Dios." What are these days to me? But that far-off day of my romance, when from between the blue and white bales in Don Ramon's darkened storeroom, at Kingston, I saw the door open before the figure of an old man with the tired, long, white face, that day I am not likely to forget. I remember the chilly smell of the typical West Indian store, the indescribable smell of damp gloom, of locos, of

7. Ford, "Seraphina" (Unpublished typescript, Olin Library, Cornell University, Ithaca, N.Y.), 50.

pimento, of olive oil, of new sugar, of new rum; the glassy double sheen of Ramon's great spectacles, the piercing eyes in the mahogany face, while the tap, tap, tap of a cane on the flags went on behind the inner door; the click of the latch; the stream of light. The door, petulantly thrust inwards, struck against some barrels. I remember the rattling of the bolts on that door, and the tall figure that appeared there, snuffbox in hand. In that land of white clothes, that precise, ancient Castilian in black was something to remember. The black cane that had made the tap, tap, tap dangled by a silken cord from the hand whose delicate blue veined, wrinkled wrist ran back into a foam of lawn ruffles. The other hand paused in the act of conveying a pinch of snuff to the nostrils of the hooked nose that had, on the skin stretched tight over the bridge, the polish of old ivory; the elbow pressing the black cocked hat against the side; the legs, one bent, the other bowing a little back—this was the attitude of Seraphina's father. . . .

Then for the first time I saw Seraphina, looking over her father's shoulder. I remember her face of that day; her eyes were gray—the gray of black, not of blue. For a moment they looked me straight in the face, reflectively, unconcerned, and then traveled to the spectacles of old Ramon.

This glance—remember I was young on that day—had been enough to set me wondering what they were thinking of me; what they could have seen of me.[8]

There is certainly nothing offhanded, nothing left to chance *here*. In "Seraphina" what was "rich and strange" is now an itemized list of the contents of a West Indian storeroom. Seraphina's "superior merits of face and figure" have given way to those wonderful eyes and their first unforgettable glance. The reader gets everything at once, the rich atmosphere, a glimpse of the main characters, and an immediate sense of Kemp's feeling for the past. Each detail is fixed in space and time forever by this impressionist's memory. For better and worse, this fiction has acquired weight.

Though Conrad and Ford knew it sounded a little overwritten, they offered an excuse in the very psychology of memory. Kemp says at the end of the opening tableau quoted above, "Well, that is my yesterday of ro-

8. Ford and Conrad, *Romance*, 11–12.

mance, for the many things that have passed between those times and now have become dim or have gone out of my mind."[9] So the scene in Don Ramon's storeroom is like a Pre-Raphaelite painting, unselectively vivid in every detail, only because it is one moment carefully chosen from a thousand, a moment irradiated by memory. Other times "have become dim." The novel is lavish with realistic, brightly illuminated detail, but at every point the authors emphasize that these details have been selected by the strange processes of the mind re-creating its own past.

But, once they were working together, Conrad and Ford went even further with the possibilities inherent in a story thus remembered. They took the question of how man remembers and what reality looks like from the point of view of hindsight and they added an entirely new existential question. What, they asked, if these exotic, remembered moments were never in themselves unusual or dramatic? What if there is no intrinsic meaning to any experience? What if the idea that this story is romantic comes only from the effect of memory? What if all of our magical feelings come from our distance or unfamiliarity with particular things which to others have no interest at all? Here are the philosophical questions begged by the more literal manifestations of realism during the nineties. Is a dream less real than a drunken fall? Is the subjective view of experience measurable against some objective absolute? Is realism anything more than telling what being human feels like, using even the most abstract symbolism?

Ford had asked these questions inadvertently when he made his Seraphina just one more Spanish girl at the dance, interesting to Kemp only because she is a bit more pretty than the others and quite different from the girls at home. It is typical of their different temperaments that Ford at first made Seraphina mundane, thus emphasizing that she is not necessarily more romantic than any other pretty girl, while Conrad changed Seraphina into someone very special indeed and then questioned the universal existence of specialness.

Finally, the witty synthesis in *Romance* between romance and realism can be seen in a broader context as only one of a number of ways that Edwardian writers tried to bring these two mainstreams of English fiction together. Many novels in the period try to transform the mundane in romantic ways, and Ford himself was to explore, at some length, the frontier

9. *Ibid.*, 12.

between these two literary kinds with very mixed tonal results. In 1898, in a letter to H. G. Wells praising *The Invisible Man*, Conrad hailed Wells with the words "O Realist of the Fantastic!" which could well be taken as a sort of rallying cry for much that was to be written in the next decade.[10]

WHAT FORD LEARNED ABOUT TECHNIQUE

Winding Tight the Tension

Conrad knew that somehow he and Ford must get their hooks into the reader so that *Romance* would not have the listless, unfocused quality of "Seraphina." This was an adventure story and the reader must be constantly driven forward by an excitement, an edge of tension in every event. Nothing Ford had formerly written had had this sort of tension in any degree. It must have been a revelation to him when Conrad instructed him, "You must invent. You have got to make that fellow [Kemp] live perpetually under the shadow of the gallows."[11]

This kind of writing must have been hard for Ford at first, always one as he says, "to suppress the melodramatic incident and the sounding phrase."[12] But this overdose of structure, working within a controlling design, must, nevertheless, have provided him with a profound lesson: he learned how a story can gather, through the gradual development of a few themes, an intensification of effect. In their long nights of technical discussion and revision Ford and Conrad came to call this *progression d'effet*.

Conrad also taught Ford the related technique they called the time shift, in which incidents are reordered to move them inexorably forward. When Conrad broke the usual order of events, his purpose was to give them an even tighter organization; even though he broke his materials apart into impressionistic bits, his stories maintain a strong linear movement.

Ford took away from the collaboration a good understanding of the mechanics of this technique. He had learned from Conrad to break reality up "in little shreds" and to reorganize these to achieve both surprise and psychological truth. "Life did not narrate," they agreed, "but made impres-

10. Jean-Aubry, *Joseph Conrad*, I, 259.
11. Ford, *Joseph Conrad*, 43.
12. *Ibid.*, 43.

sions on our brains."[13] However, in Ford's hands, time shifts and impressionistic juxtapositions do not inexorably lead to a tighter, more
controlled march towards the denouement. When his *progressions d'effet*
work—which is not always—they work in a quite different way from Conrad's. He uses the time shift they devised together to create a field of experience with all its parts of potentially equal importance. Indeed, the impact of Ford's thematic materials is never like a noose around the neck; his
linear movement is never strong. The power of his effect comes, instead,
from tone and pattern.

However, in a novel like *Romance*, Ford's obliquity and his delaying
tactics are fatal. One sympathizes with André Gide who wrote in his jour-
nal after trying to read the novel:

> Read with some impatience and a serious fatigue toward the end *Ro-
> mance* by Joseph Conrad and Ford Madox Hueffer. Should like to
> know the latter's role and his share in that collaboration. I naturally
> attribute to Conrad himself certain excellent parts; but it seems that
> toward the last third of the book he gave the floor to the other, who
> is too discursive and finical. It drags on and the judicial misunder-
> standing becomes boring. Three literary manners are unbearable to
> me: the Garibaldi (and this is why I dropped Nostromo, though Ar-
> nold Bennett, who is a good judge in the matter, considered it to be
> Conrad's best book), the Musketeer manner, and the "*Caramba!*"
> manner. If I made a real effort, I think I should find still a fourth.
> . . . But let's drop it and find relaxation in Gibbon.[14]

The end of the novel is, indeed, mostly Ford's, and he promises an excitement he then cannot offer. In the tedium of the final court scene, the
reader begins to sympathize with the weary old judge who shuts his eyes
"with an air of a man who is going a long journey in a post-chaise."[15]

From being forced to write in the *Caramba!* manner, Ford learned a
great deal about how to get excitement, conflict, movement and a feeling
of unity into his work. However, at the same time, his subtle, delaying,

13. *Ibid.*, 203, 194.

14. Justin O'Brien (trans.), *The Journals of André Gide* (New York, 1951), VI, March 12,
1943, 188–89.

15. Ford and Conrad, *Romance*, 377.

and perhaps also "too discursive and finical" temperament left its mark on the experiment. Once again, Ford was learning lessons he could only put to use in an entirely different manner and context from those of his mentors.

Making a Larger World

It was not only the plot of *Romance* that got a new shape and movement during the collaboration. The whole world of the second novel is a vast enlargement of that of the first. James called *Romance* "an immense English Plum Cake which he kept at his bedside for a fortnight and of which he ate a nightly slice."[16] And in spite of the novel's exotic qualities, this is just what it is, full of cameo characters and carefully elaborated, detachable incidents.

Together they called the writer's task of filling in the necessary background to give characters and situations life "the mystic word 'justification.'" Justification is the process of making a novel's scenes and people so complete that what happens seems right and inevitable. Even if the action is no more than what occurs in so many of Ford's later novels, what he called "the gradual coming together of [a] thousand small circumstances,"[17] each of these small circumstances, according to the law of justification, must come from somewhere; each must have its own independent life and development and its own denouement. One of Ford's most treasured memories of the collaboration is of the praise Conrad gave him when he provided one of the pirate rabble with a vocation and history in the phrase "Excellency, a few goats."

At other times, justification was more tedious and less successful. Did Ford and Conrad carry justification too far? Does it sometimes contribute to what longueurs are to be found in their novels? Ultimately, these questions can only be answered by individual readers for individual books, though certainly some of their novels were better conceived to carry the extra weight of justification than others. In all cases, however, one needs a taste for this kind of elaboration. It is a species of realism that comes into and goes out of fashion. Undeniably there is always some degree of strain in a "justified" style, a strain that comes from the very arduousness inher-

16. Ford, *Thus to Revisit*, 114.
17. Ford, *Joseph Conrad*, 218.

ent in this sort of labor. As Ford said of Conrad, "he was never convinced that he had convinced the reader."[18]

From the first, Ford shared Conrad's insecurity, his compulsion to explain and justify. Conrad tried to teach him how to use his immense energy for discursive writing to enrich rather than diffuse intensity. Working together on *Romance* with extraordinary tenacity and devotion, Ford and Conrad squeezed more blood out of the subject of "Seraphina" than that little story had ever had. Naturally, the result was funereal, though, at moments, *Romance* is an amazingly vivid corpse.

Oddly enough, a corpse is just what the original typescript of "Seraphina" was not. Though Conrad infused believability and depth into the characters and incidents in the process of transforming the frivolous, disorganized "Seraphina" into *Romance*, in Ford's version issues were raised, if not developed, that were more complicated than any in the later book. In "Seraphina" Ford mentioned money and how Kemp has to struggle and compromise to earn it; he mentioned the incompatibility of beliefs and temperament between Kemp, an English earl's grandson, and Seraphina, a Spanish lady; he mentioned the issue of the mixed marriage between them. In an adventure story these issues seem out of place, but in 1898 when "Seraphina" was written, such vibrant topicalities were becoming an important element in fiction. In "Seraphina" Ford described at length one of Kemp's money-making schemes: he will kill hummingbirds and send them to London to be stuffed and sold as curiosities. No trace of this entrepreneur Kemp remains in *Romance*, but one can recognize him in the novels of Bennett, Wells, and Galsworthy. Conrad did indeed elaborate Ford's thin rough draft, but for all the layers of detail, character analysis, and plot complexity he added to it, he may, at the same time, also have simplified it.

The rich complexity Conrad is able to generate around characters and situations usually resolves itself into a general truth about social impotence. Ford wrote of him, "He was a politician, but a politician of the *impasse*."[19] All revolutions, Conrad told Ford, resolve themselves into palace intrigues. Because no one can control a significant portion of the circle swept by his actions, political struggle is at best foolish, at worst criminally destructive.

18. *Ibid.*, 221.
19. *Ibid.*, 44.

This tendency of Conrad's to posit a universal similarity behind the most chaotic of human differences throws a new light on his revisions of Ford's work. For while Ford agreed with Conrad's general doubts as to whether or not a human being has any chance of controlling his own affairs—indeed, in many respects, he carried the idea of social dislocation and helplessness further and embodied it more completely in his style—he was interested in the particulars of social issues in a way that Conrad was not. In his books, local detail is honored for itself. Reality presses in on the characters without resolving itself into clear shapes. Social life remains itself because it has no symbolic escalator by which to climb out of itself.

Speaking of all Conrad's early books as "political parables," Ford described the otherworldliness of Conrad's social vision, so different from his own:

> The Republic of Costaguana, as portrayed in Nostromo, is a study, really, of some immense Nowhere. . . . The Secret Agent, again, is a study in comparative detectives of another wonderfully projected Nowhere. There are policemen of a kingdom that is not the united one of Great Britain and Ireland; there is the Agent Provocateur of a kingdom whose seaboard touches on that of the kingdom of Bohemia; . . . and there is a London that may be seen in Malaysia, but in few other places.
>
> And this London of The Secret Agent lets us into a secret of Mr. Conrad's immense appeal to his fellow men—into the secret of his universality. Other writers would render a London that is just London. Mr. Conrad gives us the Eternal City that floats in the minds of an immense company of men. . . .
>
> That, of course, is not the London of the Londoner who, self-protectively bent upon his personal errand, observes nothing since everything is familiar, ordinary—and indispensable to make up the immense, quiet thing that, to the Londoner, London is.[20]

It was Ford who described from the inside that Londoner for whom London is mundane home. In this Ford shares with so many of the other Edwardian realists an interest in the texture of everyday life. But unlike many of them, he saw an insidious implication of the social changes to be

20. Ford, Thus to Revisit, 91–92.

seen on a familiar London street: they were leading everyone, inevitably, to a more subjective, limited point of view. The way it felt to look at things was being transformed. To the modern Londoner, there could be no spiritually authentic overview of an Eternal London: "We are losing more and more the sense of a whole, the feeling of a grand design, of the coordination of all Nature in one great architectonic scheme. . . . We have to face such an infinite number of little things that we cannot stay to arrange them in our minds, or to consider them as anything but as accidents, happenings, the mere events of the day. . . . we are thrown more and more in upon ourselves."[21] Ford always wrote of the people "thrown more and more in upon themselves" with sympathy and a close attention towards the specific conditions of their predicament, while in Conrad, he always honored the grandeur of outline, the symbol-making power, the ability to project with confidence a more or less private universe—all qualities so different from his own.

But finally it would be a falsification to make too much of the contrast between Conrad's "grand designs" and Ford's less assertive power of imagination. Though Conrad could create complete worlds, they are still private ones in a way that, for example, George Eliot's, are not. The collaborators shared the experience of being "thrown more and more in upon [them]selves," and in the passage above Ford is describing Conrad's spiritual crisis as much as his own. They both felt the increased importance of a limited and self-conscious point of view. How else could one be realistic about a social situation that seemed to be proliferating and changing at an accelerating rate? How else could one escape mere randomness in one's selectivity from among "an infinite number of little things"? But, finally, the contrast between the two writers holds. Conrad, under pressure, reached for the symbol, for the archetypal London street. Ford, feeling the same pressure, tried as so many Edwardians were to do, to write about that street as it felt to walk along it.

Developing a Point of View

Conrad's temperament demanded a narrative method that could erect a protective screen between himself and his own depression, isolation, and

21. Ford, *Memories and Impressions*, 69.

scepticism. He evolved a number of techniques to maintain this controlled distance between his material on the one hand and both himself and his readers on the other. Some of his most beautiful and exciting effects come from this layering process. White men go into jungles where they meet black men who tell them stories about the distant past. Then the white men go home and retell these stories years later, when they have become a memory of a memory.

Ford, too, was attracted by distancing devices. He found it difficult to dramatize conflict directly and he was particularly interested in the way experience gets diffused by thought. Nevertheless, for "Seraphina" he chose the most direct and painfully revealing point of view of all, the first person narrator as hero. No novel Conrad wrote alone has a narrator as self-exposing as Kemp. Indeed, it is interesting that Conrad accepted Ford's original conception and agreed to leave *Romance* in the direct first person. Perhaps he felt that the filtering effect of time would serve as well as a detached narrator in creating a controlled perspective on events. The dense exoticism of the second novel also creates an effect of distance absent in the first draft.

Nevertheless, when they decided together to keep Ford's original form of narration, they kept something of Ford's temperamental approach to point of view, which is quite different from Conrad's and which remains an important element in *Romance* in spite of all Conrad's major changes. The difference is evident in a comparison between *Romance* and *Lord Jim* which was being written during breaks in the collaboration. Jim's moment of cowardice, which in Ford's hands might have been potentially embarrassing and absurd, becomes a fatal and epic moment by means of the layered narrative technique by which it is told. We circle the moment with a circumspection that gives it the appearance of cosmic significance. We hear about it indirectly, reported by Marlow and then by the informants of Marlow. In this way Jim's crisis becomes magnified, a moment important enough to be refracted through many minds. Jim's own relative inarticulateness has the effect of further enlarging the mysterious importance of his act since it must pass through various phases of interpretation by others.

In *Romance*, John Kemp, who shares Jim's unformed and untested character, tells his story directly. What is absurd in it he must either excuse or bear in his own person. The older Kemp, who is the writer, makes fun of the younger Kemp, who had made childish and embarrassing errors in judgment, but he does not altogether hold aloof from his younger self. There is an immediacy in the feelings of the narrator about his story that is absent in Conrad.[22]

This closeness, which was natural to Ford, between his own temperament and that of his narrating personae, had exciting potential for the most immediate and searing kind of writing. Though he saw Conrad as brave, as the one who was "for inclusion and hang the consequences," in fact, Ford was able to face a form of self-exposure that Conrad found intolerable. Ford joins his characters in their run from pain and forces his readers to join in too by showing us things from a point of view that becomes almost claustrophobic in its subjectivity. In *The Good Soldier*, for example, Conradian narrative layers, instead of creating a dispassionate and judicious distance from events, have the opposite effect. Here the most elaborately distanced and contained point of view paradoxically brings the unhappiness described in the story closer and closer to the reader. Conrad, in his need to generalize and, finally, to judge, could never have created a narrator like Dowell, whose sufferings, mistakes, and confusions are the central subject of his story and whose judgment of his own life's meaning is not seconded by any voice in the universe.

At the end of "Seraphina," the falsely accused John Kemp is acquitted of piracy at the Old Bailey. As is the case with so many Ford heroes, Kemp's sufferings create a screen of confusion around him so dense that he cannot even hear the verdict. After it is pronounced, he is overcome. "What did I think—what did I say?—I think I thought nothing, so weary was my mind, and said nothing, but just stood holding Seraphina's hand and noting little cracks in panellings and scraps of paper on the benches."[23] Here, in this early version, is the Ford hero with his subjective point of view. The crisis of the novel leaves him too overcome to appreciate its magnitude. Finally, it is in little things that the memory of that great day lives.

22. An interesting exception, which ultimately proves the rule that Conrad creates narrative screens to place his material at a distance, is *Youth* (1902). Marlow tells his own story of his first responsible position at sea directly, as Kemp does. Written during the heart of the collaboration, *Youth* has a number of similarities to *Romance* that make it a possible example of a story by his undeflectable mentor on which Ford may have had a fleeting influence.

23. Ford, "Seraphina," 171.

Creating Characters

In creating characters, Conrad can be said to have worked in such a hard medium that his people are sometimes like military statues in a park, distinguished by their particular deeds, but frozen into one eternally repeated characteristic gesture. For example, the death of Nostromo is like the crashing down of an enormous, symbolic totem pole. It is tragic, but not only tragic: one thinks of Conrad's contemporary, Henri Bergson, who defined comedy as "something mechanical encrusted on the living."[24] Nostromo is described as strong to provide the sceptic with the exquisite irony of finding him, nevertheless, weak.

Conrad placed great value on authorial indifference. In a letter of 1901 to John Galsworthy he advised, "before all one must divest oneself of every particle of respect for one's character." A writer's success depends on "scepticism, the tonic of minds," not on "fidelity to his personages."[25] Younger writers like D. H. Lawrence were, in a sense, to agree, but to them indifference was meant to defuse judgment as they made their way into the subjectivity of their characters. Freud's insights changed the rules of character. While Conrad's people are often overshadowed by their destinies, younger writers such as Virginia Woolf played down both individuality and destiny in their new, intense interest in the play between the conscious and unconscious.

Ford stands in his usual ambiguous and uncomfortable position in relation to this evolution of the idea of character. He knew nothing of Freud during the years of the collaboration, but he was painfully sensitive to the erosion of what he called the Victorian Great Figure, whose disappearance he celebrated and mourned between one breath and another. As an old man he wrote of the centrality of character in fiction, "we are all kings—if only over a kingdom of our own minds."[26] But he had always worried about what a small kingdom the mind could be—nothing to an empire, nothing even to a public world in which one had an established sense of role and place.

Both Ford and Conrad took refuge from this sense of constriction in

24. Henri Bergson's "Laughter" (in Wylie Sypher [ed.], Comedy [Garden City, N.Y., 1956] was written between 1884 and 1900, Conrad's formative years as a novelist, and it describes a French aesthetic of comedy to be seen in many of the comic elements of Conrad's work. "Indifference," Bergson said, is comedy's "natural environment."

25. Jean-Aubry, Joseph Conrad, I, 301.

26. Ford, Portraits from Life, 90.

technique. If the moral components of character were unclear, at least technique guaranteed some kind of faithful reproduction of the confusion. And so in *Joseph Conrad* Ford writes sections about "surprise," "cadence," "style," even "philosophy," but never one titled "character." "Character," that great category of Victorian writing, was a category no longer.

Ford criticized the conventional prewar novel for, "without pausing to look aside," telling stories "too confined to [their] characters."[27] Ford, of course, was always looking aside; but, ironically enough, while casting out the old character-centered novel, he found himself clinging to his characters' points of view and particularities as the only bearings in a maze.

Conrad's imaginative strengths, technical skills and official indifference ruled *Romance*, while Ford's more tentative view of life was submerged. However, because of the technical lifeline Conrad threw to him—the carefully limited point of view—Ford was eventually able to write his best studies of subjectivity. There character was, in a sense, to matter since each one was trapped in his or her own mind, from which issued a world, however absurd or small.

《 》

It may help to clarify the difference between Conrad and Ford's treatment of character to look at one interesting example, their treatment of women. At first it may appear that the loaded example of women characters clouds the more general issue of characterization since we know of a fundamental difference of opinion between the two writers: Ford was a suffragist and wrote a suffragette pamphlet in 1913; Conrad was a misogynist who openly mistrusted women as an anarchic force in nature and who believed they must be denied the vote because their "power is of the night."[28] But, in fact, these differing attitudes are typical of their differences of approach towards character building in general and towards the placement of characters into a world.

Ford made various efforts over the years to describe and explain Conrad's profound lack of interest in women characters. In 1921 he wrote:

> It has been said somewhere—and Mr. Conrad has somewhere corroborated the statement if we do not mistake—that Mr. Conrad

27. Ford, *Joseph Conrad*, 204.
28. *Ibid.*, 54.

cannot draw a woman. But that is not true. . . . If we said that Mr. Conrad's world is a man made world we should be more near the truth.

For the women in Mr. Conrad's books are omnipresent and various. . . . It is only that, in their functions they are extremely unimportant to the story. They are the chattels of the hearth, the occupants of deck-cabins; they hold torches or they soothe. . . . relations of the sexes do not come into his working life—and by life the writer means, of course, not the life that Mr. Conrad has lived, but the life that he has given us.

Here Ford gives, in a footnote, a passage illustrating his point from *Heart of Darkness*: "Girl! What? Did I mention a girl? Oh she is out of it—completely. They—the women—I mean—are out of it—should be out of it. We must help them to stay in that beautiful world of their own, lest ours get worse."

To descend for the fifth of a moment to reminiscences, the writer well remembers a speech that Mr. Conrad inserted into a collaborated work. . . . It was to the effect that there are men who will derogate from the most sacred duties of friendship: "For a little money or some woman!" and the disdain expressed in the last three words was overwhelming. In Mr. Conrad's world, in fact, woman is just "some woman."[29]

In the 1930s, once more trying to explain Conrad's women to the world, Ford compared him to Frederick Marryat, "Conrad's first master." "Marryat, realizing that a world of men without women is in truth a world of only a half-horizon, got his heroes' young women as often into his books as he could. Conrad, sensing the same thing, left women, for a great part of his writing career, altogether out of his books and supplied their place with the epicene great waters, attributing to them all the passions and pretty ways of he-male rages and feminine coquetries."[30] The absence of women left a blank to be filled either with symbolic platitudes ("they hold torches or they soothe") or with a richness of sensuous detail ("the epicene great waters") that distracts us from noticing the less-embellished surface of character itself.

29. Ford, *Thus to Revisit*, 98–99.
30. Ford, *Portraits from Life*, 85–86.

Though women can do nothing in Conrad's world they can cause things to happen. As Ford described Conrad's idea, man, "the solitary, cynical, not impracticable dreamer is brought down by his womankind, his relations, his servants, his hangers-on, his household."[31] Conrad's women either arouse passions they can never fulfill, leading men away from their proper comrades (*Karain, Outcast of the Islands, Heart of Darkness*), or they live in a kind of impermeable innocence that is a fatal doctrine for any man who must live in the world (the fiancée in *Heart of Darkness*, Miss Haldin in *Under Western Eyes*). Powerless but often fatally dangerous, these women personify the paradox of Conrad's great art. They are menacing, suggestive, magnificent, yet also static and unknowable. They do not change.

The history of Ford's efforts to depict women characters has quite a different shape. From his first novel, he could never remain consistent in his representations of idealized, romantic females of the Conradian type. The elevated woman of romance, opaque and perfect, or to use a phrase of Conrad's, "occult and mysterious, . . . like all natural forces,"[32] becomes too human in Ford's books, breaking the delicate balance of romantic illusion. "Seraphina" provides another example of this interesting failing of Ford's. Like everything in the manuscript, the women are undeveloped, but at the same time they are given complete histories, which are told with empathy. In fact, several female figures leap for a moment from the novel's immature prose. The book opens with a long section devoted to the life story of Kemp's mother, a passionate and powerful woman, whom Ford's Seraphina resembles.

A great deal has been written about how Ford's women are menacing figures, witches who, like Conrad's women, make a man suffer.[33] But, though Ford could certainly write about women as dangerous and perfidious—Florence and Sylvia are monstrous, frightening women—he could also write about women like Kemp's mother, Seraphina, Maisie Maidan, and Valentine, women who have difficulties, who experience conflicts, who are, very simply, immersed in the contradictions of human existence along with everybody else. These women can have a subjective life impossible in a Conrad novel.

31. Ford, *Joseph Conrad*, 60.
32. Conrad, *Chance* (1912; rpr. New York, 1924), 327.
33. Arthur Mizener and Caroline Gordon typify this critical view.

In Ford's rough draft, Seraphina smokes "her own cigarettes." She makes jokes. She is coquettish and excitable. When she has Kemp's enemies at her mercy (they are in a drunken stupor), she wants to kill them all with her knife and is restrained only with difficulty:

> "Seraphina," I said, "you must understand me. I could not marry a murderess."
> "You are a coward," she said.
> "I am an Englishman," I answered, "and you must be an Englishwoman."[34]

And so the hero and heroine fight on for several pages. They have different temperaments, backgrounds, and religions. They fight the war between the sexes. They enact classical marital misunderstandings. Yet at the end of the novel, when Kemp has been captured and is being taken away in an English ship to be tried as a pirate, Seraphina jumps into her canoe and paddles after him for miles into the open sea. Her passion is a romantic cliché and her character is hardly developed, but her actions are something else again. She is athletic, full of life, an amazon in love. There is more vigor in her little finger than appears in any woman in the published version of the novel, on which Conrad's influence lies so heavy.

Turning from "Seraphina" to *Romance*, we see the heroine transformed, or rather, reversed. All that was active, impulsive, and rather charming in her is gone, and she has become impassive, delicate, humorless, ideal. There are no more arguments between hero and heroine. They are not two people facing the world anymore. Instead, Kemp has become the active principle, Seraphina, the passive. He struggles a man's struggles and she supports him invisibly. When he is in difficulty and is tempted to act unmanfully, Kemp writes: "I ran to Seraphina. 'Put out your hand to me,' I panted in the darkness, 'I need your help.' I felt it resting lightly on my bowed head! She did not even ask me what I meant; as if the greatness of her soul was omniscient. There was, in that silence, a supreme unselfishness, the unquestioning devotion of a woman."[35] Indeed, the Seraphina of *Romance* never asks what is meant. When this second Seraphina runs away with Kemp, one of her retainers informs him that her foot has

34. Ford, "Seraphina," 93.
35. Ford and Conrad, *Romance*, 301.

never before touched the common ground. These are all Conrad's images, of course. Ford could never have written them and the fact invites one to speculate about the way in which the collaboration failed to make use of the things he knew.

In spite of their shared doubts and aims, Conrad wraps his characters in an insulating cocoon of symbol and emotive detail while Ford's walk relatively naked. The divergence is of generation, of temperament, of sensibility. Ford's people are often as static as Conrad's but in them this quality is immediately painful, a direct source of frustration and sadness.

« »

It is idle to speculate about how things might have been different if Ford had had a different sort of mentor. Nevertheless, one can wonder if Conrad's method, so concentrated on detail, so calculating and carefully limited, did not in fact impose not only a much needed order but also a drag on Ford's more volatile psychological imagination. Would Ford have been able to create characters more in motion if he had not so slavishly adopted Conrad's standards of thoroughness? He immediately recognized D. H. Lawrence as a genius who was cutting loose and creating a world of internal realities without Conrad's sometimes almost intolerable sense of strain. But Lawrence first crossed his path in 1908 when Ford had been laboriously building character from a texture of carefully limited impressions and details for ten years. Or perhaps, to imagine still another kind of mentor for Ford, might his chattering verbal energy have led him to set characters talking and doing and encountering the world more as they do in the novels of Wells and the plays of Shaw if Conrad's painstaking, symbolical constructions had not first presented themselves to him?

The point here is not to wish Ford different. Ford and Conrad had a subtle and complicated affinity for one another and Ford's response to Conrad's methods is in keeping with something static and impersonal that was already present in his work before he met Conrad. In fact, Ford already relied heavily on detail and felt the need for certain kinds of distancing devices in his earliest writing. One can perhaps say, however, that Conrad confirmed and encouraged Ford in his laboriousness and that when they worked together they created characters who often move somewhat woodenly, monoliths in an otherwise shifting shimmering world.

In 1909 changes, old contradictions, bitternesses stored for years erupted into a serious quarrel: Ford and Conrad were never to be close again. For both, the collaboration—in its broadest meaning as an intimate sharing of work and ideas—was one of the great periods of their lives. Angry as Conrad was, he mourned, and guilty and bewildered as Ford was, he continued to celebrate Conrad's genius and the honor and joy of having been his friend for the rest of his life.

It is a queer and fantastic world. Why can't people have what they want? The things were all there to content everybody; yet everybody has the wrong thing. Perhaps you can make head or tail of it; it is beyond me.

FORD, *The Good Soldier*

Part III

EXPERIMENTATION

How they come back to me after a quarter of a century . . .
the savoured, half-humourous, half-deprecatory words, the
ironically exaggerated gestures, the workings of the closely
shaved lips, the halting to emphasize a point, the sudden
scurryings forward, for all the world like the White Rabbit
hurrying to the Queen's tea-party . . . along the Rye Road,
through the marshes, from Winchelsea. . . . I walking
beside him and hardly ever speaking, in the guise of God's
strong, silent Englishman—which he took me really to be.

FORD, remembering his walks with James in
Portraits from Life, 1937

«4»

THE ROMANCES: COMEDY, IRONY
AND HENRY JAMES

SOURCES FOR THE WRITING OF ROMANCE

WHEN Millais has his blind girl sit by the roadway in her homely
clothes (borrowed from a beggar and painted painstakingly from
the life) with her back to a rainbow so beautiful that it distills the experience of all lovely skies, of all intense colors, his Pre-Raphaelite picture
successfully brings together the supernatural and the everyday. The pathos
of the blind girl's presence in the midst of all that visual splendor is an
almost literary statement of what Coleridge described as the romantics'
goal of "awakening the mind's attention from the lethargy of custom and
directing it to loveliness and the wonders of the world before us." Similarly, Ford wrote works in which the mystery and surprise hiding beneath
everyday life are stunningly revealed, though when, in his novels, he
breaks through "the lethargy of custom," he usually finds, instead of the
"loveliness and the wonders of the world," a frightening underlife of passion and disorder.

After the Pre-Raphaelites, Conrad was, of course, the other early influence on Ford who dramatized for him the possibilities of romance. Con-

rad's unstated but profound romanticism had as much impact on Ford as did his mentor's more vocal concern with Flaubert and the French form in general. For him, to read *Almayer's Folly* for the first time "was to come into contact with a spirit of romance, of adventure, of distant lands, and with an English that was new, magic, and unsurpassed. It sang like music; it overwhelmed me like a great warm wave of the sea."[1] Conrad's particular way of mixing the realistic and the romantic impulses was of great importance in Ford's developing concept of how to balance his own twin desires, to be both historian and romancer. Here is Hugh Walpole's contemporary analysis of how Conrad made this blend: "Joseph Conrad, from the very first, influenced though he was by the French novel, showed that Realism alone was not enough for him. . . . upon recorded facts Conrad's imagination, without for a moment deserting the truth, worked beautifying, ennobling it, giving it pity and terror, above all putting it into relation with the whole universe, the whole history of the cycle of life and death."[2] Walpole goes on to say that the idea of romance (in his very Jamesian definition of the term as a subtle imaginative shaping and heightening of fictional material) became increasingly important during the last years before the war as the Russian influence eclipsed the French. There was debate about the proper relation between realism and romanticism during those years, and it was common among Ford's contemporaries to try for some kind of self-conscious amalgam of the two.

Ford's particular mixture of comedy and seriousness has everything to do with this exploration of what is in fact a basic theme of English literature, what Dickens called in the preface to *Bleak House* "the romantic side of familiar things." Most of Ford's books deal in some way with the dissonant and sometimes apparently ridiculous clash of idealized with more realistic versions of experience. In the nine historical novels he wrote, this project often became in Ford's own estimation "nothing more than a *tour de force*, a fake more or less genuine in inspiration and workmanship."[3] Conrad's practical suggestiveness as to how the romancer operates is visible primarily in these historical romances, from which comic ironies are almost programmatically absent.[4] It was finally in Ford's romances of con-

1. Ford, *Memories and Impressions*, 250–51.
2. Walpole, *Joseph Conrad*, 110–11.
3. Ford, *Joseph Conrad*, 186.
4. Of the nine historical romances Ford wrote, eight were written in the ten-year period initiated in 1903 by the publication of *Romance: The Fifth Queen*, 1906; *Privy Seal*, 1907; *The Fifth Queen Crowned*, 1908 (these three were a trilogy about Katharine Howard); *The "Half*

temporary life that the project of yoking realism with romance stripped of scholarly archaisms, of what James called mere costume, became potentially comic, thematically urgent, and tonally complex. Moving from the often richly wrought and earnest but seriously flawed historical novels to Ford's romances of the present, the influence Conrad had on Ford is eclipsed by the next major figure in his writing life, that most subtle of comedians, Henry James.

As Ford himself said, no novel of his can be called a direct imitation of Conrad's style, but Ford owns at once to having tried to write Jamesian novels.[5] After spending hours with Conrad working on refinements of style, it was to James he turned for an idea of how one might appropriately describe modern life, describe it at a recognizable and fitting pitch. And Ford turned to him not just for the how, finally, but for the what. Unlike Conrad, James stimulated Ford towards an increasingly subtle conception of contemporary subject matter. As he compared his two mentors, "Mr. Conrad is probably the more consummate artist, in the sense that he is the greater poet and has paid more attention to technical details; but his stories deal so much less intimately with the normal products of our day that, in this particular department, he scarcely comes, Oriental as he is, into comparison with the great writer from the West."[6]

Unlike Conrad, "the great writer from the West" was never an intimate of Ford's, and James dropped him from his visiting list in 1908 when he heard of Ford's adulterous liaison with Violet Hunt.[7] All the same, Ford's admiration for the Master (Ford's word) was constant, though his critical perspective about what James was actually doing in his novels underwent some interesting changes. In 1905 when Ford wrote The Benefactor, his imitation of James's renunciation theme was slavish and essentially un-

---

Moon," 1909; The Portrait, 1910; Ladies Whose Bright Eyes, 1911; The Young Lovell, 1913. Ford's only historical romance written outside of this period, A Little Less Than Gods, was published in 1928. Certainly the commercial appeal of writing such books must have been strong. The Forest Lovers (1898) made Maurice Hewlett rich and famous. In addition, the form had immense prestige, particularly during the Edwardian years. Conan Doyle was ashamed of his Sherlock Holmes stories and hoped instead to be judged by his long, romanticized tales of chivalry, The White Company (1891) and Sir Nigel (1906).

5. See Ford, Joseph Conrad, 187–88.

6. Ford, Henry James, 81.

7. See James's letters to Violet Hunt, Hunt Papers. James begs Hunt to keep him in ignorance and signs one letter, "Believe me then, in very imperfect sympathy, yours, Henry James." Certainly there can have been little significant contact between Ford and James after November, 1909.

illuminating. In 1907, with *An English Girl*, Ford again imitated Jamesian themes slavishly, without transforming them to his own purposes, but the writing itself had become more subtle in ways that are distinctly Jamesian. By 1910, with his last James pastiche, *A Call*, he was writing prose that sometimes sounds like wonderful Henry James but that never runs the risk of being mistaken for it. It was only after 1910, after his period of writing direct Jamesian pastiche, that Ford began to see the more general possibilities James held out to him. *The Good Soldier* was the novel he wrote that finally incorporated James's example in a way that did no injury to Ford's different temperament and quality of observation. In *The Good Soldier*, Ford made full use of James's tragicomic ironies to express his own particular species of bewilderment.

In 1913, the same year he was writing *The Good Soldier*, Ford wrote his book on James, perhaps in part as an acknowledgment of a fully assimilated influence. It is not a very thorough or even a particularly perceptive study of James. (One gets glimpses in it of how Ford had been misunderstanding his mentor's intentions all along in ways that led his own imitations astray.) It does contain, however, some general statements about the Master that show how Ford then defined James's general importance to him as a model: "He is the only unbiassed, voluminous and truthful historian of our day. And, in our day, the greatest need of society is the historian who can cast a ray of light into the profound gloom, into the whirl of shadows, of our social agnosticism."[8] In *The Good Soldier* Ford himself had just become for the first time a successful historian of "the whirl of shadows" and of a moral relativism that can well be called "social agnosticism."

After the war, with a new distance from the society he and James had tried to describe from the inside, Ford came to see more clearly just what the "historian" James was trying to distill from his observations. He wrote in 1921 that "what [James] knew he rendered, along with its amenities, its gentlefolkishness, its pettinesses, its hypocrisies, its make-believes. He gives you an immense—and an increasingly tragic—picture of a Leisured Society that is fairly unavailing, materialist, emasculated—and doomed."[9]

With the hindsight of 1921, it was evident that the "Leisured Society" had been doomed indeed, but Ford had already pictured it in *The Good*

8. Ford, *Henry James*, 66.
9. Ford, *Thus to Revisit*, 119.

Soldier, much as James had pictured it, as a world where tragedy had become a very small and personal matter, had become, in fact, sadness, and where the old social forms were so rotten that "doom" was bound to overtake them sooner or later. In fact, it overtook them sooner, and one wishes that one could know what the Master himself would have said in 1921 about the changes in the world he had so attentively described before the war. Certainly Ford speculated about this, for he said that he first began thinking about *Parade's End* by wondering how James "would have treated that intractable subject," the war.

By 1921 Ford could already see prewar social reality placed within a frame, and could recognize the way in which both he and James had always romanticized it. In what he wrote before the war, Ford emphasized James's realism; James the social historian is the central image. After the war we hear more about James the romancer, a man who described an ideal, a vision of a civilized state that could never be realized: "It was possible that James never wanted to live outside tea-parties—but the tea-parties that he wanted were debating circles of a splendid aloofness, of an immense human sympathy, and of a beauty that you do not find in Putney—or in Passy! It was his tragedy that no such five-o'clock ever sounded for him on the timepieces of this world."[10]

Whatever the reality had been, for Ford the world of the tea party had begun to seem far away, a romantic dream, by 1921. A few years later, in *Parade's End,* he began to take earnest measure of just how completely the world of the tea table had disappeared from the life Tietjens leads during and after the war. In the tetralogy Ford is both historian and romancer. He has an ideal vision he continuously projects onto his descriptions, but the descriptions themselves are detailed reportage of what the war must indeed have felt like for a man with Tietjens' species of almost feudal romantic beliefs. In this subtle mixture of realism and romance he shows himself to be truly James's disciple.

Finally, in the thirties, in his last essay on James, Ford wrote his own romantic fantasy of what James had been to him. This essay, "Henry James, the Master," opens, "I will begin this work with a little romance in the style of the Master."[11] Though this late vision of James has the notorious Fordian faults of being somewhat self-serving and often inaccurate and

10. *Ibid.*
11. Ford, *Portraits from Life,* 1.

digressive, it has, too, some of Ford's best insights into the shape of James's career. Here Ford sees that the early James romanticized the English ruling class, while the late James lived under a cloud of disillusionment about these "good people," who, as Ford explains, are not to be confused with people who are morally good. He sees the kinds of abstraction James imposed on social history and the kinds of romantic elegy he was capable of writing—though how entirely without Ford's sentimentality!—about a declining class. James the historian had suggested to him a way of looking at contemporary detail; James the romancer had given him a myth of a moral decline, of a class's tragedy.

This myth misled Ford as often as it guided him to solutions, but what the Master taught him about how to listen, how to pitch his voice appropriately, how to schematize, helped him to bypass, by means of local accuracy and brilliance, some of the recurring deficiencies in his overall conception of his times. James's view of the contradictions between the surfaces of life and the depths, unlike Conrad's, was essentially social. He offered Ford more appropriate subjects than Conrad could do and his novels suggested a range of attitudes towards social experience which left their traces on all Ford's work.

FORD AND JAMES, THE MODERN COMEDIANS

"These atmospheres, nuances, impressions of personal tone and quality *are his subject*," wrote Ezra Pound of Henry James. "In these he gets certain things that almost no one else had done before him. These timbres and tonalities are his stronghold, he is ignorant of nearly everything else." [12] Pound complained that art can be trivialized when tone becomes subject. But, though this trivialization does sometimes happen in both Ford and James as they turn inward and write art that explores its own attitude towards itself, at the same time, writing about tone was the expression of a general cultural change. Twentieth-century novels in the modernist tradition of James, Ford, and finally Joyce are often about tone, about the emotion behind the act of observing and synthesizing. It is a self-conscious art, an ironist's art, always concerned in some way with the question of its own mixed motives. It is, in short, the elaborate, the defensive art that is a

12. Ezra Pound, "Henry James," in T. S. Eliot (ed.), *The Literary Essays of Ezra Pound* (Norfolk, Conn., 1954), 327.

common product of modern, pluralist, industrial society. Earlier, we observed a distinction between Conrad's comic irony, which was a device, and Ford's, which was an inescapable habit of mind. James, the eldest of the trio, was closer to Ford than to Conrad in his unavoidable complexity of voice in general and of comic voice in particular.

Their contemporary, Henri Bergson, theorized that comedy is essentially a socializing form, designed to control the inappropriate or antisocial tendencies of individuals.[13] Laughter is a corrective directed at those who confuse or ignore the social contract. Thus comedy, as Bergson defines it, has a dual nature: it pretends to undermine social differences only to reconfirm them by reducing the tension these disparities have caused. We break free and laugh but we are also, at the same moment, being disciplined by the joke to fill our proper places in the social order. However, in describing this mixed phenomenon, this resolution of opposites, of the bitter and the frothy in life, Bergson was postulating a society in which the norms are more or less agreed upon and the categories of human types more or less stable. What happens to comedy when these categories are no longer sharply defined, when serious conflict is undermining them?

In his tale "The Author of Beltraffio" James portrays a peculiarly modern young woman (she is wearing a medieval dress, an appropriate expression of her modish nostalgia for a more structured time): "Her laugh was modern—by which I mean that it consisted of the vocal agitation serving between people who meet in drawing-rooms as the solvent of social disparities, the medium of transitions."[14] This modern laugh is not the traditional comic release of tension, a moment of reconciliation with immutable social structures. Instead, it is quite disturbing, a "vocal agitation" which is used as a "medium of transitions." Laughter cannot confirm the modern young lady, or us, in a sense of order and decorum that is not there. Instead it strains to be a "medium of transition," to bring things together that are, in fact, falling asunder.

Though James tries to use comedy in the tradition Bergson describes, as a criticism and tonic for social life, in the end, laughter fails to restore him to a sense of a healthy social order. His novels move away from comedy towards a more spiritual solution for the individual character. Reconciliation with the social order, laughter in which loss and acceptance can both

13. See Bergson, "Laughter."
14. Leon Edel (ed.), *The Complete Tales of Henry James* (London, 1962), V, 318.

be accommodated finally seem to James impossible. His novels leave the sphere of comic social criticism and reach for some other kind of synthesis.

Ford takes James's scepticism about the ultimate sustenance to be found in social life even further. His comic effects don't even pretend to criticize the divergence from socially agreed upon norms. Instead, his strained, uneasy laughter can land anywhere, and his hero is as likely to be the butt of a joke as his most venial, two-dimensional grotesque. He has a vision of social norms that has been elevated into a realm of timeless romance that is clearly unattainable, and no joke can bridge the gap between him and this idealized world. The absurd or the ridiculous in Ford measures this gap without being able to close it.

Ford found himself as a comic writer at the moment when things that had formerly been the appropriate subjects for laughter—the class system, the role of women, the social and economic stability of the middle class— were all in the process of rapid change. Yet the old forms were still vivid in everyone's memory, so that there was a cultural moment of nostalgia and increased rigidity as the old order scrambled to maintain itself against change. This was fertile ground for romance and Ford kept trying to use comedy as a weapon against social insurrection, but with little success. The joke is a leap towards order that in Ford's novels, as in the novels of so many of his contemporaries, falls short. In these novels, comic tone becomes a bewildered outcry, in several keys, against the loss of the old norms that formerly gave laughter its social meaning and its pleasure. In this kind of comedy, comic elements are stripped of their comic feeling.

THE SHAPE, SCALE, AND VOICE OF COMEDY IN JAMES AND FORD

The essential shape of a Jamesian comic romance, such as, for example, The Spoils of Poynton, moves from satire and comedy of manners to a serious lament over personal limitations and universal cultural deprivation. The simpler, satiric jokes tend to be clustered near the beginning and these gradually give way to more ambiguous and upsetting kinds of comic effects. At the same time, James arrays his characters on a wide spectrum from what he called "fixed" to "free," in other words from primarily comic to more complex in meaning and tonal resonance.[15] The free are often,

15. Henry James, The Art of the Novel, ed. R. P. Blackmur (New York, 1934), 131. Richard Poirier, in The Comic Sense of Henry James: A Study of the Early Novels (New York:

also, the romantic; they have the rich consciousness that is the stuff of ideals and dreams.

Even at a glance it is clear that Ford's spectrum of characters running from fixed to free is much narrower than James's. At one extreme, there is no one in a Ford novel as successfully above reproach or above the reach of simple ridicule as James's subtlely "free" heroes and heroines. (Ford *wished* some of his characters to be thus magnificent and irreproachable, but his doubts mingled with these idealizations, creating a more equivocal tone.) At the other end of the spectrum, there is no one as flatly presented as James's fixed fools in a Ford novel. Ford's subjective impressionism, his wandering sympathies, made it impossible for him to keep any character at such a strict distance from the reader. Even a cruelly satirized, two-dimensional character like Dowell's wife Florence in *The Good Soldier* is figuratively as well as literally married to Dowell himself: he shares her limitations which shape his own experience of life. Since Ford's characters—both grotesque and sympathetic—are closely bunched together, comic ironic tone lashes them all to some extent.

The careful differentiations in comic tone that mark people off from each other in a James story become in a Ford novel a means of vacillation *within* the presentation of one character. Hence we have a typical Ford hero viewed first with condescending and ironic pity, then with a flicker of angry satire, then with detachment. Because of Ford's sense of uncertainty about all fixed categories, each of his characters is forced to make a wavering journey back and forth between comic inelasticity and subjective insight many times. The extremes of James's moral and tonal spectra do not exist in Ford, where irony, the undercutting and reevaluating of meaning, is a constant process, inherent in the creation of every character.

But what of that other comic structure in James, the movement from satire and the comedy of manners towards a darker and more menacing vision of social life? Here Ford comes very close to James, with an affinity that runs deeper than any question of influence. Of course, in Ford's James pastiches, the movement from social comedy to a nonironic sense of loss or absurdity usually has less of the carefully plotted shape than it has in the stories of the Master. Instead, in Ford the two manners jockey each other

Oxford University Press, 1967), explores fully many aspects of James's comedy, only a few of which are relevant to my discussion of Ford. His main point is that James used comedy to give his characters life and a volatile independence from his highly structured novelistic designs.

uncomfortably, undercutting each other, so that nothing is ever as simply funny as James's comic scenes and nothing is ever as morally resounding as his tragic ones. Nevertheless, even in the rough, we can see Ford in these novels begin by laughing at social situations with a wit that came easily to him, then turn away from social relations with a despair that is very similar to James's. "The heart of another is a dark forest" was an aphorism he repeated in various contexts for years. Another favorite was "homo homini lupus."

Comedy in its character as a social corrective or even as only a reflector of social life had its limitations for James and Ford. They both felt an increasing scepticism about society's potential for supplying human beings with moral sustenance and coherence. They could write comedies of manners because they were both deeply attached to the social forms with their ancient meanings; they were interested in social conventions and believed in their necessity. But their position was painful. Increasingly, neither could write the kind of comedy that laughs at the fools and rewards the fine and sensible without ultimately undercutting it with another and contradictory vision of profound social and moral decay. They felt forced to abandon the classical form of comedy, which traditionally ends with some kind of reassurance about the continuance of familiar and comfortable social forms. Instead, in their novels, the social theme drops away, leaving the individual character to find his or her own subjective, asocial meaning for existence.

James's movement from social comedy to a profound seriousness is more detached than Ford's more erratic journeys from farce to pathos. However, in Ford's masterpiece, *The Good Soldier*, we can see his own peculiar species of triumph over this particular form. Here, for the first time, he controlled the movement from comedy to passionate seriousness using a consistent design. One of the technical miracles of that short book is the way in which the narrator develops, gradually changing the tone he takes towards his own story. He begins by being overwhelmed by his materials, and he narrates the early portions of the book with an air of innocence, mixing the important and the trivial in a way that is, at moments, very funny. Gradually, however, as he listens to himself tell his story, the jokes acquire a furious edge. Finally, though, his rage drops; the self-protective, satiric ironies that he has been using give way to a more warmly emotional treatment of his material. Increasingly his jokes are intended to rouse our sympathy; he feels more and more and makes fun less and less. Comic irony shades off into comic pathos and, finally, into a pathos which is not much undercut by irony at all.

This first sketch of *The Good Soldier* can hardly suggest the subtlety and richness of its comic structure, but what is important here is to make clear the similarities between James and Ford as they move from social comedy and satire to what is, in some senses, a more tragic idea of life. Both writers wished for a social coherence they could not find and both were capable, though in different ways, of constructing a romantic myth of absolute moral rectitude. For both, the final working out of this code became personal rather than social. James used irony like a scalpel to separate the levels of social failure. Ford, interested in making the same distinctions, could never use irony as so dispassionate a tool. Ford's narrator, Dowell, is both ridiculous and sympathetic at the same moment so that all James's careful differentiations are blurred in him. The ironic and the romantic— traditionally at odds—are, in Ford's novels, inextricably synthesized. But the similarities between James and Ford survive these differences of tonal range and narrative distance to form an essential relation: both writers were comedians who pushed the expressive possibilities of comic ironic tone to the limit and beyond, to where comic irony became something else.

The comedy of James and Ford is also crucially shaped by their conception of the scale of experience. We have already observed how Conrad's grand themes were on a different scale from any general moral pronouncements Ford felt himself prepared to make. James, too, had his own species of grandeur, his sweeping final judgments: "We shall never be again as we were."[16] But while Conrad still refers directly to the cosmic, James makes a universe out of a tea table. For James, the moral values are also counters in a parlor game. People must win or lose in the social terms of their daily lives. It is from the material of these essentially unheroic circumstances that James drew his romances with their subtle mixture of the serious and the trivial. It is the small details that make up the story, the little social exchanges. Deaths, passions, and night fears are indicated, as they are in the surface of our social life, rather than explored directly.

Ford was ultimately to transform Jamesian reticence into his own quite

16. This, of course, is the last sentence of *The Wings of the Dove*.

different form of indirectness. While James knew how to frame events, limiting the scope of each fiction, the limitations Ford placed on romance were messier, supplied by the limitations of his people's consciousness. Nevertheless, for Ford, the orderly tension in James between writing of the small social events and trying to see through them to the essential questions of virtue and happiness was intensely suggestive. He could not search for what the Master called "the tiny nugget" or "the speck of truth" hidden under all the dross of life—"clumsy Life . . . at her stupid work"—because he was always more immersed and overwhelmed by "clumsy Life" than James.[17] But, like his mentor, he was impressed by the closeness between the depths of human experience and the shallows. This grotesque juxtaposition became one of his themes and is a central component of his comic effects.

Ford responded to the controlled scale of feeling and event in James to the very full. He once listed as one of James's advantages as a novelist that "at an early age he had read the line of Musset's: 'Mon verre n'est pas grand mais je bois dans mon verre.'"[18] He has Dowell say in The Good Soldier, "Some one has said that the death of a mouse from cancer is the whole sack of Rome by the Goths, and I swear to you that the breaking up of our little four-square coterie was such another unthinkable event."[19] Reading this the first time, one cannot help thinking it absurd. What is the "unthinkable event," the death of the mouse, or the sack of Rome? Both seem out of scale to describe the elaborate intrigues and final breakup of Dowell's happiness, the "little four-square coterie." And yet, on subsequent readings, one comes to feel that this ambiguity, this inappropriate verbal decorum, is just the point. Dowell cannot decide whether his experience is universal or not. He cannot trust his own judgment in large matters or in small. "Forgive my writing of these monstrous things in this frivolous manner," he begs us.[20] Throughout the novel, his immense feelings find only petty or passive outlets. The values of his hero, Edward, become trivial on contact with modern reality. Dowell wonders: is there really something wrong with Edward or is it simply that the world has grown too small for him? Among other things, this is a question about contradictions

17. James, "Preface to The Spoils of Poynton," in The Art of the Novel, 120–21, passim.
18. Ford, Henry James, 120.
19. Ford, The Good Soldier, 17.
20. Ibid., 61.

in scale so that it is fitting that the monstrous and the frivolous are yoked in the synthesizing medium of Dowell's voice as he asks it. In this voice, with its supple variation in tone from the absurd to the pathetic, the grand to the trivial, Dowell is exploring a cultural crisis, a moment when the old virtues and meanings are losing force and scale while the new ones are still unclear. Ford's is a world of passion trivialized by confusion.

‹‹ ››

Both James and Ford are writers of great verbal wit. They share a sensitivity to the details of word choice, tone, and cadence that makes the surface of both men's narratives coruscate with sheer verbal brio. Ford only briefly fell into the error of directly imitating what he called James's "luxuriant phraseology," but his sentences try to do what James's do—to follow the mind constructing the thought. Both men wrote sentences that try to suggest by art in a rarefied and witty distillation the sinuous turnings, the changing levels of tone that are natural in thought and speech. Ford called this style in James "the treatment of mental progressions" and honored him as one of the few in Anglo-Saxondom to attempt this task.[21] Both writers were interested in colloquial speech and in finding a specifically *talking* voice, though Ford finally came to use this concept of the colloquial differently from James. His subjects did not as often lend themselves to dialogue. While James was dramatic, Ford tended to explore the colloquial voice of the mind's interior.

So far the emphasis has been on James's greater range as an artist, his greater ability to differentiate among his characters by means of narrative technique. In the sheer variety of themes he is able to handle from novel to novel, James far outstrips Ford's invention. However, when we come to talk about range of tone, Ford's own kind of variety and force of invention come to the fore. In any one story, James aims for consistency rather than variety in tone. This is not to say that Jamesian speech is all in one key. On the contrary, James can move, inside one sentence, from the highest formality to the most common colloquialism, to the ludicrous, gossipy, or chatty, but the fact remains that this movement itself becomes a homoge-

21. Ford, *Henry James*, 59, 168. I am indebted here to the insight of Kurt Oppens, friend and subtle reader of James, who suggests that James's delight in the very act of mimesis is so intense as to cast a radiance, typical of the comic imagination, over much that he writes. Ford shares this sense of narrative play in which the writer, however serious his overall theme, puts an antic disposition on in the sheer joy of verbal facility.

nized style. The most dramatic changes in James are to be found in his development of the situation, the movement of his plot. He sets up symbolically extreme, even grotesque psychological clashes. Behind the restraint and unity of his narrative surface, he is capable of melodrama, of every kind of surprise. Though the story of *The Good Soldier* has some of this melodramatic quality (which is part of the debt it owes James), it is really an exception in Ford's work as a whole. Ford's extremes, his surprises come less from incident, more from the manipulation of tone. His movement is in the voice, the narrative surface. His situations, unlike James's, are often quite static, while his style is forever diving beneath the surface in every direction, searching, by experimentation, for its own meaning.

In Ford's James imitation *An English Girl*, the hero, Don Kelleg, tries to tell his fiancée, Eleanor, and her father, Mr. Greville, his life story. He is incapable of telling the story straight. Like the Henry James surrogate figure one might imagine standing at Ford's elbow, Mr. Greville keeps exhorting Don to stick to the point, to keep the story moving, to put the emphasis in the right places. But this is just what Don (and Ford) cannot do. Unlike Mr. Greville (and unlike Henry James), Don is an impressionist. As a young man, he "had stowed himself away on a cattle-liner. . . . 'It was not a bad time that,' Don said. 'Some of the cattle hands belted us: some were quite decent and showed us how to catch the birds that live in the holds on the steers' backs. Little chaps with dabs of yellow on their heads, like fire.' He added the inconsequential detail that he still remembered the [ship] *Minnehaha* whenever he smelt a stable, and that he seemed to smell a stable whenever he saw a golden-crested wren."[22] In this passage we can see Ford using a comic mode utterly unlike anything in James. While James is always making distinctions, putting a finer and finer point on things, Ford is sometimes as concerned to blur distinctions, confuse the senses, and mix impressions. The passage above draws its wit from synesthesia, an impressionist's trick foreign to James's sensibility.

Sometimes, instead of wit, Ford uses humor. He dissolves the distance between characters, between narrator and reader, between right and wrong, and indulges in a tearful laugh or a comic cry over mankind's state of confusion. The traditional limitations placed on romance, that it be of another place or time, are supplied in Ford's novels by the limitations of

22. Ford, *An English Girl: A Romance* (London, 1907), 62.

the brain itself. Trapped inside a character's consciousness, the reader's view of reality is sharpened and narrowed to a small, romantically charged point.

Ford's way of mixing the comic and the romantic is also, finally, a departure from the way James synthesized these elements. In contrast to a typical James figure, a Ford character is often ridiculous and sympathetic in the same moment. In James, comedy tends to stay on the verbal surface, a coruscation of wit playing over hidden depths. In Ford, comedy is a more essential part of all that is sad. Ford makes both romance *and* comedy out of the same basic material, human limitation itself.

JAMESIAN PASTICHE IN SEVERAL KEYS: THREE ROMANCES

The Benefactor—1905

In going from Conrad and Ford's *Romance* of 1903 to Ford's imitation of James, *The Benefactor*, of 1905, one moves from elaborate, atmospheric and laborious impressionism to crisp verbal wit. There is an electric playfulness in the language here that was always Ford's but for which, at the same time, James's particular species of verbal daring must have offered an inspiring model. Conrad tried to make his narrator Marlow a colloquial speaker, but it was James who succeeded in creating a voice that twists and turns with the suppleness of thought and that rejoices in the pleasures of speech for their own sake.

The Benefactor is the story of George Moffat, a distinguished but underrecognized man of letters, who has spent the chief energies of his life on helping others realize their talents. As the novel develops we see George Moffat's generosity in a number of different lights. Is there something wrong with his dedication to other men's more vivid desires? Can the virtue of generosity be exercised in excess? What does one owe to others, what to oneself? These are problems many of Ford's heroes face. Ford himself was never to get far in untangling these complexities, though he did, in later novels, find more and more satisfactory correlatives for his own continuing uncertainty.

In *The Benefactor*, however, Ford's ambivalence about his romantic hero swamps his material in a confusion very unlike the carefully elucidated contradictions in the work of his mentor, James. "Like all great men," Ford writes of his hero, like "all our great figures, George, in fact, was romantic." And this figure, this patron to aspiring artists, was very dear to Ford. We know from his essays how much he wished himself to play the part of a sort of baronial uncle. The trappings of this role are a little theatrical and a little the worse for wear in *The Benefactor*, but Ford insists that difficult as it has become to assemble the traditional elements of *noblesse oblige*, George nevertheless is "the old, great man," a modern embodiment of the ideal figure of romance. Ford loves this hero's generosity, his feudal ideal of helping the weak, and he creates a sensible and fine heroine, Clara Brede, to fall in love with George Moffat and to say of him: "He was too good. People could not appreciate him. They *must* treat him badly. It was inevitable."[23] These are words that are spoken in earnest, without tonal ambivalence.

At the very moment, however, when we are most pressingly invited to take George and his kindness seriously, a note of irony obtrudes itself. George's protégé, Thwaite, is described as transparently unscrupulous. George's failure to recognize this fact and his insistence on Thwaite's excellence of character, even to the point of marrying him off to Clara's younger sister, Dora, begin to be both ridiculous and disturbing. The reader starts to wonder if George's generosity is perhaps an arcane promiscuity. The novel contains devastating criticism of George's idealism hidden in ironic little jabs made at George's grand manner or at his obtuseness. Indeed, he is "too good" and this makes him something of a fool.

George's brother Gregory acts as his foil. George says gaily to him, "Something good must result from bringing nice people in contact," to which his admiring but more worldly brother responds, "Haven't you grown out of that pathetic illusion?"[24] As the novel proceeds, George's errors in judgment become increasingly comic and pathetic until, finally, having helped all those unworthy of assistance, he finishes by rejecting the heroine, Clara Brede, who is at once the only person who really needs him and the only one capable of appreciating him for the gifted and innocently generous man he really is.

Like James, Ford probes his situation with the delicate instruments of small distinctions, ironic juxtapositions, and modulations in tone. At moments he seems to see clearly the nasty underbelly of *noblesse oblige*, to

23. Ford, *The Benefactor* (London, 1905), 51, 69, 95–96.
24. *Ibid.*, 30.

know everything about his subject, and to be capable of anatomizing it in the way James anatomizes the snobbery of the Bellegardes in *The American* or the fatal innocence of Daisy Miller. But, though Ford was the Master's faithful pupil and carefully put his George Moffat through the Jamesian wringer, he was not clear here, as James was always clear, about his own attitude towards his people. Instead, he allowed himself to fall sentimentally in love with aspects of his hero that his own irony tended to undercut or condemn. He loves his George for his ignorance of evil, as if innocence were an effective resistance to the material greed that surrounds him; yet Ford keeps noticing uncomfortably that some form of kidding is inevitable in any description of a man like George. His close authorial identification with the hero keeps drawing him into having to share that hero's humiliation at not knowing anything. The novel is full of the embarrassment inevitable in laughing at romance while adoring it.

This kind of failure of tonal and thematic clarity becomes most obvious at the end of the novel, at the point at which Ford's imitation of James is at its most overt and its least convincing. In the course of the book, all of the many obstacles, both material and moral, that stood between George Moffat and Clara Brede have been removed. In the last scene there is no reason for them to remain apart except for conventions they both are capable of rejecting. And yet, George decides for convention, for the debased world as it is, as it has appeared to be throughout the novel, a world in which the spirit of social order is utterly dead and the letter can but kill the generous of heart. Why? The denouement feels arbitrary, not inevitable. There is none of that exhaustion of all aspects of the situation that both Conrad and James thought necessary for the fully rendered tale. One cannot help suspecting Ford, at this point, of grabbing a Jamesian ending without paying for it. The end is a sort of slap in the face, a rejection of the vitality these characters seemed at some points in the story to contain in good measure.

Carol Ohmann has conjectured that Ford had another theme of which he was unconscious, the theme of George's sexual reluctance.[25] He draws back from sexual experience and from direct assertion in general. There is certainly good evidence for this reading in the text. Ford always emphasizes George's passivity in a tone that borders upon or crosses over into the

25. See Carol Ohmann, *Ford Madox Ford: From Apprentice to Craftsman* (Middletown, Conn., 1964), 41–45 *passim*.

comic: "It was as if, recognizing very fully the futility of human strivings, he were content himself to strive not at all, and had attempted to be, in a small, practical way, a tutelary of good fortune. He had tried to supply at odd moments those little bits of unexpected luck that will change a man's moods and the tide of a man's affairs."[26] This is a species of passivity yoked with fantasies of power to be found to some degree in all Ford's heroes. Impotence, both social and sexual, is one of his thematic obsessions. His heroes are always stepping aside to let the more vigorous play through. But, as Ohmann points out, in *The Benefactor* Ford is not yet aware of the importance of this theme. He subordinates it to that other great theme of English literature, the chastening of a romantic nature in the hard school of reality. But here, too, Ford's own vacillation about how much George *should* be mocked for his delusions confuses the resonance of his final gesture of renunciation. Is it a noble gesture, a recognition at the eleventh hour that he is mortal and must live as other men do? Or is it cowardly, a hysterical extension of the self-abnegating generosity which makes George act for others throughout the book but never for himself?

Ford's conscious apprenticeship to James in the writing of this novel may be responsible for some of these confusions and particularly for the unsatisfactory ending. For both James and Ford the themes of romantic self-delusion and of emotional and sexual passivity were central. Ford was deeply attracted to James's handling of materials so congenial to him. However, slow learner that he was, he tended, in *The Benefactor*, to adopt James's use of these themes somewhat literally. It was only gradually that Ford found his own version of this central myth of incapability and loss.

However, in *The Benefactor* Ford has already evolved a voice easily as complicated and colloquial in its own way as James was ever to use. Certainly the narrative surface of a James tale is not more verbally adventurous than Ford's experiments here with an elastic and lively narrative surface. But since he had the voice to speak long before he knew at all clearly what he wished to say, *The Benefactor* has peculiar tonal dissonances. Shafts of irony seem to hit inappropriate marks; solemnities disintegrate and become funny. Ford is hiding behind James. By having his hero say a too simple "No" he is evading his own important thematic question: How are men and women to proceed together when the old rules govern-

26. Ford, *The Benefactor*, 214–15.

ing their relations are everywhere being broken? This was never James's question. The falling asunder of man and woman seemed altogether natural to him. He accepted it as both psychologically true and symbolically suggestive of other failures in human beings. Ford, however, was finally to allow a later hero, Tietjens, to leave an unsatisfactory wife and live with a woman he can care about, albeit in the privacy of a country cottage. In spite of their passivity, both sexual and social, Ford's most interesting characters find themselves unavoidably in the middle of things. They wish they could say yes or are forced by life to say it, and then they pay a heavy price. This is a transaction with the experience of desire utterly different from anything in James.

An English Girl—1907

It is a pity that Ford's next romance, *An English Girl*, was written in the kind of haste its every page reveals since, at the same time that it is a far shoddier production than *The Benefactor*, it represents some interesting developments in Ford's discipleship to James. Ford began the novel very soon after making a brief and frustrating trip to New York where he had hoped, and failed, to make money. The novel bears the stamp of desperation, and at moments, it is the travelogue that would more appropriately have appeared as ephemeral journalism. But perhaps the most obvious sign of the pressure under which *An English Girl* was written is the way in which Ford took over the structures and assumptions of James's stories on the international theme whole, with hardly a gesture made towards selection, transformation, or digestion of the Master's materials. In one sense it is surprising to find Ford, with his profound self-consciousness about cultural differences, so superficial on James's great subject. One would have expected him to be able to dip down into his own particular well of knowledge on the subject of deculturation and come up with a real contribution to James's exploratory *oeuvre* on expatriate emotions. Indeed, there are flickerings of Ford's own talent for talking about the strange ramifications of nationality here and there in the book. The hero, Don Collar Kelleg, is a man who is perpetually lost and confused, a man whose cultural background is absurdly complex. Ford clearly equates these two things and feels a sympathy for his hero whose past contains such painful contradictions as a childhood spent in Hut, Montana, a father born in a Yorkshire workhouse (subsequently an unscrupulous American millionaire), and a

mother whose idea of life came from being an English lady's maid. Ford is
excited here, as he always was, by the difficulty of locating firm cultural
values, a thematic interest to which the international theme lends itself
particularly well. But the uncomfortable fact remains that in *An English
Girl* he constantly muddies the water of his contrasts. James's way of creating a complex situation by subtle indications was a dangerous model for
Ford to follow. If one is vague, as Ford was vague, about his own meaning,
speaking in telegraphic hints can only increase the reader's feeling that
nothing is clear.

Though Ford always tried to locate cultural referents amid a sea of shifting and unfamiliar impressions, it was James who had by far the greater
imagination for locating and clearly describing the specific content of different cultures. In contrast, Ford's gift was for the re-creating of the subjective experience of a culture. Strangeness never had for him the appeal it
had for James or Conrad, and in this sense he is not a romancer as they
were. He could know in depth only the familiar.

In *An English Girl*, Don Kelleg's brilliant father has died far off in
America leaving his son the richest citizen in the world. This immense
and magical wealth is like that of Newman in James's *The American* or of
Theodore Racksole in Arnold Bennett's *The Grand Babylon Hotel*. Bennett
let himself enjoy this typical situation of romance without strain and wrote
a harmless murder mystery. For him, romance was a holiday, but for both
James and Ford, it was an inescapable mode, though one which badly
needed to be transformed.

All the traits of Jamesian romance are evident in *An English Girl*. The
novel tries to deal with the slippery materials of modern life, recording a
host of impressions and making numerous distinctions, all within the classical structure of the simplest romances. The hero goes forth to a strange
place and he returns, but in the chastened, ironical romances of James and
Ford, his return has no comfortable finality. At the end of the novel, Don
cannot decide whether to return to England, social stability, and his fiancée, Eleanor, or to stay in the tumultuous, upsetting America where his
wealth was spawned and where it might actually stimulate social change.

Once again, as in *The Benefactor*, Ford borrows James's structure and
thematic preoccupations but cannot similarly appropriate his clarity of
purpose. Like George Moffat, Don is almost pathologically passive and
Ford vacillates between seeing this passivity as absurd and pitiful and

seeing it as the only honorable refuge in a world in which all action is evil. Once again, in the end Ford loves his romantic fool Don more than he criticizes him, while his tonal fluctuations reflect his thematic uncertainties. He wants to make Don a romantic, but he is not sure whether a romantic should reject America as no place for an idealist or should reject Eleanor, the English girl, because she represents convention and control instead of adventure and change. Ford never resolved this question of symbolic values in his mind and the novel flounders about as his characters saw back and forth between these two viewpoints. First, England is romantic because it is the place where William Morris socialism is taken seriously and where ladies trail around in medieval gowns and tradition is not forgotten. Then, America is romantic because it is lawless, wild, and strange and because it holds out a challenge to the William Morris idealist who would resuscitate old values in new worlds.

Ford loves Don for being a man who "hates modern circumstances," but he laughs at Don as a nineteenth-century European altruist thrown up absurdly naked on America's shores. The book is constantly satirizing Don's impractical aspirations for reform. Eleanor's father is treating Don with a sympathetic but comic irony when he says Don is "for Aestheticism right or wrong. He *does*, really, want the American people to go in for certain European virtues—for poetry and the Higher Thought and Rational Dress. Well, they can't! How can they? . . . [America] is made up of people who left Europe because they could not stand Tory restraints or poetic restraints." Eleanor wonders what Don will be able to do with the cowboys, to which Mr. Greville gives the snorting reply, "Do you think that Don is going to be able to convert *them* to medieval gowns or a love for Fra Angelico?"[27]

It is in the spoofing that goes on in such passages that Ford's novel undoes itself. He sends his hero up once too often and then cannot rescue him from absurdity at the end. For four-fifths of the novel's length, Ford seems to have written a book about a man who, while having all the money in the world, is pathologically unable to exercise any form of power, decision, or even desire. Then, at the eleventh hour, Ford turns his back on Don's grossly demonstrated inadequacies and proclaims him the new man, the poet who will have a new vision and who will rise above the

27. Ford, *An English Girl*, 268–69.

good sense and the steadiness of Eleanor to found an even more refined tradition. However, no such ending can erase our earlier impression of Don as hopelessly marginal and impotent. What we can see at the end of the novel, is Ford himself sifting his materials and making a choice for future use. He decides here, as he could not yet decide in *The Benefactor*, that he will choose his lost, absurd man over the efficient and clearheaded creatures who are at home in the modern world. With each novel Ford is becoming clearer about which side he likes best until, finally, in *The Good Soldier* the people in control, the knowing, sophisticated people like Florence and Leonora, are resoundingly rejected and the romantic idealist Edward and the lost American innocent Dowell are left as the only decent people in a crumbling world.

In *The Good Soldier* Ford's preference for the lost and superannuated over the knowing moderns works in part because he divides Don Collar Kelleg's traits into two people, Edward and Dowell. In *An English Girl* and even as early as *The Benefactor*, we can see Ford groping for this solution by giving his weak men, George and Don, various foils, strong men whom we can admire and who can speak for the hero who is speechless and confused himself. In *An English Girl* Ford's effort to put a Lancelot and a lost, impotent man in one body makes for an impossible tonal mixture. He cares about both of these types, sympathizes both with the romantic and with the emasculated, lost expatriate, but in *An English Girl* he has no device for examining these two motifs, no voice for joining them without unresolvable self-contradiction.

Henry James, while deeply involved in similar thematic questions, did not share Ford's unconscious confusion about the collision between the ironic and the romantic. Rather, he had conscious control over this collision and was able to balance within any particular story the various sides of his argument so as to keep them from undermining each other. In *The American*, for example—a novel thematically related to *An English Girl*—James does not choose to deal with all the contradictions that plague Ford's weaker book. In contrast to Don's complex and peculiar inability to leave his mark on events, Newman's failure to do so is shown as unequivocally honorable. Don's powerlessness is a mysterious and total wasting disease while Newman is powerless only because he will never fight with the dirty weapons of his supposedly aristocratic adversaries, the Bellegardes.

In a counter example, "The Figure in the Carpet," James has made a different decision about his chief character, the narrator. Sharp irony undercuts the narrator's earnest but utterly inadequate efforts to understand the mysteries of sex and of art which proliferate around him. James judges *this* powerlessness harshly. In contrast, Ford's ironies in *An English Girl* undercut wisdom as often as they undercut vice, until nothing can stand, the novel least of all.

All this is not to say James has a more simple theme or a more simple tone or technique than Ford. On the contrary, by reducing the surface noise that plays over Ford's handling of modern social complexity, James is able to say more than Ford can. In *A Portrait of a Lady*, for example, James is able to monumentalize *and* ironically undercut Isabel Archer, maintaining both dimensions. Isabel is diminished both by "modern circumstances" and by her own failure to find a significant way to live in these circumstances, but she has, too, the tragic stature that such a failure implies.

Perhaps this is just to say that James was the more skillful romancer, able and willing to abstract, simplify, and frame events while still leaving a wide field for suggestion. Ford, more mired in the contradictions of his material, had finally to create a voice one might call ironic romance. Here ridicule and pathos blend together and James's romantic moral categories get blurred.

<< >>

Ford's Jamesian pastiche in *An English Girl* is immature, but there remains one area in which the novel is an interesting advance, as an imitation, over *The Benefactor*. Though the earlier book often has a complex narrative surface, related to the middle-period James stories and novels Ford always liked best, this detailed verbal play rarely makes use of one profound element of Jamesian narration, that of metaphor. Romance relies heavily on metaphor and symbol as patterning devices. Insofar as Ford was trying to learn James's techniques for giving a significant symbolic structure to his sense of the chaotic mass of modern experience, his increased interest in metaphor is an exciting development. Here, for example, is a scene on shipboard. Don, Eleanor, and her father are on their way to America: "In the course of long wanderings in the deeper stages of the ship, with their slight but persistent odours, their slight but insistent creakings of polished wood and, their perspectives that seemed infinite, Don several times lost his way. It is indeed one of the most difficult things in the world, when you have turned a number of corners, gone down and up a number of oscillating staircases, to retain in your mind just where you are or even to realise whether you are going towards the stem or the stern." This picture of Don unable to tell if he is walking back towards the old world of Europe or forward, in harmony with the motion of the ship, towards the new world of America, carries all the feeling of Don's confusion and despair within it. He is the traditionalist who inherits an inadequate tradition, the romantic who doubts that man's potential is infinite. The "long wanderings," the "deeper stages," and "oscillating staircases" are all suggestive. Don is at sea, without a sense of direction. When he finally reaches the deck, he sees Eleanor far above him. He dives back into the maze of passages trying to join her but has trouble finding, from beneath, the exact location of the eminence on which she stands. At last he finds her and her father and, linked to them, he feels more solid. They are surefooted and "as if he had acquired their point of view . . . He didn't seem any more to float, lost and alone."[28] But Eleanor and her father are an anchor that cannot hold for Don. His uncertainty is as permanent as their solidity.

Unfortunately, Don's mind is a maze of contradictions in which the reader, too, gets lost, never clear whether he is moving forward with Don towards resolution or back with him into further doubt. Ford's use of metaphor is still muddy. He flirts with too many of the possibilities latent in the tropes he uses. But finally, in James's use of metaphoric constructions, the Master offered Ford a technique for making his materials more concrete and, at the same time, more suggestive. This process of stylistic development is at a rather primitive stage in *An English Girl*, but the novel marks for Ford an interesting beginning on the problem of making his subconscious work for rather than against him in the construction of believable and internally rich fiction.

A Call—1910

Turning from Ford's earlier Jamesian pastiches to his last, *A Call*, is a peculiar, an almost disconcerting, experience. It is not just that *A Call* is better than *The Benefactor* and *An English Girl*, for though it is, it is still a far cry from the effective complexity of Ford's best books. Rather, what is most immediately arresting about *A Call* is that it comes from the same kaleido-

28. Ibid., 112–13, 126.

scope of elements that make up the later and far better novel *The Good
Soldier*. Motifs, characters, phrases, and gestures to be found in the later
novel are already present in *A Call*, but they await a significant reordering,
a series of taps to the kaleidoscope, to make a good design into a great one.

At the same time, certain persistent immaturities in the earlier novels
are quite gone in *A Call*. Ford no longer romanticizes the passive hero;
instead, passivity is described as destructive and dangerous. Ford was later
to reintroduce his romantic affection for and identification with his passive
hero figures but never again was he to do so innocently, without full awareness of their participation in the evils around them.

A Call is the story of Robert Grimshaw who marries off the woman
he really loves to his best friend, Dudley, while continuing to offer
marriage—quite safely—to a woman he knows does not believe in marriage and is, indeed, phobic about the very idea of weddings. In consequence of his odd marriage, Dudley has a rather comic nervous breakdown
precipitated by a telephone call, and his new wife suffers. Indeed, everyone suffers because of Grimshaw's misplaced kindness and patronage. But,
in comparison to *The Good Soldier*, the end is happy, if the engulfment of
Grimshaw into the very marriage he seemed so willing to avoid can be
called happy. Certainly the couplings in *A Call* make an ironic comment
on the traditional endings of romance.

Placed next to *The Benefactor* and *An English Girl*, *A Call* is startlingly
unsentimental. For the first time, Ford seems to have decided not to identify too closely with any one character. This makes *A Call* thin in its char-
acterizations as the earlier novels are, but not for the same reason. The
earlier novels are thin because Ford identified too much with the subjective reality of his characters and failed to make differentiations from which
meaningful patterns could emerge. In contrast, *A Call* is thin because Ford
identified with no one. The earlier romances are often confused, author
and hero submerged together in a set of unexamined contradictions. In *A
Call*, Jamesian pattern triumphs over this kind of sentimental overiden-
tification of author with hero or author with romantic ideals. Indeed, in *A
Call*, Ford comes closer to having James's species of control over his materials than anywhere else in his *oeuvre*, and it remains to be seen how completely this kind of control served his ends.

Though Ford always admired how "impersonal" a writer James was,
how Flaubertian and objective, he was also always a little taken aback at
what he called "the singular pitilessness" of some of James's narrator fig-

ures.[29] A *Call* makes a serious stab, really Ford's first, at being coolly objective about what he called in the novel's "Epistolary Epilogue," "a little
episode—a small 'affair' affecting a little circle of people."[30] The "affair" is
itself a Jamesian concept, but in Ford, James's emphasis on defining frame
and focus becomes a more hectic expression of the constriction of a modern writer's subject matter: "For no one will to-day assert that his life is
really an affair of bashings of skulls, plots, conspirings, piracies, of Wall
Street panics, debauches, or the improbable rewards of virtue. And no one
will deny that his life is really a matter of "affairs"; of minute hourly embarrassments; of sympathetic or unsympathetic personal contacts; of little-
marked successes and failures, of queer jealousies, of muted terminations—
a tenuous, fluttering, and engrossing fabric. And intangible!"[31] How different from James's concept of the "affair" as a "tiny nugget, washed free of
awkward accretions and hammered into a sacred hardness." Life, for
James, is "all inclusion and confusion" while art is "all discrimination and
selection."[32] A *Call* fails in part because it tries so hard for "discrimination
and selection" when what Ford knows best is "inclusion and confusion."

◀ ▶

Ford loved James as a talker, but speech is a veil in James, hinting at what
can never be said. As Ford wrote admiringly:

> He can convey an impression, an atmosphere of what you will with
> literally nothing. Embarrassment, chastened happiness—for his
> happiness is always tinged with regret—greed, horror, social vacu-
> ity—he can give you it all with a purely blank page. His characters
> will talk about rain, about the opera, about the moral aspects of the
> selling of Old Masters to the New Republic, and those conversa-
> tions will convey to your mind that the quiet talkers are living in an
> atmosphere of horror, of bankruptcy, of passion hopeless as the Dies
> Irae! That is the supreme trick of art today, since that is how we
> really talk about the musical glasses whilst our lives crumble to
> pieces around us.[33]

29. See Ford, *Henry James*, 24–26 *passim.*
30. Ford, *A Call: The Tale of Two Passions* (London, 1910), 304.
31. Ford, *Thus to Revisit*, 36.
32. James, "Preface to *The Spoils of Poynton*," in *The Art of the Novel*, 120.
33. Ford, *Henry James*, 153.

But Ford could only write social conversation as farce. He could not take it seriously or make it portentous as James often did. Ford's interest was too much in subjective states of mind, and particularly in inner immobilization, for him to make a good dramatist. When the characters in A Call speak to each other, we may know they are suffering underneath, but what they say is absurd and distracts us from their feelings.

Ford had no intention to write farce. But because he had not yet found a way to set the superficial and banal social surface in a meaningful tension against personal feeling, A Call wanders, always in search of an adequate and expressive voice for its interesting themes. First, it is a farce that keeps metamorphosing into romance. Then, it is a psychological thriller but with characters who only at moments have anything more than caricatured psychologies. The people in A Call say very serious and portentous things to each other at times, but their passion is belied by the urbanity of the novel as a whole. Colloquial asides, full of irrelevance and charm, jockey with intense disclosures.

All of these miscellaneous elements belong in A Call and are a necessary part of Ford's vision of life. The problem lies in the fluctuating style of the novel's narration. In The Good Soldier Dowell narrates far more farcical and far more serious things than anything in A Call, and he convinces us of their appropriateness and importance through the medium of his voice. "A narrator," Ford once wrote, "being already a fictional character, may indulge in any prejudices or wrong-headednesses and any likings or dislikes for the other characters of the book, for he is just a living being like anybody else."[34] In other words, with the entrance of a perceiving intelligence like Dowell, Ford found a way to join the disparate and often cacophonous elements of his subject. The speaking voice of Dowell expresses confusions and doubts which, in A Call, readers are left alone to feel without any echo of support from the narrative itself. Dowell becomes a unifying device for the mixture of tones so central to Ford's greatest effects as an artist.

James always disliked the anarchy Ford loosed on the world with a narrator like Dowell. He speculated in the Preface to The Ambassadors about why he had not made Strether a first person narrator: "Had I . . . made [Strether] at once hero and historian, endowed him with the romantic privilege of the 'first person'—the darkest abyss of romance this, invet-

---

34. Ford, "On Impressionism," rpr. from Poetry and Drama, 1913, in MacShane (ed.), Critical Writings, 69.

erately, when enjoyed on the grand scale—variety, and many other queer matters as well, might have been smuggled in by a back door. Suffice it, to be brief, that the first person, in the long piece, is a form foredoomed to looseness, and that looseness, never much my affair, has never been so little so as on this particular occasion." James goes on to say that he preferred to have Strether talk to other characters, leaving the omniscient author to eavesdrop on these conversations, since in this way there is some kind of social control over Strether's revelations and the narration escapes "the terrible fluidity of self-revelation," hardly an escape managed by Ford.[35]

Years later, in *Parade's End*, Ford returned to the cool narrative stance of *A Call*, to impersonal narration hidden behind the mannerisms of impressionism, but by that time, he had fully understood that the subjective viewpoint was an essential element in all his work. In this, his masterpiece, he was able to tell his story from the insides of all his characters without needing to make them first person narrators.

‹‹ ››

The Benefactor, *An English Girl*, and *A Call* are all experimental stages in the development of the extraordinarily effective narrative voices of *The Good Soldier* and *Parade's End*. Critics have been rather harsh on these experimental productions. A weak 350-page experiment in Jamesian construction on the international theme does, perhaps, seem *de trop*. Samuel Hynes, for example, thinks of Ford as two different writers before and after 1913. But perhaps this impatience with Ford is misguided. Unlike his mentor, Ford did his learning with pen in hand and rushed into print works that read today like incomplete drafts that cry out to be recast, polished, deepened with another layer of feeling and ratiocination. James, a more economical and directed learner, did much of *his* experimentation in his tales. But Ford never shared the Master's genius for compression. The small "affair" left no scope for the essentially circuitous quality of his art. There is nothing that can be called a short story, or even a novella, in all his work. Instead, to explore each new idea, he wrote a long novel, often a potboiler like *An English Girl*. He suffered from his facility, writing a hundred pages as easily as twenty. But Ford was quintessentially a novelist, not

35. James, *The Art of the Novel*, 320–21.

a short story teller. In spite of their thinness, even his weakest novels have elaborate structure and their own peculiar kind of selectivity. They do not merely sprawl into their length; they circle into it, searching for their own centers. And there is method, if not clarity, in this search. Each of these novels contains moments of triumph when the experimenter makes his discovery.

Ezra Pound, also defending Ford from the impatience of critics, complained that we have not yet learned how to enjoy the particular value of "one of the finest chapters in English" if it is buried "in a claptrap novel." Ford, he said, "is still underestimated . . . [because] we have not yet learned that prose is as precious and as much to be sought after as verse, even its shreds and patches."[36] Perhaps it is unlikely for "one of the finest chapters in English" to be buried "in a claptrap novel." Novels, even the most condensed and poetic, have, finally, to do their work by accretion. But the spirit of Pound's generous remarks about Ford's "claptrap novels" contains this important truth: Ford was always a serious novelist, struggling for a form; with all their flaws, his practice pieces conceal wonders to delight and surprise the connoisseur of novels.

36. Eliot (ed.), *The Literary Essays*, 372.

Fantastic Books are not of necessity jocose books or ribald books, nor even extravagant books. . . . A book is a Fantastic Book, though time and space be commonplace enough, though the time be to-day and the place Camberwell, if only the mind perpetually travels, seeing one after another unexpected things in the consequence of human action or in the juxtaposition of emotions.

HILAIRE BELLOC, "On Fantastic Books," 1909

« 5 »

THE FANTASIES: COMEDY, IRONY, WELLS, AND CHESTERTON

EDWARDIAN FANTASY: ESCAPE AND VITALITY

FOR those romances that are primarily love stories or, in general, stories of human relationships, James was Ford's chief model during the Edwardian years. But there were other kinds of romance afoot in the land far more accessible and visible than what James was doing and more likely to lead to the making of money. Both good and bad, these books were not primarily about character. They were concerned with other kinds of exploration. Ford, always hard pressed for cash, drew the line at the kind of sentimental, formless, and unreal romances being written by Hall Caine, Marie Corelli, and the earnest but hopelessly slack Maurice Hewlett, all of which were immensely popular, critically admired, and financially successful. Even under duress, there were certain kinds of bad books he was incapable of writing. However, as one might expect of the always eclectic and suggestible Ford, good writers were able to lead him, even if hopelessly astray, when the Hall Caines of this world could not. Men like Wells and Chesterton were serious reflectors of their time in precisely the way Ford cared to be. They wrote fantastic romances because they wanted to generalize, to achieve by a shortcut an overview. For a time, Ford copied them in the hope that their means of escape from or transcendence of modern, sublunary confusion might be his.

About 1906 Ford began to spend more and more of his time in London. His last really intense year with Conrad, 1904, had been followed by mental collapse. In 1905 the success of his collection of essays, *The Soul of London*, helped him begin a process of regeneration. By 1906 Ford was, for the first time since his Pre-Raphaelite boyhood, a figure in London, a literary man about town. First the *Daily Mail* and then the *Tribune* commissioned "Literary Portraits" from him, of which he wrote forty in 1907 and 1908. These articles gave Ford a public platform. They were topical, chatty, engaged, and engaging, written in that mixture of flippancy and urbanity which is the voice of so much Edwardian ephemera. It was during this exciting period, which finally led to Ford's influential editorship of the *English Review* in 1909, that he seems to have made memorable contact with the two men whose influence was central both on his own idea of fantasy and on all Edwardians' idea of this most typically Edwardian of genres: H. G. Wells and G. K. Chesterton.

In that *annus mirabilis*, 1906, which seems to have been such a period of motion and change for Ford, he and Wells saw each other constantly, for it was in that year that Wells made his notorious bid for leadership of the Fabian society, a political move Ford seems hardly to have understood but which he noisily supported. The two men met often and Ford joined happily in Wells's criticism of the earnest Fabians, Sidney and Beatrice Webb and Hubert and Edith Bland. It was after this period of real friendship in what was usually a more uneasy lifelong acquaintanceship that Ford wrote his only real imitation of Wells, his fantasy *Mr. Apollo*.[1]

The case of G. K. Chesterton's relationship to Ford is quite different. It would be misleading to speak of his having had any direct influence on Ford, but certain shared needs and experiences connected them. The two men began to see each other regularly in 1906 when Ford started going to the monthly meetings of Chesterton's Square Club. There he discussed new books with Walter de la Mare, John Masefield, John Galsworthy, Algernon Blackwood, Edgar Jepson, Maurice Baring, E. C. Bentley, and, most importantly, with Hilaire Belloc and Chesterton himself. At the same time he was attending weekly lunches at the Mont Blanc restaurant

---

1. For a discussion of Wells's influence on Ford's satires, see Chapter 6. I shall have nothing to say about James's fantasies here since Ford was not particularly interested in them; they do not provide discernible elements in his fantasies. (See Ford, *Henry James*, 121–23.) Virginia Woolf, in her essays "Henry James's Ghost Stories" (*TLS*, 1921) and "The Supernatural in Fiction" (*TLS*, 1918), discusses how James does, and does not, fit into the general resurgence of interest in the ghostly I am describing here.

where he continued to see his older friends and influences, Edward Garnett, W. H. Hudson, and Conrad. Though Ford was always sensitive to
whatever issues were in the air, this exposure to people most of whom were
writing constantly for journals and the press brought him very near indeed
to the prevailing winds in both politics and art. It is in this context of a
shared cultural ambience that one can speak of Chesterton's influence on
Ford. Chesterton provides a frame through which to see the ways in which
Ford did, and finally did not, incorporate the Edwardian passion for the
fey, the paradoxical, and the magical.

《 》

From the 1880s onwards, the perennial English interest in fantasy had begun to develop a new side, an avidity and sometimes a desperation that
was a direct response to modern circumstances. There was a growing interest in the unseen and the unknowable. Many late Victorians hoped they
might still be found lurking behind the ever thickening veil of materialism. The popular fascination with Madame Blavatsky is but one instance
of what was a vital and varied cultural phenomenon. Fantasy, which has
always been a delicious and treasured element in English literary tradition,
grew into a new prominence. Writers like William Morris, Walter de la
Mare, W. H. Hudson, Kenneth Grahame, George Macdonald, M. R.
James, Rudyard Kipling, and Henry James wrote fantasy as an honored
part of their *oeuvres*. They were tapping both the old national taste for the
disclosure of the marvelous beneath the trappings of the everyday and also
the new, more desperate interest in sublunary spiritual manifestations as
replacements for traditional belief. These transitional writers could still
play seriously with this world of belief and they wrote fantasy with gusto.

The group that can be called (spiritually if not always chronologically)
the next generation to write fantasy, writers like Arthur Machen, Wells,
James Barrie, Chesterton, Belloc, and Beerbohm wrote of the marvelous
with a difference. Generally they tended to be either ironic and fey or sentimental. They were terribly self-conscious about their magic. One certainly feels, in reading Edwardian fantasy, that one is confronting the
hopelessly terrestrial, literal side of magic. Did the Edwardian writers of
fantasy expect to be hauled down out of the sky if they attempted flight?
Edwardian magic is much more mannered and insistent than that of earlier
generations.

Ford liked the fantasy tradition as it had come down to him in the rich examples of his boyhood and he shared his contemporaries' need of fantasy, an Edwardian bastion against modern circumstances. But he was uneasy with the new tendency of the tradition to skitter off into meretricious escapes. Pained himself over spiritual decay, he did not always trust the idealism that by-passes real experience or that too blandly transcends. He wrote typical Edwardian fantasies and he wrote denunciations of these sorts of self-serving potboilers. English taste, Ford wrote in 1921,

> takes refuge in the feebly pawky and the feebly negational—or the feebly immoral: in, that is to say, *Tom Jones*; the essays on buttered toast of Charles Lamb; the works of Lewis Carroll; nonsense rhymes in the London periodical called *Punch*; in the negational nonsense plays of Mr. Shaw, the more positive, sentimental nonsense of Sir James Barrie, the topsy-turvey Ballades of Mr. Belloc and Mr. Chesterton. This *genre* . . . is Anglo-Saxondom's sole exclusive contribution to the literature and thought of the world. Considering it aloofly from almost any philosophic standpoint you can only regard it as purely immoral, as almost always negational, as the last protest of a comfortable Class against any fine-nesses that can be achieved without the accompaniment of Comfort. But it is all these things, as a rule, in only a very gentle, gentlemanly degree and as a literature of escape for the wealthy or for those who consider that they ought by divine right to be wealthy it has no doubt its place in the world. It is England's substitute for Realism.[2]

Actually, as Ford's wide range of examples themselves attest, humor is only one in a large arsenal of "substitutes" English writers have had for realism. And though in 1922, with a grand sweep of the hand in his best lecturer's manner, Ford looks down on these substitutes, these escapes, by 1914 he had experimented with every means the English ever invented to forget the quotidian. As always, in him, we have an intensely experimental writer, one who embraces dynamically, if not always consciously, the contradictions of his time. He agreed with the disapproving Conrad that the attraction of fantasy was nothing more than "the seduction of ir-

2. Ford, "Towards a History of English Literature" (Unpublished typescript, *ca.* 1922, Olin Library, Cornell University, Ithaca, N.Y.).

responsible freedom."[3] At the same time, Wells's and Chesterton's uses of the fantasy form were suggestive to him. Though their solutions were not finally to be his, their problems were.

« »

In 1904 *Peter Pan* was the most successful play in London, playing not to children as it does now, but to enthusiastic adult audiences. Ford had a condescending affection for Barrie whose charm he saw as a sincere "yearning to see life as an affair in which little jokes will not only count but solve problems."[4] Of the class that flocked to see Peter Pan remain forever a boy, Arnold Bennett wrote, "It quite honestly asks 'to be taken out of itself,' unaware that to be taken out of itself is the very last thing it really desires."[5] Indeed, the innocence of childhood, when desires can be acted upon without much scrutiny given to motives, is a fitting image for the Edwardian decade. And using this metaphor, the war becomes, of course, adulthood.

If unserious novels were a refuge for what Bennett called "the dullest class in England," some very serious writers tried to use the conventions of escape for a different purpose.[6] Magic is a species of strong jolt, and in some writers' hands, it was used as a thunderbolt, an effort to imaginatively challenge a philistine audience on the brink of social upheavals it scarcely imagined.

This was H. G. Wells's use for fantasy. He wished to force the Edwardians to notice the latent possibilities in the material world that surrounded them so solidly. In his hands, fantasy became an imaginative projection of modern fears. He took the complacent Edwardian who resisted change and lifted him off the earth in the inhuman grip of a Martian invader. Indeed, after feeling the essential pessimism inherent in *The War of the Worlds,* in which no amount of foresight could have saved mankind and only a force as inhuman as that of the Martians themselves could come to the rescue, one can perhaps look on Edwardian escapism as at least as desperate as it was blind or tawdry. The Edwardians recoiled from the dissolv-

3. Conrad, "John Galsworthy" (1906), reprinted in Wright (ed.), *Joseph Conrad on Fiction,* 89–90.

4. Ford, *The Critical Attitude,* 85.

5. Arnold Bennett, "Middle-class," in Bennett, *Books and Persons: Being Comments on a Past Epoch, 1908–1911* (London, 1917), 73.

6. *Ibid.,* 75.

ing universe science was beginning to depict; they took refuge in visions of the past to escape T. H. Huxley's idea that evolution was cyclical and might, at any point, begin its downward curve. In *The War of the Worlds* Wells tells us offhandedly that the first to die in one of the early military assaults on the Martians, a man we never meet, was one Major Eden. Indeed, many Edwardians were suffering from an indefinable sense of loss. They had not known Eden, but they imagined its loss all the more poignantly for that very reason. Huge structural changes took place in English society and hence in English social ideas during the decade, and fantasy was one of the probes some of the most socially responsive and aware Edwardian writers such as Wells used to project themselves into the new worlds that were coming into being.

In *The Invisible Man* Wells's hero gives an elaborate pseudoscientific explanation of how he made himself invisible. It is all perfectly logical. We can follow him step by step. But at the end of his discussion, a more primitive sense of awe at the idea of conquering the ancient intractability of matter overcomes him. "I could be invisible!" he cries. "To do such a thing would be to transcend magic."[7] Certainly for some Edwardians, science had completely replaced magic; but for others, science was itself a kind of magic. Large masses of people were benefitting from electric lights, telephones, and medical discoveries, and most had no idea how these worked. For them, Wells's science-magic made perfect sense.

In Wells two powerful streams of thought merge or, rather, lie close enough together to engage in a dialectical conversation as they run along. One stream is the Victorian romance with science. Wells was as thunderstruck by science's potential and could be as moved and engaged by its power as the most sunny optimists of the 1850s, who beheld English technical achievements and saw only that they were good. The other stream of Wells's thought is the underbelly of this Victorian romance with technology. At night the scientist goes home. He muses on the explosion of new knowledge. He dozes in his chair only to find himself having nightmares: *The Time Machine* (a bad dream about evolution running down like a tired clock), *The Island of Dr. Moreau* (a bad dream about the moral questions accompanying scientific experimentation and improvement of the species), *The Invisible Man* (a bad dream about scientific discovery in the

7. H. G. Wells, *The Invisible Man: A Grotesque Romance* (London, 1898), 167.

hands of a madman), *The War of the Worlds* (alien technology as a killer of man). These stories, while obviously coming from the pen of one entranced by science, are nevertheless expressions of deep ambivalence towards discoveries that must sometimes have appeared to the popular mind to be as slippery and out of control as magic itself.

In the expression of this ambivalence towards the powers of science, Wells comes much closer to people like Chesterton and Belloc than at first appears. Modernity alarmed him as it alarmed them. The earnestness of Wells's scientific romances tends to obscure his similarity to a farceur like Chesterton, but at the same time that Wells was writing these serious fantasies, he was also playing Chestertonian magic tricks in novels like *The Wonderful Visit* and *The Sea Lady*. These more directly expressed the popular bewilderment about the boundaries between science, magic, materialism, and spirituality, and they expressed it in a typically Edwardian way. The tone is often cozy, the magic lumberingly earthbound. In these novels one can hear the voice of so much of the ephemera of the period, a voice that is both charming and fatuous and always a trifle self-congratulatory. In Wells's case, however, behind the hearty righteousness lies anxiety and an angry, often ugly struggle for intellectual closure, for final solutions.

« »

In Chesterton, a related tone of voice has a different history and meaning. In him, Wells's hidden dangers are, instead, hidden promises. In a typically Edwardian image of Arthur Machen's, a respectable north London neighborhood appears to certain people as a wildly beautiful garden rather like Eden. This kind of magical transformation was perfect for deprived urbanites in search of relief and recalls Chesterton's remark that "a street is really more poetical than a meadow, because a street has a secret . . . the fact that all romantics know—that adventures happen on dull days, and not on sunny ones. When the chord of monotony is stretched most tight, then it breaks with a sound like song."[8] Of all the Edwardian writers who can be said to have tried to use fantasy as an expression, not of escape, but of positive values, G. K. Chesterton is surely the chief. Escapist he would immediately have owned himself to be, but he would have quickly added

8. G. K. Chesterton, *The Napoleon of Notting Hill* (1904; rpr. Harmondsworth, Middlesex, 1946), 66, 16.

that the blighted, materialist quality of modern life made active efforts to escape the only honorable and responsible occupation.

In Chesterton's case the Edwardian canard about the grayness of modern life and the necessity of discovering some spring of magic beneath it acquired spiritual and moral passion. The contrast between modern surfaces and the vivid spirituality those surfaces can deaden or obscure but can never destroy is always his great subject, the subtext of his every novel, story, and essay. When he looked for a tone that would best express this interest in transcendence amid modern circumstances, he found paradox, childlike playfulness, and nonsense were the literary voices that came most easily. In his dedicatory poem in *The Man Who Was Thursday*, Chesterton described the things he had hated in the eighties and nineties, the materialism and the decadence, and offers his own kind of gay, laughing spirituality as the proper cure:

> TO EDMUND CLERIHEW BENTLEY
> A cloud was on the mind of men,
> And wailing went the weather,
> Yea, a sick cloud upon the soul
> When we were boys together.
> Science announced nonentity
> And art admired decay;
> The world was old and ended:
> But you and I were gay;
>
> . . . .
>
> Fools as we were in motley,
> All jangling and absurd,
> When all church bells were silent
> Our cap and bells were heard.[9]

The sounds of cap and bells, "all jangling and absurd," were major voices in Edwardian literature. Using this slippery contemporary idiom, Chesterton wandered back and forth between Peter Pan nonsense—that is, a nonsense in which childhood innocence is a sentimental pose, a form of what Conrad called fantasy's "irresponsible freedom"—and a greater nonsense

9. G. K. Chesterton, *The Man Who Was Thursday: A Nightmare* (Harmondsworth, Middlesex, 1908), 7–8.

that is as much Christ-like as childlike and which genuinely contains freshness of vision.

It was of course Chesterton's Catholicism that saved him from the difficulties that weighed down the fantastic flights of many other Edwardian writers. Often the magical creations of his contemporaries could hardly hoist themselves up on their rainbow-colored wings: Wells's mermaid in *The Sea Lady* has great trouble managing her large, scaly tail and Kipling's phantom rickshaw is more solid than any phantom can be and still deserve the name. But the greater earnestness of Chesterton's magic did not finally protect him from the complexities of Edwardian ambivalence. Like his contemporaries, when he wished to be serious, he could find no way to be serious *enough* without some kind of comic or ironic exaggeration. He tried to make a virtue of these tonal contradictions, but he could only rescue Edwardian drollery from its own shallowness some of the time.

Nevertheless, Chesterton's struggle to combine significance and horseplay permeates his work. This is a combination that was always suggestive for Ford. He must have been interested in the virtuosity with which Chesterton combined glib Edwardian playfulness with the serious paradoxes of Catholic belief. With a good faith few of his contemporaries could share, Chesterton was always on the lookout for ways to reintroduce the unseen, the mysterious, and hence the divine into descriptions of the modern world.

Ford had no such spiritual anchor. He, too, was Catholic, but without the temperament for certainty. When he wrote about the experience of imaginative impoverishment in modern circumstances, he often made use of the ironic and the ridiculous, but behind the mask of lightness, there was serious doubt and pain. Chesterton, in contrast, could still really laugh. Forced into laughter as he was by an age that laughed perhaps too much or for shaky reasons and put on the defensive as a man of faith by an age of confused and unstable beliefs, he nevertheless embraced the voice of Edwardian gaiety as a positive weapon. In him, laughter is still a rebellion against, rather than an acquiescence in, the reduced scale of modern life.

An appropriately silly quotation provides a final example of how Chesterton uses the often self-indulgent devices of Edwardian fantasy to play joyfully with the idea and the hope of spiritual renewal. The passage is from *The Club of Queer Trades*, which is a series of sketches revolving around men who have found new and unique ways to earn a living. In this particular story, a Major Brown has been much bothered when stumbling by chance on the activities of Club of Queer Trades' member Northover whose special work it is to provide surprise, adventure, and romance to modern men. Northover explains his work:

"Major," said he, "did you ever, as you walked along the empty street upon some idle afternoon, feel the utter hunger for something to happen—something, in the splendid words of Walt Whitman: 'Something pernicious and dread; something far removed from a puny and pious life; something unproved; something in a trance; something loosed from its anchorage, and driving free.' Did you ever feel that?"

"Certainly not," said the Major shortly.

"Then I must explain with more elaboration," said Mr. North-over, with a sigh. "The Adventure and Romance Agency has been started to meet a great modern desire. On every side, in conversa-tion and in literature, we hear of the desire for a larger theatre of events—for something to waylay us and lead us splendidly astray. Now the man who feels this desire for a varied life pays a yearly or a quarterly sum to the Adventure and Romance Agency; in return, the Adventure and Romance Agency undertakes to surround him with startling and weird events. As a man is leaving his front door, an excited sweep approaches him and assures him of a plot against his life; he gets into a cab, and is driven to an opium den; he re-ceives a mysterious telegram or a dramatic visit, and is immediately in a vortex of incidents. A very picturesque and moving story is first written by one of the staff of distinguished novelists who are at pres-ent hard at work in the adjoining room. Yours, Major Brown (de-signed by our Mr. Grigsby), I consider peculiarly forcible and pointed; it is almost a pity you did not see the end of it. . . .

"We believe that we are doing a noble work," said Northover warmly. "It has continually struck us that there is no element in modern life that is more lamentable than the fact that the modern man has to seek all artistic existence in a sedentary state. If he wishes to float into fairyland, he reads a book; if he wishes to dash into the thick of battle, he reads a book; if he wishes to soar into heaven, he reads a book; if he wishes to slide down the banisters, he reads a book. We give him these visions, but we give him exercise at the same time, the necessity of leaping from wall to wall, of fighting strange gentlemen, of running down long streets from pursuers—all healthy and pleasant exercises. We give him a glimpse of that great morning world of Robin Hood or the Knights Errant, when one great game was played under the splendid sky. We give him back his childhood, that godlike time when we can act stories, be our own heroes, and at the same instant dance and dream."[10]

The critical literature reels in confusion over how to take this non-sense, Hugh Kenner calling Chesterton a great philosopher, a true Tho-mist, while Stephen Spender sees him and all his works as the "collapse into self-parody" of all serious nineteenth-century efforts to revivify past traditions.[11] And these extremes of response are understandable. Chester-ton certainly did flirt with all that was meretricious in the large Edwardian literature of escape. In this short passage, Whitman's "driving free" is triv-ialized; knight errantry is an old chestnut; and modern man's need to slough off the alienation of industrialized, bourgeois society is reduced to a mere game. The imagination is short-circuited and therefore takes a short-cut: spiritual relief from the dullness of modern life comes, not through clarity and power, but through a mystified and meaningless "vortex of inci-dents" as conceived, of course, by some Edwardian hack writer of fantasy, "our Mr. Grigsby." The layers of irony, playfulness, seriousness, cuteness keep coming off in a dizzying striptease. This is a dance Ford performed too. But while Chesterton's single-minded Catholic purpose showed clearly through the topsy-turvy world of fey ironies that endlessly turn back on themselves, Ford was mired in these ironies and had more diffi-culty resolving them.

« »

Ford observed the problems Wells and Chesterton had in bringing angels to the earth. To dramatize such magical events with verisimilitude, they had to write in a comical, ironic, playful tone. This was the only voice for

10. G. K. Chesterton, *The Club of Queer Trades* (London [1905]), 43–46.
11. Hugh Kenner, *Paradox in Chesterton* (London, 1948), *passim*; Stephen Spender, *The Struggle of the Modern* (Berkeley, 1963), 210.

peopling Edwardian London with supernatural visitants. To write serious fantasy about the limitations of materialism, one had first to acknowledge the ludicrous aspect of the contrast between the magical and the material London. The literary results were, predictably, uneven. Perhaps the Edwardian conjurer was slightly ashamed of himself for trying to map the unseen. Certainly he made few distant journeys into truly unknown regions.[12]

Wells's tone begins with this typically Edwardian coziness that conceals a hidden danger and develops into a righteous, unironic proclamation of that danger. In Chesterton and Belloc the same conflict is resolved in a different key. They saw modern life as an unfortunate episode, a moment of confusion like a sickness from which recovery was certain. For men of Chesterton's ilk, and there were many among the Edwardians, science was a bad modern joke and its claim to answer the riddles of the universe merely ridiculous. Here, for example, is *phantaste* Arthur Machen:

> Common sense tells us that Achilles will flash past the tortoise almost with the speed of the lightning; the inflexible truth of mathematics assures us that till the earth boils and the heavens cease to endure, the tortoise must still be in advance; and thereupon we should, in common decency, go mad. We do not go mad, because, by special grace, we are certified that, in the final court of appeal, all science is a lie, even the highest science of all; and so we simply grin at Achilles and the tortoise, as we grin at Darwin, deride Huxley, and laugh at Herbert Spencer.[13]

It is hard for us to imagine now how earnestly the Edwardians wanted to laugh at Darwin, at Huxley, at Spencer. Science had won the battle for acceptance as a source of truth and power. The only weapon left on the losing side was derision. But there was something grim in this science that made it hard to laugh playfully, openly, without irony. The strained jocularity in so much Edwardian writing, particularly in fantasy, comes in part from the difficulty of breaking the ever tightening link with logic. These fantasies were straining to get free from science and from the bounds of earth to find a more spiritually satisfying species of order. In this sense,

12. There are exceptions, Kipling notable among them.
13. Arthur Machen, "The Terror" (1917), in *Tales of Horror and the Supernatural*, (1948; rpr. New York, 1973), II, 213.

Edwardian fantasy is a part of a larger revolt against modern organization, against blue books and rational bureaucratic planning, a retreat from the realities of the modern industrial state.

Why, asked Belloc, are modern men without the pleasures of ritualized festival? When men were "secure of their philosophy and social scheme," they could delight in Saturnalia, in topsy-turvydom, in turning these sound traditions on their heads for a time: "They have always done this in healthy States, and if ever our State gets healthy they will begin to do it again." That the state is ill appears, said Belloc, "in the irony which is an increasing feature of our letters."[14]

FORD'S FANTASIES: FALSE HILARITY, TRUE MELANCHOLY

Ford wrote in 1907, "Though I love fairy-tales, and love realism, cheese and sherbet do not mix."[15] This mixture may indeed be confusing to the palate, but Ford mixed them often, as did so many of his phantasmagorical contemporaries. After his early fairy tales of the nineties, Ford's novels of magic are *The Inheritors* (1901, with Conrad), *Mr. Apollo* (1908, close in idea to Wells's *The Wonderful Visit*), *Ladies Whose Bright Eyes* (1911, Ford's version—Pre-Raphaelite medievalism added—of Mark Twain's *A Connecticut Yankee in King Arthur's Court*), and *The Young Lovell* (1913, another Pre-Raphaelite vision of medievalism).

In *The Inheritors* a frightening woman comes from the fourth dimension to take over England, a notion Wells made popular a few years earlier in *The Time Machine*. But *The Time Machine* is a story about science. For Ford, the romance of the fact, which so excited Kipling, Wells, and others, had absolutely no allure. "In those days," he wrote, "no one bothered his head about Science. It seemed to be an agreeable parlour game—like stamp-collecting. And I am bound to say that it still seems to me like that. One did very well without it in those days; one will do still better without it in the not-distant future when it will be dethroned."[16] This millennial ring, so exactly like Belloc's, is a recurring element in much Edwardian

14. Hilaire Belloc, "On Saturnalia," in Belloc, *On Everything* (London, 1909), 40–41.
15. Ford, "Literary Portraits: VI Miss May Sinclair," *Tribune*, August 31, 1907, as excerpted in David Dow Harvey, *Ford Madox Ford: A Bibliography of Works and Criticism* (Princeton, 1962), 152.
16. Ford, "H. G. Wells," in Ford, *Portraits from Life*, 145.

art. Fantasy lends itself particularly well to time traveling of this sort. Wells, the scientist manqué, travels forward in anticipatory anxiety while Ford and Belloc travel backwards, trying to imagine time as a reassuring circle that can return one to a treasured past.

In *The Inheritors*, Ford's only excursion into Wells's species of futurity, all danger is concentrated in the loss of the past. When Ford's Fourth Dimensionist takes over England, life becomes grayer than the already alarming modern grayness before. The hero's penalty for helping the invader, whose goal it is to wipe out all remaining trace of past values, is to live "like a ghost in a bottomless cleft between the past and the to come," locked in bewildered subjectivity for eternity.[17]

This is not Wells's kind of magic. Ford's Fourth Dimensionist is just a weary device to describe the descent of a final materialism, the end of *all* magic. The strangeness, the fantasy, comes, not from the Dimensionist's unconvincing presence, but from the mind of the hero who is plunged into a darkness that is, finally, more profound than that into which Wells's time traveler goes on his last journey.

Again, in *Ladies Whose Bright Eyes* Ford uses magic to traverse time, and once he has arrived at his locus of interest, in this case the fourteenth century, his purpose is social criticism of the Edwardian present. He uses verbal archaisms to suggest the past, but otherwise he practices a strict, untranscendent realism in his descriptions of the medieval world, akin to Pre-Raphaelite realism in paintings like *Christ in the House of His Parents*.

The mysticism of *The Young Lovell* is more profound. Ford took this novel very seriously and his medieval knight, Lovell, is caught between a dying social ideal, perfect feudalism, and an undying perfection, *la belle dame sans merci*, who finally seduces him away from all worldly struggle. The novel collapses into a dream. Lovell is in a sorcerer's trance for six months and the action of the novel revolves around this motionless monolith, a man dreaming of a perfect beauty and experiencing a perfect love. He is in another form of Edwardian never-never land.

Finally, however, it is in *Mr. Apollo* that we can see most clearly how Ford reacted to the general interest in the fantasy novel that surrounded him. Conrad, who always disliked the form, spoke of it as soaring, but "on

17. Ford and Conrad, *The Inheritors: An Extravagant Story* (1901; rpr. Garden City, 1923), 211.

goose's wings," finding in advance the perfect critical metaphor for Mr. Apollo.[18] The first section of the novel is a description of how the arrival on earth of the god Apollo appears to the constable in Anglesey Square who first sees him, descending slowly through the air, wearing impeccable evening dress. He appears to be travelling down a wire—"The constable had seen the like at the play."[19] And so have we seen the like, but has a god ever come as stolidly to earth as this Apollo comes?

Wells's The Wonderful Visit begins with a similar scene, but his angel's descent is more magical. The tone of the novel is light, its purpose mildly satirical. In The Wonderful Visit we know where we are. Though Wells was afraid of the potential for evil in nature, in man, and in the hidden future of both, his comedies and scientific romances still have an attractiveness, a chattiness, that implies a comfortable familiarity with the everyday. In contrast, Ford's Mr. Apollo is not charming, but imperious, suave, and powerful. The greater brutality of Mr. Apollo comes, in part, from Ford's greater satiric seriousness, but it comes, too, from his inability to maintain the unstrained gay-heartedness of the form. He was uncomfortable with the literal magic he was imitating from Wells.

Indeed, all purely spiritual transcendence was essentially foreign to Ford. A number of critics have written of Ford's Catholicism and have seen in his work a serious religious vision, but in fact, there is no more temperamentally agnostic writer than Ford.[20] He had his absolute beliefs, but these were essentially secular. He often takes a doctrinaire tone in his essays and memoirs, but on further examination his pronouncements are more likely to be on the subject of garlic, of saffron, or of art, than about the nature of the Godhead. The variety of spiritual quests proliferating during all his formative years never preoccupied him, and indeed, when he did treat of them, it was always with a gently mocking irony.

Nevertheless, with his usual patient and intelligent response to the quality of those books he was imitating, Ford touches all the bases of Edwardian fantasy in Mr. Apollo. The set pieces of the genre, the gray London streets for a moment irradiated, the lover of facts confounded by

18. Conrad, "John Galsworthy" (1906), in Wright (ed.), Joseph Conrad on Fiction, 90.
19. Ford, Mr. Apollo: A Just Possible Story (London, 1908), 6.
20. See particularly Caroline Gordon's A Good Soldier: A Key to the Novels of Ford Madox Ford, University of California Chapbook, No. 1 (1963), and Robert J. Andreach's The Slain and Resurrected God: Conrad, Ford, and the Christian Myth (New York: New York University Press, 1970).

miracles, the materialist middle class shown up in all its spiritual impoverishment—they are all there in Mr. Apollo. Even the particular tone
of the genre is, at moments, lovingly reproduced. Ford was a wonderful
mimic. He used Chestertonian paradox, for example, in Apollo's criticism
of the skeptics he meets, who are so bent on not knowing God that they
even deny the evidence of their own senses that the impossible is
happening.

In spite of paradoxes, the usual horseplay, and the mild jesting one
comes to expect from Edwardian fantasies, Ford's set pieces on middle-
class life, on materialism and on science keep shading off into a satire more
serious than can easily be contained by this tone or by this genre. His verbal play becomes dense and demanding. Here, for example, is his description of Mr. Apollo's first view of the cramped physical life of the middle-
class house:

> The stone steps of the staircase that they climbed as if it were an
> Alpine ascent reverberated and echoed coldly in their footsteps.
> They appeared to aspire to eternal height, the immensely high and
> blank walls were a flat and glooming surface of shiny, dark wall-
> paper, enormously tall at the turns and landings.
>
> They stopped, however, at the first floor. In a room uncomfort-
> ably too tall for its breadth—a room so tall that a little old woman
> beside a tea equipage had an aspect of toys set out for the play of a
> giant's child, and the pictures on the walls were so near the floor
> that it appeared that there could not have been in the house a lad-
> der up which to climb and hang them—the light from the north
> was dim and chilly even on that July afternoon. Immensely high
> windows occupied the whole of one narrow wall, and through
> them, as if at a weary distance, the sun made a haze of light upon
> the foliage of the spindly plane trees with their black and piebald
> barks. The whole room—the whole house—had the air of having
> been built for tall, cold-blooded, and spindly creatures; like the
> plane trees themselves, that in the triangular gardens were "drawn
> up" towards the light and air, so that the little old woman seemed
> not so much to sit on the floor of a room as to be encamped at the
> bottom of a well.[21]

21. Ford, Mr. Apollo, 54–55.

The hero and heroine of Mr. *Apollo*, Alfred and Frances Milne, are interesting characters who could almost have come out of a novel by Gissing. Impecunious teachers, they live the bleak life of the educated who cannot afford, in time or money, the pleasures of the culture they have so painstakingly acquired. They live in a dreary, stuffy hole at the top of a graceless block of modern flats, and it is Mr. Apollo's final miracle, a typical Fordian extravaganza of incongruity, to topple all the houses opposite and create a green park so that the Milnes can at last look out of their windows like human beings and see and breathe. Before Mr. Apollo invades the Milnes' hearts, they are wise and kind but beaten down by the utter dullness and impoverishment of their lives. The entry into this daily grind of *anything* glamorous or unusual would always have for them something of the character of a miracle: "It must be remembered that neither Alfred nor Frances Milne had any touch, either by birth, tradition, or upbringing, of that romantic strain that makes many of us believe in a special providence—a special providence who will cause an indefinable 'something' to 'turn up.' Nothing that would turn up entered into their scale of ideas: they calculated solely upon their own efforts. Life for them was cause and effect."[22]

The plot of the novel gives the Milnes a happy ending: they are to live as Apollo's happy worshippers. But what really interests Ford about the Milnes is that unlike Apollo, the god, they live in a perpetual state of intelligent doubt. The Milnes' fate, to be Apollo's priests, can hardly capture our imaginations after we have experienced the rich texture of their personalities and their lives before this most unlikely change.

In fact, Ford's convincing miracles are never magic or religious. What is truly fantastic in all his novels are the wild connections he makes between thought and thought. His adventures are of trauma, memory, repression—things to make an Edwardian godly miracle look simple indeed. He shared the Edwardian love for the often buried fact, the hidden reason, the convoluted relation between cause and effect so typical of everything that happens in a modern industrial state. The world is a mysterious maze to his characters. The style with which Ford renders the dull life of the Milnes at home is more amazing in its daring and fecundity than anything Ford invents for his tin god Apollo to do on earth.

To illustrate, it is necessary to quote at length since, unlike Apollo,

22. *Ibid.*, 163.

Ford grows his mental gardens in the urban wasteland slowly. In the following passage, for example, we can see the complex life of Frances Milne unfold gradually. Her mind circles and travels and circles again until finally it finds a distant resting place:

> Frances Milne was preparing for supper a rabbit which she had bought from a barrow in the Pimlico Road. She had cut the pink carcase into four pieces, had rubbed them with salt, sprinkled them with chopped bay leaves and the fine shreds of onion cut into little squares, and was preparing to place them, one by one, in a brown earthenware jar. . . . She was meditating, at one and the same time, as to what she could add, without noticeable cost, to the ingredients of this ragout, and on the teaching of geography to children of nine and less. For, on the one hand, the series of papers that she was writing for a Parents' Home Teaching Association journal was coming to an end; on the other, she was trying to persuade the proprietors of *Home Whispers* to let her contribute to its columns a series of recipes called: "Eightpenny Dishes for Gas-stove Users."
>
> She stood in the tiny kitchen that was also a bathroom, tall and unhurried, wiping the fragments of chopped herbs from the steel blade of the chopper. Against the light of the frosted window she had the air of a Madonna of domesticity; a tin clock ticked on the wooden table at her side; she glanced at it, and observed that in five minutes she must set the rabbit upon the gas stove.
>
> And yet she was hardly a Madonna of domesticity any more than her husband was an inspired teacher. It was what came to her hand. If making the bed, sweeping the floors, shaking the rugs out on the roof, washing the plates, and executing the cookery took, as a rule, three hours of her day; if meditating a great deal upon how it was really best—as distinguished from the educational fashion of the day—to teach small children the rudiments of knowledge so that, in after life, with awakened intelligences they might assimilate these knowledges—if these actions and meditations occupied the greater part of her day, she would have preferred to be able to meditate upon other things. . . .
>
> . . . she had seldom more than a page and a half of a large handwriting to show for a day of restraint and of effort. And, though it was all in the day's work, it is not to be thought that she did not

sometimes remember a long poem on the history of a wood that, in
a drawer of the sideboard in the dining-room, had a line added to it
day by day, sometimes at intervals of many weeks.

It allured her, this History of a Wood of hers, though she was
never concerned to think whether it would allure any other soul in
the universe. It allured her because, when she could write long
lines, and still more, when she could think the big thoughts, she
seemed to be turning in, off a lane, in between the boles of huge and
tranquil trees into thick, peopled, and historic undergrowths. It
brought her thoughts of the scampering tails of rabbits, of the harsh
cries of jays, of pheasants that ran furtive and noiseless before the
footstep. It gave her inklings of the thoughts that the trees would
have, reaching up, as if asleep and dreaming, to the stars of winter
nights. It gave her thoughts of the woodcutters, of the hurdlers
shaving spiles, of the cottages hidden between coppices; of the gods
these men had created, the dryads, the nymphs, the fauns, of the
little people and of the gods that had created these men, these trees,
and the little wood-flowers that, for years and years, slept beneath
fallen leaves until, the woodcutters letting in the light, frail and
crowded blossoms for a time looked again out at the skies and heard
the night-cry of the foxes. And so for years they would go to sleep
again, the flowers; the unnumbered leaves would fall, the uncon-
sidered men would die.[23]

Here, then, is Ford's version of the magic woods in the city. In spite of
his inclusion in Mr. Apollo of so many of the standard elements of Edwardian fantasy, it is finally as an impressionist that he is magical. For him the
link between the mind and the world was tenuous, dangerous, misleading,
and mysterious. Only impressionism, he believed, could render how real
life, as we actually experience it, is drenched with our illusions, our past
and our dreams:

It is . . . perfectly possible for a sensitised person, be he poet or
prose writer, to have the sense, when he is in one room, that he is in
another, or when he is speaking to one person he may be so intensely haunted by the memory or desire for another person that he
may be absent-minded or distraught. And there is nothing in the

23. Ibid., 157–160.

canons of Impressionism, as I know it, to stop the attempt to render those superimposed emotions. Indeed, I suppose that Impressionism exists to render those queer effects of real life that are like so many views seen through bright glass—through glass so bright that whilst you perceive through it a landscape or a backyard, you are aware that, on its surface, it reflects a face of a person behind you. For the whole of life is really like that; we are almost always in one place with our minds somewhere quite other.[24]

For their different reasons, most of the Edwardian writers of fantasy were writing in more or less conscious rebellion *against* Ford's particular kind of mental magic. In spite of their *folies d'esprits*, they were ultimately defenders of some kind of spiritual and mental certainty. For example, Wells believed there was a solid, stolid mass of immovable stupidity which only his rare mind could irradiate with surprising thoughts, unexpected connections. He constructed a clear duality—there was the familiar, the expected, the respectable and then there was what no one dreams of, the hidden reason, the stolen bacillus, the extraterrestrial visitor. It is precisely because Wells found magic and surprise too rarely in the common man that he vacillated between trying to awaken his readers' dormant imaginations and despairing of their ever seeing the light.

In spite of his admiration for Wells, Ford understood the limitations of this idea of the unseen and wrote what is, beneath the joshing surface, a disparaging and at moments savage criticism of Wells's scientific fairy tales:

And we welcomed Science—Mr. Wells's brand of Science— with acclamations. Fairy tales are a prime necessity of the world, and he and Science were going to provide us with a perfectly new brand. And he did. And all Great London lay prostrate at his feet.

Mr. Wells struck the Empire with all the impact of Mr. Kipling. He struck everybody. He delighted the bourgeois profane with his imagination, and we intelligentsia snorted with pleasure at the idea of a Genius whom we could read without intellectual effort. And with immense admiration for his 'technique.' One could ask no more. The other idols of the intelligentsia of those days were a little forbidding—Ibsen and Bjornson and the Nordics generally, and

24. Ford, "On Impressionism" (1913), in MacShane (ed.), *Critical Writings*, 40–41.

Hauptmann and Sudermann. Gloomy and forbidding. So we de-voured Mr. Wells.

He liked the process; nevertheless, inspired with the gospel of Science, he snorted a little on the side . . . not loudly, but with meaning. We, his snorts said, we who delighted hilariously in his works were poor idiots towards whom a dark shadow was swiftly drifting. Science was going to devour us as the underground working populations of one of his stories crept out and at night devoured the butterfly beings of the planet's surface. Good for Mr. Wells; good for Science; good for everybody. Particularly good for us intelligentsia because we began to see that Mr. Wells too was a pessimist. We slapped each other on the back hilariously. The note of the world of those days was hilarity. It was good to think that our pet Genius was going also to develop into an Intelligence.

So Mr. Wells went snooping about the world, emitting from time to time a prophecy in the form of an entertaining and magnificently machined gem of fiction.[25]

Chesterton shared Ford's urbane disdain for Wells. In *The Napoleon of Notting Hill* he describes all the mad varieties of prophecy that burst out everywhere at the beginning of the twentieth century. The common man, says Chesterton, listened attentively to all these prophecies and then proceeded to play his own ancient and creative game called "Cheat the Prophet," the object of which is to make a future no one has imagined.[26] But, though Chesterton believed, as Wells did not, in the mental and spiritual depth within each human being, he feared the moral anarchy of Ford's kind of impressionism, for Ford substituted subjectivity and uncertainty for false prophecy. He refused to fill in the spiritual gap left by the nineteenth-century materialists with religion or with any consistent doctrine at all. His style, impressionism, is an acceptance of the mind's limitations and mysteries; it offers no reliable form of transcendence.

To many Edwardians and to Chesterton in particular, the amoral quality inherent in this style was anathema. Here, for example, is Chesterton's indictment of impressionism from *The Man Who Was Thursday*:

25. Ford, "H. G. Wells," in Ford, *Portraits from Life*, 146–47.
26. Chesterton, "Introductory Remarks on the Art of Prophecy" in Chesterton, *The Napoleon of Notting Hill, passim*.

The sun on the grass was dry and hot. So in plunging into the wood they had a cool shock of shadow, as of divers who plunge into a dim pool. The inside of the wood was full of shattered sunlight and shaken shadows. They made a sort of shuddering veil, almost recalling the dizziness of a cinematograph. Even the solid figures walking with him Syme could hardly see for the patterns of sun and shade that danced upon them. Now a man's head was lit as with a light of Rembrandt, leaving all else obliterated; now again he had strong and staring white hands with the face of a negro. The ex-Marquis had pulled the old straw hat over his eyes, and the black shade of the brim cut his face so squarely in two that it seemed to be wearing one of the black half-masks of their pursuers. The fancy tinted Syme's overwhelming sense of wonder. Was he wearing a mask? Was anyone wearing a mask? Was anyone anything? This wood of witchery, in which men's faces turned black and white by turns, in which their figures first swelled into sunlight and then faded into formless night, this mere chaos of chiaroscuro (after the clear daylight outside) seemed to Syme a perfect symbol of the world in which he had been moving for three days, this world where men took off their beards and their spectacles and their noses, and turned into other people. That tragic self-confidence which he had felt when he believed that the Marquis was a devil had strangely disappeared now that he knew that the Marquis was a friend. He felt almost inclined to ask after all these bewilderments what was a friend and what an enemy. Was there anything that was apart from what it seemed? The Marquis had taken off his nose and turned out to be a detective. Might he not just as well take off his head and turn out to be a hobgoblin? Was not everything, after all, like this bewildering woodland, this dance of dark and light? Everything only a glimpse, the glimpse always unforeseen, and always forgotten. For Gabriel Syme had found in the heart of that sun-splashed wood what many modern painters had found there. He had found the thing which the modern people call Impressionism, which is another name for that final scepticism which can find no floor to the universe.[27]

27. Chesterton, *The Man Who Was Thursday*, 126–27.

These flickering, misleading visions, these shifting lights and shades, are the essential elements in Ford's style. Looking out through what should have been a clear pane of glass, he found himself gazing at the reflection of a person behind him. Unlike Chesterton, he never cleared up this mysterious, disturbing, and at moments absurd multiple vision, never resolved his flickering forms into one great and clear whole. Instead of constructing Chestertonian controlled opposites, he proliferated jangling, mismatched images. He took the pane of clear glass, that mimetic ideal of the nineteenth-century novelists, and on it he superimposed so many reflections that the view on the far side of the window was forever called into doubt.

Ford could never compete with Chesterton as a writer of fantasy. If the universe has no floor, the concepts of real and unreal are no longer satisfyingly distinct. When, as in Mr. Apollo, Ford pretends to be enraptured and soothed by dreaming of the possibility of a god's visit, he utterly fails to convince. Though he has moments of being appropriately lighthearted, we feel his depression and discomfort underneath.

Chesterton filled his London with an air of magic; it is always possible that on the next street corner something wonderful will happen to show that the world of prose and gray pavement is very close to the world of magic. In contrast, there is nothing less likely than that Ford's woman in her kitchen, cooking and thinking about her writing, is, at the end of Mr. Apollo, to be transformed into a priestess of the god. This is simply not Ford's kind of transition.

If real wonders happen in Ford's novels, they are the wonders of style, things juxtaposed to reveal the absurd incongruities of human life. Ford was a romantic and, like so many Edwardians, his romantic impulse, disassociated from a direct spiritual concept of a God ruling the world, became instead a search for spiritual power in art. Faith in form does not really lend itself to the creation of a popular blueprint for daydreams. Nevertheless, fantasy that leans on form for its magic dislocations rather than on content is a radical conception, one for which Ford was almost but not yet fully ready. First, he needed to get rid of his Wellsian god Apollo; he needed to write satire about a world that could not be transformed by magic, a world whose resistance to spiritual life is the measure of its recalcitrant, mad deadness. It is an indication of Ford's potential strength that, try as he might in Mr. Apollo, he could not successfully escape what depressed and preoccupied him. That necessary material kept returning and eventually led to the ironic treatment of the romantic personality that we see in *The Good Soldier* and, with hope replacing despair, in *Parade's End*, that great fantasy about the last good man, whom Ford likens to an Apollo among modern midgets.

For a man who is at all interested in the manifestations of his day, any connected thought is almost a matter of impossibility.

FORD, *The Critical Attitude*, 1911

«6»

THE SATIRES: FROM FABIANS TO VORTICISTS

SATIRIC IRONY: NEW INFLUENCES, NEW VOICES, 1910–1914

IN 1909 Ford achieved his first real literary eminence. It had eluded him as a novelist and came to him instead as the editor of the *English Review*. His financial incompetence and his constant misunderstandings with writers who found his business habits erratic put a quick end to this season of glory, but glory it was. Ford was a great editor, and nowhere is his pivotal position as a transitional figure so clear as in a glance at the strange bedfellows to be found in a typical issue of the *Review*. Ford could publish Hardy and Wells and Bennett and, as it were, in the same breath, discover, promote, and publish Lawrence and Pound.

The years 1910 to 1914 have been gradually recognized as culturally and politically distinct from the Edwardian years before.[1] Samuel Hynes has wittily described the situation by saying that in 1901, with the death of the queen, the English had a sense of an ending. But it was not until 1910, with Edward's death, that there was a sense of a beginning.[2] This leaves

1. My debt is to the following discussions of the years 1910–14 as a radical departure from Edwardian culture: William Wees, *Vorticism and the English Avant-Garde* (Toronto: University of Toronto Press, 1972); C. K. Stead, *The New Poetic: Yeats to Eliot* (Middlesex: Pelican, 1964); John R. Harrison, *The Reactionaries: A Study of the Anti-Democratic Intelligentsia* (New York: Schocken, 1967); George Dangerfield, *The Strange Death of Liberal England, 1910–1914* (New York: Capicorn, 1935); Samuel Hynes, *The Edwardian Turn of Mind* (Princeton: Princeton University Press, 1968).

2. Samuel Hynes, "A Note on 'Edwardian,'" in Hynes, *Edwardian Occasions* (London, 1972), 1–12.

the Edwardian years as a sort of Sargasso Sea in which no cultural current predominated and there was no group sense among artists. There were several famous Edwardian quarrels, but only after 1910 were there manifestos; furious, rival little magazines; and once again, as in the nineties, inconclusive but passionate discussions of the purpose and meaning of Art.

The *English Review*, standing significantly as it does on the threshold of this new cultural phase, was, like its editor, a bridge among several literary worlds. It was started, as Ford remembered in 1921, "to afford a nucleus for some sort of Movement that should combine some of the already Eminent with some of the Young who were then knocking on the doors of our Athenaeum. . . . We aimed at founding an *aube de siecle* Yellow Book." Of course the image of a new *Yellow Book* was much too *passéiste* for these futurist young. As Ford remembered the one-year history of the *Review*, "We fell back in the end altogether on *Les Jeunes*, and Les Jeunes made a very pretty movement for themselves, only the war cut it short."[3]

Indeed, in hindsight, the cultural and political upheavals of the years 1910 to 1914 look minor when compared to that truly great historical divide, the war. For Ford's own development both as thinker and artist, the rebellious excitement was all too brief. By 1914 he had only begun to assimilate the new possibilities of having "some sort of Movement" once again after the long Edwardian isolation and of having an idea of art that seriously challenged his own innovations with Conrad. Impressionism had been their earlier revolution, and Ford made way for "Mr Pound and his explosive-mouthed gang of scarce-breeched filibusters" with an openness and generosity that nevertheless could not entirely bridge the gap between his generation and theirs. As Ford remembered it in 1937:

> For those infants—Mr. Pound and his disciples, Mr. T. S. Eliot, Mr. Frost, Miss Doolittle, and the rest of the London-transatlantic crowd, as for Mr. Norman Douglas, Mr. Tomlinson, or Mr. Wyndham Lewis (Percy), or for poor D. H. Lawrence, the Impressionists were fairly old stuff. Lawrence merely grunted with absent-minded half-contempt when I suggested that he might with profit read *Bouvard et Pécuchet*; when I mentioned Conrad to Mr. Tomlinson he said he had never heard of the feller; the London transatlantics whooped with delight when they heard that Mr. Robert Bontine

3. Ford, *Thus to Revisit*, 58, 59.

Cunninghame Graham had called the Master [James] 'Henrietta Maria' . . . that would be already in 1910 when Impressionism had hardly had twenty years of a run and had only just really conquered the Intelligentsia.[4]

In another late memoir Ford defines this difference between his impressionism and the new doings of the imagists and vorticists by inventing a sort of comic composite futurist-cubist-vorticist young artist. This figure, symbol of obnoxious youth in general and of the spirit of 1910 in particular, "blasts" Ford in the following imaginary monologue:

> Your generation has gone. What is the sense of you and Conrad and Impressionism. [sic] You stand for Impressionism. It is finished, Foûtu. Blasted too! This is the future. What does anyone want with your old fashioned stuff? You try to make people believe that they are passing through an experience when they read you. You write these immense long stories, recounted by a doctor at table or a ship captain in an inn. You take ages to get these fellows in. In order to make your stuff seem convincing. Who wants to be convinced? Get a move on. Get out or get under.[5]

Though Ford laughs at this young idiot, he recognized that there might be ways to cut through difficulties with sharper, harder implements than his own tortuous ironies and elaborate explanations. Pound always remembered Ford as a teacher, one who asked the right questions. Though Ford could only begin to participate in the spirit of 1910 himself, he cared for these younger artists' experiments. He understood what Pound and the imagists were doing, and in his opinion, the war, by ending their "explosive sounds," had performed its single most destructive act.[6]

After the war Ford returned from the front to find the map of English culture so changed that he could no longer find his way about. The particular prewar revolutions in art he had known had moved to Paris, and he followed them there, where, later, he was to make his intellectual peace with them. Before the war, however, there was more frenzy than clarity for Ford in the *empressement* of the new movements. At this stage in his development, the new ideas served primarily as a way to gain some critical

4. Ford, *Portraits from Life*, 289.
5. Ford, *Return to Yesterday*, 400.
6. *Ibid.*

distance on the Edwardian life being so universally sloughed off between 1910 and 1914.

A personal crisis in Ford's life hastened and contributed to the process by which he found himself critical of his own past associations. His marriage to Elsie Martindale, in trouble from as early as 1906 when he abandoned the simple life of the country, in other words Elsie's life, for the pleasures of literary life in town, finally foundered. In 1909 Violet Hunt became his mistress and Elsie began what was to be a long, painful and public process by petitioning for restitution of conjugal rights. Between 1909 and 1913, Ford and Violet Hunt managed to offend and upset almost everyone from the old life of literary teas, of visits to Henry James, and of socially desirable garden parties. At South Lodge, Violet's roomy house in Kensington, a new social life had to be constructed from scratch. With their passion for what was good in art and their immense and generous social energy these two managed to turn South Lodge into a center for the younger generation who cared not at all that their hosts were unmarried and that their names had been dragged through the courts. Edwardian London mingled here with something new. For a time, before the war, South Lodge must have been, along with places like the Poetry Bookshop, the Café of the Golden Calf, and T. E. Hulme's salon, one of the most odd, fascinating, and important places for a young artist to visit.

In fact, however, Ford himself was not always at South Lodge. During these years, in his efforts to escape the scandal that dogged his and Violet's steps, he spent months at a time in Germany trying first to establish German citizenship and then to get a German divorce from Elsie. These efforts, never clearly planned or consistently carried out, failed, and Ford spent many months of these crucial writing years depressed and lonely in furnished rooms at German spas or visiting paternal relatives who were disapproving of his anomalous position.

After his shift to London in 1906, Ford's small producer persona had receded and that of Tory gentleman, an old pose, had become more prominent. The rural politicoes, anarchists, Fabians, Simple-Lifers who had surrounded him in the neighborhood of the Five Towns were replaced by the more urbane Galsworthy, by Belloc and Chesterton, and finally, all these political influences, this strange potpourri of radical reactionaries and reactionary radicals, were placed for Ford at a critical distance by the public and private upheavals of 1910–1914. The new revolutionaries were industrial workers with whom Ford had no living contact and for whom his class had little sympathy. The militant suffragettes he was more able to understand, but it was finally the new breed of reactionary who offered him a social analysis of the Edwardian years with which he could identify and to which he could cling.

The novels Ford wrote between 1910 and 1914 are satires, criticisms in the mixed mode, the full plate of satire, of contemporary life. Irony is traditionally one of satire's voices: in Ford's case, this irony is a central expression of social ambivalence and goes very deep. In these books Ford began to ask questions about his times he had been incapable of posing earlier.

«»

If only it were possible in good faith to analyze seriously the tone and meaning of Ford Madox Ford's political writings, since they are the necessary and proper preamble to discussing his satires. Even Graham Greene, one of Ford's most steadfastly friendly critics, admits that his is a personality "which calls both for respect and mockery." While recognizing as serious Ford's suggestion in *Provence* that civilization's only hope is to find a way to return to the Dark Ages, Greene sees that "nothing in Mr. Ford's hands remains too serious. As in his fiction he writes out of a kind of hilarious depression."[7]

"Hilarious depression" is an oxymoron that well captures the voice of Ford's cultural analyses both in fiction and in essays. Some of Ford's biographers and critics, reading his many volumes of sociology and history and finding there unembarrassed self-delusions and pained disorder, have hastily explained the confusion by saying that Ford was nothing more than an assemblage of self-dramatizations, assumed selves, anxiously developed personae. Though this is one source of Ford's inconsistencies and though he could indeed be, on occasion, an outrageous poseur—the country gentleman pose, the Tory landowner pose, the bohemian artist pose, the poor-old-horse-whom-nobody-loves pose—this psychological mechanism of his cannot finally elucidate the peculiar mixture that makes up his political thought or the strange agglomeration of tones in which he expressed these thoughts. Instead, Ford's role playing was often symptomatic; his

7. Graham Greene, Review of *Provence*, *London Mercury*, XXXIX (December, 1938), 217–18, quoted in David Dow Harvey, *Ford Madox Ford*, 422.

political confusions reflect a cultural crisis. His social essays and satires are accurate barometers of the ways in which a whole class was uncertain about its destiny. Obfuscation was central to this class's way of life. Unclear thinking was, during the Edwardian years, an epidemic. Other writers besides Ford were affected, became feverish, changeable, and "hilariously depressed."

In his fantasies, Ford was elusive and subjective; he played with his characters' mental lacunae, hiding some kinds of causes and effects while heightening others. One might expect that in turning to Ford's social satires one would be turning away from this kind of subjective impressionism, but this is not the case. On the contrary, in the satires, Ford is as capricious as elsewhere in both method and tone, even in what are ostensibly his most earnest political and social pronouncements. The mad rush of attenuated, associative thinking becomes, if anything, more pronounced when he is stringing together a sociological or historical train of thought. Indeed, in some grotesquely self-contradictory cases, for example in moving from his pro-German essays of just before the war to his anti-German essays of 1915, one cannot avoid the feeling that Ford's descriptions of culture are a kind of fantastic bedtime story he is telling to soothe himself into sleep.[8] The tone of Ford's essays is authoritative, bold, but their imaginative leaps are in fact quite precarious. If one tries to follow his dizzy mental course, one discovers gaps, hidden pitfalls. His logic often disintegrates under any sort of scrutiny, and if one is still in doubt over how seriously to take him, his tone finally gives the game away. Here is a man, this tone would seem to say, who goes rushing along with an élan that obscures the embarrassing fact that he is running for his life. He pretends only to be making one more innocent, Chestertonian ramble, while in fact there is nothing restful in this writing.

In 1911 Ford wrote The Critical Attitude, a book of essays clustered around the main idea that clear and objective thinking is a lost art in England and needs to be revived. The book itself is like a parody of clear thinking, a send up of objectivity in a cloud of unfocused, subjective hysteria. This was not, however, Ford's intention; under the anxious patter, he was quite earnestly trying to explain why the England of now seemed to him to be so much less satisfactory than the England of then. His argu-

---

8. Contrast The Desirable Alien (1913) with When Blood is their Argument and Between St. Dennis and St. George (both 1915).

ment circles back on itself because he could see no way forward. Its structure is purely associative rather like the conversational style of Mark Tietjens' mistress in *Parade's End*. It pretends to discuss causes and effects, but
causes recede into a realm of vagueness while effects loom large and most
of Ford's rushing energy is lavished on their description. Roughness and
haste appear, too, in the way that important points and shifts in ground
are often buried in the structure of the argument. Some logical links are
fudged, others passed over altogether.

Conclusions are always Ford's weakest point. In *The Critical Attitude* he
rails for pages about the loss of the Victorian Great Figure and about the
yellow press which forces "the relatively unimportant things, in a perpetually flickering cloud of small claims upon the attention, into the fore-
ground."[9] He concludes that thought has died because the Boer War gave
rise to this popular press. As cures for the diseases of thoughtlessness and
confusion he diagnoses in modern man, he offers visions of a glorious future for democracy when the Great Figure will return, presumably once
again to guide mankind. But this is really only an aside in his train of
thought. Unlike his contemporaries, Wells and Shaw, he projects few
ideal solutions. He does not begin to analyze the content of the new opinions, which he sees only as a random proliferation, an anarchic bombard-
ment, containing no helpful hint about new directions emerging from a
changing culture.

Ford's mourning for a lost elite, with its educated fineness, remained a
constant throughout his intellectual life, but even in this primary tenet of
his social ideas there is an underlying irony. He was not the public-school
boy, the country gentleman, the Tory aristocrat he often pretended to be.
Instead, he was part of the very class that had so little respect for artists
and that so eagerly read about itself in the morning paper. Indeed, the
seemingly aimless, polyglot mixture of modern experience fascinated him.
Or at least, he sometimes recognized his own immersion in this confusion
and saw his rendering of the "gnat dance" of modern emotions and experiences as his most bona fide social role as an artist.

As for Ford's direct political ideas, in his argument he flirts with every
shade in the political spectrum of his time. He is the practical Fabian, the
anticapitalist, the Tory elitist, the hopeful democrat, and finally, the fas-

9. Ford, *The Critical Attitude*, 122.

cist who dreams of an authority strong enough to control the life of the mass and give it meaning.

Finally, however, Ford gives up on politics altogether and even on thought. It is art he cares about and wants to preserve. He finds himself unable to discriminate in these other matters and wants only to render in art, rather than to analyze, what is. This decision could not, however, rescue him from his confusion. His uncertainty followed him around and nagged him. He was constantly tempted in essays and novels to grapple once again with "the sharp facets of facts," which for him usually remained "hardly at all related the one with the other."[10]

In 1921 when Ford came out with yet another of his volumes of criticism and hopelessly circular cultural analyses, Ezra Pound wrote him a wonderful letter in which he complained about the quality, sources, and expression of Ford's ideas:

> WOT you dont bloomin' see is that wot you do with ideas is just as bad for the reader's morale as wot Bridges does with langwidge.
>
> I.E. you hang onto a lot of old tarabiscotage Sancte Foi Catholique, Tory party, etc. O the hell of a lot of it; and that not only is it necessary to have the mot juste, and the order of words simple, without interjected digits obstructing, and grampion hills gramping etc., it is equally necessary that the writer shdnt have his *citron* filled with semblable clots of ancient furniture sentimental, traditional, purely decorative et bloody cetera. (even if one isn't treating the same in immediate paragraph it, the clutter, causes a slide-around just as deliterious as the slide-around (verbal) in the Times lit sup).
>
> . . . .
>
> I admit it is better to meander than to put up a fake structeure in rectangles pretendus (kipng and H. G.) [Kipling and Wells]
> No, mong cher, you are full of suppressed forsooths and gadzookses of ideation. . . .
>
> AND it aint any use, not to you it aint, no more than my early clingin to "forloyn"s and swevyns. . . . I send my analyst's dossier, fer wot it is wurf. As my belief as to why you don't swat the bead-sighted fly at thirty yards.

10. *Ibid.*, 125.

. . . .
You are all right as long as you are talkin abaht prose or style, when
you get off that you go all right until you strike a bit o somfink deco-
rativo, after which you rabble like a bloody brebis.[11]

"Semblable clots of ancient furniture," an overdecorated space—that was
the mind of Ford Madox Ford when he sought to analyze the culture of his
time. What were the "sentimental, traditional, purely decorative" elements he inherited from the cultural attic? And what did Pound and the
new men really have to offer him in the way of critical distance from and
insight into the cultural and social life of England before the war?

《 》

Here, though to be taken with a grain, is one of Ford's own descriptions of
his political history, this one written in 1931:

> I never took any stock in politics. But political movements have
> always interested me. I have only once voted. It is one of my most
> passionate convictions that no one individual can be sufficiently in-
> telligent to be entrusted with the fortune or life of any other indi-
> vidual. . . . I don't believe a creative artist can have any intellect;
> he is an observer and a recorder. He may have passions but he must
> mistrust them.
>
> My own predilections have always been towards the Right. I like
> pomp, banners, divine rights, unreasonable ceremonies and cere-
> moniousness. It seems to me that when the world was a matter of
> small communities each under an arbitrary but responsible head
> then the world was at its best. If your community did not prosper
> you decapitated your chief. Till then he was possessed of divine
> rights. Presumably you cannot better the feudal system.
>
> So I was always a sentimental Tory. But inasmuch as the Tories
> stood in the way of Home Rule for Ireland, I never voted or wrote
> for that Party. . . .
>
> It has from my earliest days been my fate to be regarded as a
> brand to be snatched from the burning by the Left. From my earliest
> days in darkest London! I never quite knew why.[12]

11. Ezra Pound to Ford, May 26, [1921], in Lindberg-Seyersted (ed.), *Pound/Ford*,
58–60.
12. Ford, *Return to Yesterday*, 81–83.

In one sense one can sum up Ford's lifelong lucubrations on social matters with his sentence here, "Presumably you cannot better the feudal system." That "presumably" is the shrug of the shoulder given by one who is in no position to make judgments or to be, like his childhood relations on the Left, doctrinaire. How, this tone would seem to say, should a man presume who admits that his political "predilections" come largely from a liking for "pomp, banners, divine rights [and] unreasonable ceremonies"?

But Ford's species of Toryism, his interest in feudal control, has roots much deeper than any mere affection for pomp and banners. It is also one of the most typical responses made by Edwardians to a breakdown in the liberal tradition. Both the Left and the Right as Ford describes them shared at least one thing—the idea that liberalism in general, and the Liberal party in particular, represented a species of both humanism and laissez-faire capital which were utterly bankrupt solutions to the social and economic difficulties of post-1873 England.

Ford and most of the writers of his generation had some kind of groping awareness of the material basis for the crisis of liberalism. Indeed, what is amazing is how unified the artists were—Left, Right, and Center—in their understanding that the middle class was living on borrowed time and that the plutocracy of the period was worse than vulgar—it was dangerous. But as the reconciling and reforming power of liberalism waned, the Edwardian middle class was particularly dependent on not letting the right hand know what the left was doing. In this mental state of avoidance, the artists were placed in a difficult position. It was traditionally their job to make connections, to see sources, to put their fingers on the pulse of culture. But, as middle-class Edwardians, they shared some of their class's fear of probing too deeply into the implications of their precarious position. In Ford, in Shaw, in Wells, in Galsworthy, the workers are mentioned but they are sentimentalized or abstracted or feared. Who were these people who made the wealth but did not get any of it? And how long could they be bought off by Liberal reforms or by the thin promises of those reforms? The artists were as nervous about the answers to these questions as everybody else. Here, for example, is Ford describing his nerves before meeting the plebian D. H. Lawrence, while at the same time he snobbishly lengthens the supposed class difference between them:

> It was . . . with a certain trepidation that I awaited the visit of Lawrence. If he was really the son of a working coal-miner, how exactly

was I to approach him in conversation? Might he not, for instance, call me 'Sir'—and wouldn't it cause pain and confusion to stop him doing so? For myself I have always automatically regarded every human being as my equal—and myself, by corollary, as the equal of every other human being—except of course the king and my colonel on—not off—parade. But a working man was so unfamiliar as a proposition that I really did not know how to bring it off.[13]

Compare this absurd and precarious condition to Dickens' state of mind. In the nineteenth century it was possible to be middle class and yet write *Great Expectations*, a novel that uncovers the true source of the money in the sweat and suffering of an invisible class. Though Pip becomes a gentleman and can only remain one forevermore while Magwitch can only die, at least the connection has been faced, the painful link between the classes dramatized.

In *Character and the Novel* W. J. Harvey implies an organic link between the health of Victorian liberalism and the ability of the Victorian artist to explore a full range of difficult and contradictory human relationships. He describes the English novel as an essentially liberal form. The novelist is a pluralist; he is ambivalent, ironic, constantly undercutting one point of view with another. For Harvey, the richness of the great English novels is a product of their ability to encompass a wide range of perspectives. They contain living dialogues among viewpoints. This is the liberal tradition at its best, a balancing of rival claims.[14] It is the Gladstonian liberalism Ford idealized in *The Critical Attitude*, a liberalism secure enough in its values and in its ability to make ends meet to look at all sides without being swamped by a plethora of undigestible opinions or irresolvable demands. It is a liberalism that can still dare to explore conflicts and to acknowledge contradictions in relatively stable ironies.

But by 1910 the last thing the plutocratic upper middle class wanted was an exploration of conflicts. No one rich *or* literary wanted to look at where the money was coming from. The artists were sensitive to the dangers of this avoidance while continuing to be ambivalent about how much they wanted to know. In 1909 H. G. Wells wrote *Tono Bungay*, in which a man gets puffed up into a great plutocrat who can command immense

13. Ford, *Portraits from Life*, 99–100.
14. W. J. Harvey, *Character and the Novel* (London, 1970), 24–29, *et passim*.

credit based merely on the foundation of the slick advertising of a quack
medicine. We are shown waste, disorder, chicanery. But Wells doesn't
once show us the people who are tricked into buying the sham medicine.
Where does the money come from? He fails to ask this question forth-
rightly. By 1911 he had stopped asking it at all: in *The New Machiavelli* he
averted his eyes from both capitalist and worker and began to concentrate
on what was to be a new elite, an educated class of superior planners.
"Muddle" is the real enemy, says his hero, as he quotes Kipling—

> All along o' dirtiness, all along o' mess,
> All along o' doin' things rather-more-or-less.[15]

It is easy to dismiss Wells as a peculiar renegade among more canonical
socialists, as the man whom Ford blithely joined in 1906 in assailing the
orderly workings of the Fabians. But Wells's mixture of socialist opinions,
utopianism, elitism, and finally, fear of workers is a typical combination of
the period, and these elements appear in some kind of conjunction, sprinkled from end to end of the political spectrum of writers. Wells's conflation
of views from both the extreme Left and extreme Right, far from being an
isolated case, is a touchstone of the times.

Shaw, on the other side of Wells's debate with the Fabians and far more
clear than he about the material basis for social realities, nevertheless was
capable of reaching conclusions closely related to those in *A Modern Uto-
pia* or *The New Machiavelli*. In *Major Barbara*, he faces the implications of
militancy—blood and fire—as Wells cannot, but he waxes romantic about
his enlightened despot, Undershaft, in exactly the way Wells was to do
about his utopian saviors in *The Shape of Things to Come*. Wells is disgusted
by the disorder of the workingman while Shaw, in contrast, sees the weaknesses of the worker as a natural outgrowth of an unequal distribution of
wealth. But though Shaw says that man will be good, safe, and happy if
only he has enough, in Undershaft's mighty cannon factory, the old class
hierarchy applies as rigidly as ever. Only expansion, hence war, can provide a reliable abundance of wealth so those on the bottom will not starve.
No one questions the power of Undershaft, the man, to provide a better
world. The future hope, indeed, comes from him; in other words, it
comes, just as in Wells, from the top of society, not the bottom.

15. H. G. Wells, *The New Machiavelli* (1911; rpr. Harmondsworth, Middlesex,
1946), 107.

« »

As always, then, in thinking about the Edwardians one finds opposites col-lapsing into confluence, paradoxes and ironies resolving themselves into even more surprising unities. Certainly, presumably socialist writers like Wells and Shaw demonstrate the peculiar condition of social criticism in Edwardian England. Like the Liberals they despised, these writers were confused and self-contradictory, victims, like everyone else, of the breakup of a liberalism that had formerly succeeded in defusing essential contradic-tions and could do so no longer.

At first glance Ford would seem to have essentially different political views from those of Wells and Shaw. One can place him easily in the Chesterton-Belloc camp among those who looked back towards feudal order rather than forward towards an order scientifically designed by a technocratic elite. But of course, these forms of human organization have structural similarities. In general, Ford was not conscious of these links. Certainly he always criticized Wells's idea of an elite class of scientific ex-perts without recognizing in it any analogy with his own desire for an aris-tocratic class. For of course, Ford had his own elite, his own Undershafts, his own utopias, though with a difference. Shaw and Wells believed in a future while Ford, with Chesterton and all those who believed in the Fall or in some version of an ideal past, dreamed only of a return to yesterday. Macdonald, the hero of Ford's satire *The New Humpty-Dumpty*, is an ideal man, Ford's own particular Wellsian expert, more romantic and vague than Wells's leaders but easily as brilliant and superior to other men. But his fate is to be plowed under by inferior, modern people. He is a leftover from the glorious, aristocratic past, a Great Figure who, in modern cir-cumstances, is either distrusted or invisible.

Few literary periods can so abound in revisions of the present or ver-sions of escape from the here and now as the Edwardian; few writers can have felt so called upon—even, as in Ford's case, against their wills—to be sociologists evolving new worlds for old. "The novel became a vehicle for every kind of 'ism'; a small but noisy minority backed Imperialism and bank-holiday patriotism, but the serious novel as a whole interested itself almost solely in sociological questions," wrote Ford.[16] One has only to

16. Ford, *Portraits from Life*, 177. See also Hynes, *The Edwardian Turn of Mind*, *passim*, about how highly politicized was much of the writing in this period.

compare satire as it was written by Shaw's mentor, Samuel Butler, with the sort written by Ford's generation. Butler criticizes extremes; his highest ideals are good sense, compromise, tolerance, and moderation. In *The Way of All Flesh* Ernest's slow emergence from the harshness of Pontifexism brings him into a glowing light of humanism. He rejects authority and embraces liberalism.

Satirical Edwardians, of whatever stripe, do just the opposite. Their satires court the extremes that may rid the age of its vagueness, its hypocrisy and—strange, new word—its inefficiency. (The failures of the Boer War first alerted the English to this new worry: the state was a rat's nest of privilege, overlapping influence, inefficient offices.) The breakdown of old compromises, old conventions, old alliances had by 1910 forced everyone into a kind of accelerating dance of speculation. But perhaps the word *extremes* must be qualified. The true extremes came later, with thinkers like T. E. Hulme, who rejected the ideal of humanism altogether. Edwardian extremes, in contrast, are the end points in continuous oscillations. Ford's circular, self-contradictory, and inconclusive sociological arguments are caricatures of what was typical. He and his contemporaries were painfully and actively a part of the failure of the liberal synthesis. Like Herbert Asquith's government, they tried to reconcile furious opposites by vaguely pretending they were not opposites at all; also like the government, they had difficulty in reaching conclusions. They were oblique, ironic, tortuous because they could not be, were afraid to be, clear.

« »

Perhaps more than any other major writer of the Edwardian period, Ford floundered around in a painful spiritual state of unknowing. He had a hundred masks for this confusion, but his contemporaries have recorded that they found these unconvincing. Certainly, in the arguments in *The Critical Attitude*, there is a failure of cohesion in his proliferating and grandiose social ideas. Worse, they lack decorum. He often offers a small solution to a large problem with no sense of any inappropriateness of scale, or he can speak grandly of bringing back feudalism to achieve better eating habits.

But put him next to a writer like Galsworthy, and one begins to see that Ford has his own form of seriousness as a sociologist: "Galsworthy believed that humanity could be benefited by propaganda for virtue of a Christian order," Ford wrote, "whereas I believed that humanity could only be brought to ameliorate itself if life as it is is presented in terms of an art. And the business of Art is not to elevate humanity but to render."[17] Like Galsworthy, Ford wanted to see humanity "ameliorate itself"; unlike Galsworthy, liberal visions of what this amelioration might look like gave him no intellectual or emotional sustenance. Galsworthy's biographer, Dudley Barker, lists the humane causes for which Galsworthy campaigned: he organized a protest letter to try to persuade governments to agree to ban the use of airplanes as weapons of war; he was for the reform of the House of Lords, for votes for women, and for a revision in the divorce laws; like Gladstone, he helped prostitutes; he helped ex-convicts. But Barker ends this list: "The campaigns in which he was most absorbed were those to do with animals."[18] The contrast with Ford is striking. It is inconceivable that Ford could have seriously engaged himself in any of these liberal projects. Neither his dissatisfactions nor his intellect could ever have been assuaged by such reforms. His hopes for both art and society were more sweeping, though by very reason of that sweep he ran the risk of having his own particular shallowness, a too easy despair.

If, like Ford, one refuses to confront, as Wells and Galsworthy confronted, immediate and practical political questions, one must either establish some higher ground from which to comment on the world or retreat into subjectivity. There is a phrase in Ford's book on James which exactly describes how Ford hoped to combine these extremes. He wanted to find a voice "dominated with that vibration—with that balancing of the mind between the great outlines and the petty details."[19] Wells covered the middle ground between these extremes, the social life, the public life, the conscious life. Ford, suffering from a species of alienation now all too familiar to us, felt hopeless about the public sphere as he found it. He could only dream of absolute and enormous social reversals or, alternatively, fixate on the small details, the atomizations, the "flicker of small vitalities" or "the dance of midges" which is modern life.[20]

Finally, however, it is impressive to see how Ford found a way to express and universalize his bewilderment in both the tone and structure of his satirical writing. His uncertainties and his techniques for their expres-

17. Ford, *It Was the Nightingale*, 51–52.
18. Dudley Barker, *The Man of Principle: A View of John Galsworthy* (New York, 1963), 154–55.
19. Ford, *Henry James*, 155.
20. Ford, *The Critical Attitude*, 185–86.

sion seem to evolve together. His essays of social speculation are interspersed with novels that grope for their own voice in a constant oscillation between expressions of grand notions and of tiny, frustrating distractions. He elevated to the status of theory his feeling that he could not see life steadily or render it whole. "It is obviously best if you [the imaginative writer] can contrive to be without views at all; your business with the world is rendering, not alteration. You have to render life with such exactitude that more specialised beings than you, learning from you what are the secret needs of humanity, may judge how many white-tiled bathrooms are, or to what extent parliamentary representation is, necessary for the happiness of men and women."[21] Change will come through the agency of "more specialised beings" (again those expert officials), but it will be the artist who shows the way by rendering the truth of what is. Thus, by a feint typical of his subtle mind, Ford makes a case for art's importance as a social force while still insisting that the artist has no business with "views." Like Wells, Ford wanted to stuff into the novel all the odd and mismatched bits that made up life. But unlike Wells, Ford was not going to sum these little bits up. He could draw no conclusions.

In this drawing back from any direct judgment of the social present while still insisting on art's power to direct reality through a sort of educative mimesis, Ford set up a typically Edwardian paradox. Wells called this state of mind a "dignified dexterity of evasion" and connected it with the decline of liberalism.[22] A number of literary tones evolved from this "dignified dexterity of evasion," but they are closely related under the skin. In Wells we hear proliferating declarative sentences, a flurry of judgments. Each statement is firm in itself and the moment of synthesis repeats itself. In reaction to the aesthetic of Ford and Conrad, Wells insisted on his right to adopt a flat tone, to be a "journalist": "I write as I Walk because I want to get somewhere and I write as straight as I can, just as I walk as straight as I can, because that is the way to get there."[23] But from book to book Wells keeps changing his judgments. He reaches for consistency and order but is wracked by perpetual doubt. Taken as a whole, his works exhibit as much desperation and confusion as Ford's do.

Ford's "dignified dexterity of evasion" has a very different voice. He

21. Ford, Joseph Conrad, 223.
22. Wells, The New Machiavelli, 258.
23. Wells, Experiment in Autobiography, II, 623.

used constant vacillations in tone to express the same confusion which Wells tried to anatomize by intellect. If Ford declares anything at all with any consistency it is that art is the only resting place while life is thus disorderly. Ford could be very literal-minded about the social function of art. If, he reasoned, the French had read Flaubert's *Sentimental Education* seriously and in sufficient numbers, they would have known enough to avoid the Franco-Prussian War. Art was going "to beat the Blue Book out of the field."[24] Such hopes, such declarations, could only be precarious bravura in the mouth of an Edwardian novelist. Like Lloyd George's oratory, Ford's words conceal a multitude of difficulties. Like Asquith's statesmanship, they try to postulate a settled condition of things which is fast disappearing.

« »

Between 1910 and 1914, Ford participated in a great deal of talk at South Lodge and among the newly agitated young about materialism, philistinism, and industrialism. What to Wells had been "muddle" looked much more sinister to these younger writers. They had none of Wells's or even Ford's more wavering confidence in an artist's power to guide the sensibilities of the state. Nor had they any confidence that the future could be utopian on Wells's model. In the paintings of Wyndham Lewis one can see their love-hate relationship to modern industrial society: it is both beautiful and terrible in its inhuman hardness. Certainly to the vorticists, liberal reforms were laughably soft. The modern state was out of human control. Significant change could only be radical change, but in what direction? One route was back in time, and a great nostalgia swept some members of the 1910–1914 literary generation, that generation cut off, ironically enough, by that final herald of the new times, the war. As Stephen Spender describes the state of mind shared by such as Ezra Pound and Wyndham Lewis: "When nostalgia of this intensity is applied through action to contemporary history, it is—or it was—Fascism. The attraction of Fascism for these writers was that it seemed a programme for using entirely modern techniques to impose upon twentieth-century society the patterns of preindustrial society. The sirens of nostalgia sang the speeches of Mussolini."[25] The vorticists took Ford's paradox of the role of the artist to its

24. Ford, *Henry James*, 119.
25. Spender, *The Struggle of the Modern*, 219.

furthest point of exaggeration: on the one hand the artist is a sage, the only man who knows enough to save the state; on the other he is a powerless and maligned creature who, to preserve himself, must utterly separate his work and life from the alarming, debased flux of modern society. Rather as the pope was declared infallible at the moment when he was losing his real political powers, these artists proclaimed art as absolute and supreme at the moment when it was losing its earlier organic connections to a large reading public. They defensively fetishized form; they rejected humanism as the source of muddle. "Les Jeunes" stood instead on the only firm ground they could find: they would make form for its own sake.

In their different way, these writers were as intensely concerned with political questions as were Wells and Ford, but their solutions were far more drastic. The liberal compromises, the gentler confusions, to be found in Ford and Wells give way in Pound and Lewis to a more violent and polarized set of positions. What in Ford is still a sentimental and rather unfocused conjunction of feudalism, socialism, and Toryism is in them a more desperate and furious rejection of all pluralism. The new men felt they could not afford the luxury of Ford's maunderings on social subjects; confusion was a self-indulgence of the liberal age that must be swept away to be replaced by all that is sure—by a strong state to control society and by the hard-edged line, the formal innovation, or the original and powerful structural idea to control art.

Ford dreamed the dream of these young, of using modern methods to control human messes, but he never had the brutality to imagine the cataclysm necessary to reduce industrialism to a pulp. Unlike most of the vorticists, he was no worshiper of the clear outline with no blur or detail. Instead, like the romantic Tory swamped by late liberalism that he was, he flirted more easily and sweetly than Pound with visions of a future life and never lived to hear the speeches of Mussolini:

> For myself, I look forward to a day when the automobile being as nearly extinct as is today the railway, men shall live in great or small but intensively cultivated areas. Once or twice a week men shall fly to the power centers, do their three hour shifts, superintending the actions or executing the repairs, of the power-supplying machines . . . or their field work in the great grain centers and ranches. The rest of the time they will occupy with the agreeable and unhurried

labour of their own soil or with their own benches, chisels, easels, fiddle bows, lasts . . . and with whatever form of night life they shall find agreeable when the day is over. Occasionally even they will take a read in a book.[26]

A TONE FOR SOCIAL BEWILDERMENT: THREE SATIRES

The Simple Life Limited—1910

W. H. Auden wrote, "Satire flourishes in a homogeneous society where satirist and audience share the same views as to how normal people can be expected to behave, and in times of relative stability and contentment, for satire cannot deal with serious evil and suffering. In an age like our own, it cannot flourish except in intimate circles as an expression of private feuds: in public life the evils and sufferings are so serious that satire seems trivial and the only possible kind of attack is prophetic denunciation."[27] His generalization is helpful when we come to look at Ford's satiric novels. The Simple Life Limited, the first and by far the best, is Ford's sunniest and most successful comic novel. The two that follow, The New Humpty-Dumpty and Mr. Fleight, are more ambitious in their critical range and suffer as a result the trivialization of their themes that Auden predicts for authors who try to ridicule or wittily anatomize "serious evil and suffering." These two novels raise issues Ford had no way of facing either intellectually or technically. But The Simple Life Limited is Auden's modern exception, a book intended for and written about an "intimate circle" and making fun of what were, for Ford, "private feuds" in an enclosed world. Though no one escapes Ford's jibes in the novel, a well-defined fringe draws most of his fire—the Limpsfield socialists, the Fabians, the anarchists, the health cranks and Pre-Raphaelite aesthetes he had known in his youth. For a moment, in The Simple Life Limited, he abandoned his more usual critical voice, his "hilarious depression," and thoroughly enjoyed ridiculing the world he had known so well during his small-producer, pig-raising years in the country.

There are two aspects to the satire of The Simple Life Limited: the critical argument of the novel as a whole—crude, confused and self-

---

26. Ford, The Great Trade Route (1937), quoted in Paul Wiley, Novelist of Three Worlds: Ford Madox Ford (Syracuse: Syracuse University Press, 1962), 45.
27. W. H. Auden, The Dyer's Hand (New York, 1968), 385.

contradictory to the point of absurdity—and the local comic details and portraits, which are funny and filled with charming vitality. As Ford always knew about himself, it is in rendering that he makes his discoveries, and his renderings here of the ironies and absurdities inherent in any pretension towards being "Advanced" are irresistible.

The Simple Life Limited is the record of the growth and demise of a communal effort to live the simple life in the quasi country of Kent under the leadership of two very different hypocrites, Gubb, who plans to make the simple life pay, and Bransdon, the pseudomystic guru of the movement, who plans to sit still and do nothing under cover of spouting poems that typically begin,

> Oh, Ulalune lost! . . . Girl of the grey
> eyes and the milk-white feet: no more beside
> the love rath nor upon the lorn hillside shall
> thy silver hand beckon me to pursuit—
> Unseen of thee shall all the little foxes
> play by the Corrighan Ghu.[28]

What utter joy Ford clearly feels in sending up the pseudoarchaism of the Pre-Raphaelites!

These two hypocrites, Gubb and Bransdon, each have a child, Ophelia Bransdon and Hamnet Gubb. The novel opens with the entry into their world, which is made up of such things as roughly printed tracts on "Mother's Milk" and horribly ill-made garments, of the gentle Tory landowner, Gerald Luscombe, who decides to rent his villagers' cottages to the Simple Lifers as a sort of benevolent social experiment. The Lifers move into Gerald's cottages, and the plot of the novel is a series, first, of revelations of what their true relations are to each other, second, of reversals in these peculiar relations as everyone becomes more truly what he or she really is, and finally, of contrasts, for as people become themselves their differences are thrown into relief and become very funny indeed.

Hamnet and Ophelia begin as two obnoxious products of the Simple-Life system of education. Hamnet introduces Ophelia and himself to Luscombe. "'Our name,' the boy said, 'is "Bransdon," and we both have the Celtic temperament. That is what you might expect, for Ophelia's father is the great Mr Bransdon and mine is his chief disciple, Mr Gubb. We have

28. Ford, *The Simple Life Limited* (London, 1911), 144.

neither of us tasted flesh meat or alcohol in our lives and we are compiling a book called "Health Resides in Sandals."'" As it is raining very hard, Gerald Luscombe tries to get Hamnet and Ophelia to stop orating and to come in out of the wet. They feel, however, that they must first tell him to whom he is offering hospitality. They are proselytizers: "The young girl raised her hand as if she were addressing a meeting. 'We object,' she began, 'to all such things as individual property, marriage, revealed religion, the unequal distribution of wealth . . .' 'Oh, well,' Mr. Luscombe said, 'You don't seem to object to rain. Come in and we will have a fire lit.'"[29]

That is always Gerald Luscombe's voice in the novel, good-hearted, deflationary and modest. Unlike the madly hyperactive Lifers, "he had no predisposition to discontent, but he was accustomed to think rather sad, commonplace thoughts about social injustices."[30] His very different kind of simplicity becomes a touchstone by which the far from simple Lifers gradually reveal themselves. The process begins at once when Ophelia and Hamnet come into the civilized comfort of Gerald's world out of the rain. Ophelia is taken upstairs and offered the pick of Mrs. Luscombe's wardrobe from which her natural opulence prompts her to choose the most gorgeous dress in the closet. The true Ophelia is sensual, powerful, self-centered. No matter that she claims to have chosen Mrs. Luscombe's best dress because, like Simple Life garments, it is all of one piece. Ophelia belongs in this magnificent dress instead of in the gray, shapeless Simple Life outfit, or "convicts' suit," as one outsider calls it, and she carries the new clothes off instantly, enjoying the look and feel of her body in these beautiful things with a natural, animal pleasure. Indeed, as Ford repeatedly intimates, it is natural to be artificial. Both the absurdities and the amenities of civilization are a natural outgrowth of egotistical human activity and to reject them is to reject a part of oneself.

There are two kinds of voices in *The Simple Life Limited*, the voices of the Gerald Luscombe type, vague, well-meaning and nondoctrinaire, and the voices of the strident Lifers, egotistical, self-satisfied, and uncompromising. Clashes between these two kinds of people are mediated by a third voice, Ford's voice as author, a voice that narrates the backgrounds and the real but hidden motives of the characters with the most unam-

29. *Ibid.*, 17, 7.
30. *Ibid.*, 11.

bivalent irony in all Ford's *oeuvre*. Here was a case in which, for once, Ford knew quite clearly where his sympathies lay—with the gentle, confused, but essentially sound Gerald Luscombes of this world—while at the same time he was distant enough from the cranks and monomaniacs of the Simple Life to feel a certain detached affection for them, too. His tone in this novel is a consistent and lighthearted irony that indicates tolerance, calm, and the confidence and settled conscience he so rarely felt in relation to his more upsetting subject matter elsewhere.

Few figures in all Ford's novels have the vulgar, exciting life force of the Simple Lifers Gubb and Bransdon, Ophelia and Hamnet. Bransdon, for example, that dirty old charlatan and author of the best seller *Clotted Vapours*, is capable of making up the Simple-Life aphorism, "Whoso eateth of his fellow-creature, though it be but a chicken, wrings the bosom of the angels," capable of seeing it printed up and sold as a postcard by his daughter Ophelia, and finally, capable of knowing how silly and pretentious it all is. Naturally someone so free of scruple finds it easy to lead the twenty households of the colony, people who, as Ford describes them in phrases typical of the aphoristic wit of this novel, suffer from a sort of "bewildered anaemia" and chiefly resemble "chewed string."[31]

But for once in a Ford novel, the characters who have a more tolerant, conventional, and humane view of society are as spiritually muscular and gay as the Simple Life leaders. In most of Ford's novels, his favorites are anemic and powerless while his villains are vigorous, and the distance between them is painful and great. But in *The Simple Life* the people of good sense reclaim the liveliness of the best Lifers and bring all that egotistical energy into their own camp, into the Luscombe world of Toryism, civilized manners, kindness, and toleration. The neurasthenic ironies of novels like *An English Girl* or *Mr. Apollo* give way to a more direct, less guilty or ambivalent ridicule. The uneasy intellectual vacillations of *The Critical Attitude* are here rendered fictionally as an aspect of Gerald Luscombe's character and hence as a state of mind to be both laughed at and sympathetically understood.

« »

If one were disposed to judge the internal logic behind the charm of *The Simple Life Limited* harshly, one could say of its political ideas that they

31. *Ibid.*, 90, 132, 286.

embody decadent liberalism at its worst. Ford's ridicule of all active political efforts, his adulation of laissez-faire individualism, and his utter indifference to social cause and effect are as evident here as they were in his essays and in the English political scene in general in the few years before the war. One by one, the lively characters of the book pull away from the hypocrisies of the uncooperative and backbiting communal life of the colony and set up for individualism, money, nice clothes, clean hair, and scepticism about all ideals. As Gerald Luscombe sums up what had been wrong with Simple Life doctrine, "I don't say they haven't discovered the secret of eternal happiness and brotherly love—if it weren't for human nature."[32]

And what is "human nature" for Simon Bransdon? As if waking from a long sleep, he rises up one night against some villagers who have always taunted the Simple Lifers and thrashes one to within an inch of his life. Violence is human nature and human nature is the central good. Chesterton said much the same thing in his criticism of Shaw: man is the measure of all things and Shaw's supermen will never be adequately human to be suggestive for mankind.[33] At the same time there is also an element of T. E. Hulme lurking in Bransdon: humanism is a bankrupt and hypocritical ideal. Violence and materialism are in man's nature since the Fall. One must accept these things in man. Ford certainly never resolved the contradictions between these two generations of conservative thinkers, but in the closing scenes of the book, Ford gives Bransdon even more good lines than his kind Tory, Luscombe. Bransdon's tone is vigorous and sincere; the cant of the Lifers has been burned out of his speech. Ford has simply stopped being ironic about him. By returning to his natural violence, Bransdon has purged himself of false simplicity and become a real and hence a wise and tolerant man!

Bransdon joins with Luscombe in praising a new apostle to the *real* simple life, Hamnet Gubb, transformed at the end of the novel from the obnoxious hobbledehoy Lifer into what they all call—some in praise, some in blame—an individualist. Ford gives this transformed Hamnet the last word. At the end of the novel, he is living simply and happily in the woods, and all factions join in feeling that somehow he is the wisest and most natural of them all. Bransdon, Luscombe and the rest make a pil-

32. *Ibid.*, 173.
33. See G. K. Chesterton's "Mr. Bernard Shaw," in Chesterton, *Heretics* (1905; rpr. London: John Lane, Bodley Head, 1928).

grimage to visit Hamnet, who tells them: "It isn't the money that's a bad thing, it's the getting it, just as it isn't the working that is the bad thing, it's the way you scamp your work in order to get money. The point is, that it's not right that the two should be connected. I cure dogs and horses and someone else puts money through a cracked window for me. That's the way it ought to be. That's the way to be at one with Nature."[34] This sounds like a joke, but in spite of Hamnet's gaiety and in spite of the utter absurdity of his calling the arrival of a fifty-pound note through his window being "one with Nature," Ford means this seriously. And yet earlier in the novel, similar cases of not letting the right hand and the left see each other's doings are treated with ironic hilarity. *The Simple Life Limited* is the liberal tradition of the novel run riot. The tone undergoes the "slide-around" that worried Pound in Ford's sociological essays. He is first ironic about fools and then he embraces them. What it all comes down to, in this satire particularly but to some extent in all Ford's novels, is that everyone is a fool but there are the fools Ford likes and the fools he doesn't. The latter have the illusion they can live by "movements" and "advanced ideas"; the former tend to give up on human social organization. In other Ford novels, this enforced isolation can become a fearsome thing, but here, though individuality places people at mad cross-purposes, they are ultimately joined again in an air of general hilarity.

The New Humpty-Dumpty—1912

In 1906 Ford published a fairy tale, "Bingel and Bengel," that provides a psychological clue for understanding his satires:

Once upon a time there were two little boys named Bingel and Bengel. One day, they were sent into the woods by their mother to pick up sticks. Bingel came upon a wood-dwarf whose beard had become trapped in the cleft of a tree. "Help, help," he cried, but Bengel told the wood-dwarf he would only help him if the dwarf promised him the pot of gold at the end of the rainbow. The dwarf promised and Bengel released his beard from the cleft of the tree and took the pot of gold. Along came Bingel, looking for sticks, and met the same wood-dwarf with his beard caught crying "Help, help." Bingel helped the dwarf at once without mincing words. As a reward for his goodness, the dwarf tapped Bingel three times on the left side,

34. Ford, *The Simple Life*, 386.

a gift better than the rainbow gold, for now, the dwarf said, "Your heart is in the right place, and you will find that very useful." And so it proved, for when Bengel made mistakes, his mother beat him severely but Bingel's mistreadings she forgave because, she said, "Bingel's heart is in the right place." She even gave Bingel a cake to eat and Bengel nothing at all. So Bengel took his pot of gold to buy sweets, but as he offered the shining coins to the grocer, the sun set and there was nothing left in his hands but dry leaves. Then the grocer beat Bengel even more severely than his mother had done and he returned miserably home to find Bingel sitting happily on the doorstep, eating his cake. "So Bingel gave Bengel some of his cake because after all his heart *was* in the right place. I don't know that this story has a very good moral; but that is the way of the world. Some people cannot do anything at all without being most severely punished. But you can do anything whatever that you like, so long as people will say that about your heart. It's as well to make sure beforehand, though."[35]

This tale is revealing, a real spiritual autobiography telling the sort of truth about how Ford felt about himself that one sometimes glimpses in the configurations of dreams. Of course Ford is both Bengel and Bingel; he feels sorry for himself as Bengel and self-satisfied as Bingel. Particularly, the story is a statement of Ford's longing to be above reproach, to be seen by everyone as essentially honorable and good. The world is often unkind and takes a stick to him unfairly, mistaking him for Bengel, but he is really Bingel and worthy of every benefit of the doubt.

The New Humpty-Dumpty, the satire Ford wrote after *The Simple Life Limited*, is a retelling of the "Bingel and Bengel" story for grown-ups. It is not appropriate here to describe the psychologically interesting sort of badness that characterizes most of this novel. Suffice it to say that Ford creates a Bingel—Count Macdonald, a true aristocrat—in a world full of Bengels. He gives his count a wife who, like his own wife Elsie, still clings to simple-life socialism, which the count, like Ford, has outgrown. This wife, also like Elsie, drags the count through the first stages of a painful divorce. The novel is all retribution heaped upon the heads of the un-grateful wretches who have failed to recognize or be worthy of the good count's generosity. He is a prophet without honor and the tone of the novel arises out of what seem to have been Ford's hurt feelings over the

35. Ford, *Christina's Fairy Book* (London [1906]), 43–44.

fate of the *English Review* and the scandal of his divorce. Swirling out come Ford's embarrassments over money (the count is above caring about it) and his desire to be seen as a gentleman (those in the know know the modest count is from one of the best families in Europe). In the count, Ford hopes to be revenged upon the whole pack of them.

His tone is a thin crust of bravura over still-raw emotions—humiliation, wounded pride. There is none of *The Simple Life*'s good humor or its sassy confidence in human nature, only a sore self-pity. The tone has that particular kind of flatulence that comes of bad faith. Ford is always protesting too much about his Bingel figure's virtues and about his Bengel's bad principles. This becomes particularly distasteful when the contrast between the two is drawn along purely class lines. Count Macdonald is the aristocrat; Mr. Pett (a nasty portrait of Wells, who Ford believed had betrayed his *English Review* efforts) is the plebian who can never act out of honor and whose heart, by virtue of his very birth, can never be in the right place.

Indeed, so exaggerated and distasteful is Count Macdonald's snobbery that one looks for a note of irony in his portrayal, but Ford is entirely in earnest here. Macdonald is his hero; Macdonald is a true aristocrat; Macdonald can do no wrong. Even the pettish Mr. Pett comes round to singing Macdonald's praises. He says to Macdonald's termagant wife, whom he finds lying in wait to throw vitriol in her husband's face:

> The whole of the trouble comes from your being a member of the shopkeeping classes. That's what you are, a shopkeeper's daughter. That's what's in the blood; that's what's in the profession. Your father was a tailor. If a customer brought him cloth to make a suit of clothes he would steal a yard and a half of cloth and justify himself because it was the custom of the trade; that's like you. . . . That's all you care about. . . . The difference between you and gentlefolk like Macdonald—Good God!—the difference between both you and me and him is that we haven't got a spark of generosity in us. We've both conspired to injure that fine gentleman mortally. I'm ready to say that I'm Judas. . . . We aren't either of us fit to loosen the shoe latchets of Sergius Mihailovitch. That's how the world has always been. That is how it will always be. If you manage to get your vitriol on to him, he'll still be fifty thousand fathoms above the heads of

you and me. We're the lower classes, that's what we are, because we
haven't got in the whole of our compositions a spark of generosity.[36]

This is hysterical and exaggerated but not ironic. Pett's reasoning here is
the reasoning of the novel as a whole. Ford's ambivalence, which was elsewhere such a rich source of ironic constructions, is here to be found instead in the insistent, straining tone in which Ford tries to convince us
earnestly of the impossible and tiresome virtue of his hero. There is a note
of desperation in this effort to convince that tends to obliterate the comic
ironies that are indeed latent in the absurd plot; the count's ideas are
laughable, but the reader, rarely invited by the tone to laugh, can only
scoff.

In *The New Humpty-Dumpty* Count Macdonald, half Scottish, half
Russian, and entirely of good family, fired by *noblesse oblige*, has begun in
London as an anarchist, then become a Fabian, then a Russian revolutionary, and when the book opens, has finally decided to abandon all these
advanced causes and fight instead for the forces of reaction. A little gut-
tersnipe social thinker named Pett is to provide the ideas for this counter-
revolution, and Macdonald, man of action and honor, is to carry these
ideas out by reinstating a king on the throne of Galizia. Pett's idea is very
simple: the socialists are making a mistake; they are leveling everything
down to the values and culture of shopkeepers and navvies when what
they should be doing is leveling everything *up* to the values and culture of
the ancient, fine, and educated ruling class. The restoration of the king of
Galizia is to be a move in the direction of bringing back a hierarchy to the
world with an enlightened elite at the top.

That in 1912 the House of Lords had just lost its veto power and the
class it represented was in serious economic trouble seems only to have
fired Ford to further defense of an abstract aristocratic ideal. One of the
few openly comic scenes in the book shows the former queen of Galizia to
be too much of an idiot to read the new constitution, but Macdonald is
undaunted by this seeming unworthiness of the hereditary elite. Instead,
he says that all great movements have had flawed or unworthy leaders.
Though Macdonald is surrounded by plutocrats, fools, and peasants—all
comically unlikely revolutionaries—Ford is concerned to keep his hero
untouched by any satirical attack himself.

36. Ford, *The New Humpty-Dumpty* (London, 1912), 426–27.

The novel is thus split down the middle. On the one side is all that Ford is capable of seeing about the complexity of social change and about the strange and often unideal sources of such change. On the other side is Ford's desire to forget these satirical insights and to write, instead, a serious and romantic elegy for the ideal man who is destroyed by the absurdities of this unideal world.

Once again one sees here that peculiar trait of Ford's, that he can see absurdities, write screamingly farcical plots, employ subtle irony, yet finally draw back from some of the implications of these forms into a more romantic view of his material. *The New Humpty-Dumpty* pillories political idealism; at the same time, it celebrates its political idealist, Macdonald.

There is always this tension in Ford's novels. On the one hand is his antic disposition that sees incongruities, pettiness, jarring detail and that pricks the balloon of pretensions, of idealism, or of anything that puffs itself up or makes any claim to be on a grand scale. On the other hand is his intense romanticism, his grand beliefs in *noblesse oblige* or in the absolute value of art, ideas which blur details, ignore incongruity, and make their own pretentious claims to grandeur. In Ford's best novels he seems to have had some kind of dynamic control over these two sides of his imagination, though there does not appear to be a conscious process of thematic balancing even there. In weaker novels like *The New Humpty-Dumpty*, the elements of satirical criticism, absurdity, farce, idealism, and romance get scrambled together in a way that often provides moments of intense local excitement but that weakens the novel as an effective whole. The satire of *The New Humpty-Dumpty* and its romantic melancholy jockey each other throughout, but as usual in a Ford novel, by the end Ford comes down firmly for a romantic ideal. Macdonald dies an absurd death, shot in the back after his revolution is a success, by a man he earlier had mortally insulted by speaking derisively of the novels of Dumas! A martyrdom for standards in art? A death for a man of taste, while the lovers of the novels of Dumas inherit the earth? The incongruity of this death is ignored by the tone of the novel's last pages. The very funny chain of causes and effects that leads to it is entirely forgotten, hidden behind the pile of laurel wreaths that the last scenes heap upon the dead man's corpse.

We are left then with the fairy tale of "Bingel and Bengel." Ford has written a political satire but in it the individual heart remains king. Bingel is the ideal ruler because, though he can make mistakes, he cannot offend against the essential spirit of his people. They follow him not because of his ideas but because of his properly positioned heart. (Indeed, here, as in so many Ford novels, ideas keep being dropped into a medium in which they have no chance to survive.) It was certainly the Liberal party's hope at this time that somehow the people could be persuaded to take the intention for the deed, the symbolic gesture for the basic change. Like Shaw, Wells, Chesterton, and Ford himself, the Liberals desired to find a state of heart that would unite everyone under one benign Great Figure. But in *The New Humpty-Dumpty* the cozy social circle of *The Simple Life Limited* is gone. People are alone in a large, cold public arena. ("The heart of another is a dark forest" is the count's favorite saying.) Here Ford inquires into that "serious evil and suffering" which Auden says is so hard to encompass within the bounds of satire, and as Auden warns, he fails to cast any critical light on the painful political contradictions of the public life he describes.

Mr. Fleight—1913

Mr. Fleight is the most overtly political of Ford's satires. It tells the story of how Mr. Blood, an old-fashioned man of good family, decides to promote the political career of a parvenu Jewish millionaire, Mr. Fleight. Like *The New Humpty-Dumpty* it is based on a set of oppositions drawn between these two types of men, each symbolizing, as Pett and Macdonald did in the earlier novel, possible responses to the tendencies that Ford saw in modern life. Here, however, the polarization between the two is less extreme. Blood and Fleight have a respect for and interest in each other that makes the contrasts between them far more subtle and believable than anything that passes between those Bingel-Bengel fairy-tale creations of *The New Humpty-Dumpty*. Both men in *Mr. Fleight* have their hearts in the right place, and the novel has a genuine melancholy about it because of the way each one suffers his own particular disappointments in the social and political world they inhabit together.

Similarly, the contrast that was so sharp in *The New Humpty-Dumpty* between farcical and romantic elements in both plot and tone is far more muted in *Mr. Fleight*. There are comic scenes and exaggerated and antic moments but none of the driving, mad absurdity of the earlier two satires. Instead, the structure of *Mr. Fleight* is loose and episodic. As always, Ford puts the burden of the political situation onto the private life. The relatively rare satirical dialogues between Blood and his protégé, Fleight, which seem to be the novel's *raison d'être*, are as meandering as the plot; they are rather like a political argument in *The Critical Attitude*.

If the plot is episodic and the didactic satirical sections unfocused, is there anything to be said for *Mr. Fleight*? In fact, yes. The novel has a great appeal to any lover of the Edwardian period. Ford has rendered here the aura of that time (around 1912) with great richness and feeling, though, because the novel is built around a number of set pieces on Edwardian political issues that can have little resonance for readers not steeped in the history of those years, it is dated. It takes for granted, for example, an understanding of the national rebellion against Liberal party politics from both Right and Left, a crisis which the novel echoes without in any way dramatizing, except perhaps in the general angst of its characters.

Therefore there are two separate things going on in *Mr. Fleight*: on the one hand, Ford offers short spurts of political conversation which if strung together become a recognizable chain of values—anti-Liberal, antidemocratic, antiplutocratic, proaristocratic—while on the other, he creates characters who are suffering their loss at varying levels of self-consciousness. He offers both a didactic version of social changes and an atmospheric evocation of these changes. Between them these two elements do not carry the novel along with any kind of structural power, but from time to time, a resonance is indeed set off between argument and incident.

Mr. Blood's reactionary views are Ford's, as they were so many others'. Yeats similarly romanticized the class war and the ideal isolation of workers. Indeed, as the strike waves of 1910 and 1911 reached their peak, it became a commonly expressed sentiment of the middle class that the working man was another and quite alien race. Ford's satire in *Mr. Fleight*, which both embraces and flees from the idea of class struggle, is a typical product of its time, and as Mr. Fleight says of Mr. Blood, Ford is "perfectly in earnest."[37]

At the same time, Ford is not as sure of himself as his Mr. Blood. He farms out another side of himself, his melancholic bewilderment, onto his Mr. Fleight character. By a fluke, Fleight wins his seat in Parliament; by a bribe, he procures a gentile wife. The bitterness of these hollow victories in a world stripped of hope or romance provides a brief moment near the

37. Ford, *Mr. Fleight* (London, 1913), 251.

end of the novel of true pity and terror. But ultimately, Ford robs Fleight of any such pretensions to tragic grandeur. At the end he reminds us of what a mournful little creature Fleight is. "I don't in the least know whether in the long run I'm to be a Tory or a Socialist, or a Liberal Individualist for the matter of that. . . . it really has become extremely difficult for me to decide what my intentions are, or whether it's even possible to have any intentions at all."[38] Here is the voice of John Dowell in *The Good Soldier*, the voice of the modern man adrift. Mr. Fleight is Jew and plutocrat— types Ford abhorred—yet this figure is the most sympathetic character in the book because Ford cannot help loving the stranger, the man lost between cultures, the confused man. Alongside the Macdonald and Blood figures, he often places these others. The Mr. Blood in Ford pontificates. The Mr. Fleight flees, ducks, and hides. One of Ford's successes in this novel is his ability to let these two sides of himself talk to each other. Mr. Blood and Mr. Fleight are friends. In one of their arguments Mr. Fleight defends himself against Mr. Blood's criticisms by saying, "Well, I'm a modern man," to which Mr. Blood "not unkindly" replies, "So you are."[39]

‹‹ ››

At his best, Ford as a sociopolitical commentator is always giving us a specific situation, saturated with particulars which suggest the quality of life at a certain time or place. When he argues, he carries us along only if we close our eyes and leap after him from precariously balanced point to point. His arguments are vertiginous, but his evocations are reliable. It is his atmospheres which provide the social insights which are the most solid element in his satiric art.

38. *Ibid.*, 167.
39. *Ibid.*, 255.

Some one has said that the death of a mouse from cancer is the whole sack of Rome by the Goths, and I swear to you that the breaking up of our little four-square coterie was such another unthinkable event.

FORD, *The Good Soldier*, 1915

Part IV

THE GOOD SOLDIER

> If for nine years I have possessed a goodly apple that is
> rotten at the core and discover its rottenness only in nine
> years, . . . isn't it true to say that for nine years I possessed a
> goodly apple?
>
> FORD, *The Good Soldier*

«7»

FROM COMIC IRONY TO ROMANCE

DURING Ford's years of experimentation, he gradually developed his
subtle, shifting voice. Also, in book after book, he explored some
aspect of what always had to be his subjects, the tension between a detailed view of everyday life and a romantic overview, between the rival
attractions of innocence and of experience, between the past (romantic in
being orderly) and the present (romantic in being ungraspable).

His tone in these novels fluctuated in effect, undermining his intentions as often as it succeeded in expressing them. But it was difficult to find
a voice that would keep all his possible meanings alive. Indeed, it is a *tour
de force* to create a voice that can synthesize doubt and bravura, vagueness
and precision, pathos and absurdity. With this necessary baggage of contradictory material, small wonder Ford's journey in search of expressive
means was a long one.

The Good Soldier is the masterpiece that comes as the culmination of
Ford's long Edwardian apprenticeship. It is also his novel about the end of
the Edwardian way of life. Even more than most people, Ford Madox Ford
was afraid of endings; so it is in many respects a circular novel. Its narration turns in upon itself and its voice is meandering, equivocal, ironic.

The narrator, the pallid American John Dowell, tells us the story of
three sexual triangles. First he describes his marriage to Florence and her
many years of infidelity to him in the arms of his friend, the eponymous
good soldier, the seemingly impeccable ideal of a country gentleman,
Edward Ashburnham. Next, Dowell gives us the second triangle, describ-

ing the dynamics of the marriage between Edward Ashburnham and his wife Leonora, who suffers over Edward's years of infidelity in the arms of Dowell's Florence. Finally, Dowell tells us about the third triangle. Edward falls in love with the Ashburnham's young ward, Nancy, to whom he should be in loco parentis. The passions set loose by the dynamics of this final triangle kill Florence and Edward and drive Nancy mad. This leaves Dowell, who loved Edward and who was himself in love with Nancy, bereft, while Leonora stands triumphant in a now emptied field.

Ford used this story of sexual passion as a starting place for describing the decay of spiritual vigor in the Edwardian years. Social conventions are moribund; under the demanding pressure of sexuality, they collapse. The novel's painful love affairs are stages in a process that is finally to burst open the social forms that formerly hid sexual infidelity.

All of Ford's characters suffer in finding their world unable to sustain them through the course of sexual passion. Some of these characters react by making their own rules; they are carefully disguised savages in drawing rooms. Others try to live by the old rules and discover this dooms them to total deprivation. There is no nourishment left in the old forms. (Leonora waits for her rutting husband to return to her in what used to be the normal pattern for erring men of his class, but he never does, never can.)

Finally, a few of Ford's characters have the distinction of knowing that they know nothing. They can only act out of feeling. Like the others, they too are doomed to unhappiness, but their unhappiness is of their own making, a unique, asocial brew they drink down to the dregs. They do not know the meaning of life or the reason why they feel so empty, so lonely, but they search for this meaning, these reasons, and their search is what The Good Soldier is about.

Tension among possible meanings for experience keeps the novel alive, taut with the excitement of contradictory possibilities. These contradictions proliferate often with comic, often with ironic effect. Indeed, The Good Soldier is Ford's masterpiece of comic irony. We are bonded to the madly fluctuating voice of Dowell as he tries out one possible interpretation of the facts after another in a desperate chain of absurd, sad, ironic reversals.

The Good Soldier demands and rewards a kind of careful reading which Ford's earlier novels do not. Here, for the first time, he found a combination of novelistic conventions that could bring into balance his always far-flung and oddly assorted insights. Here, observations great and small, profound and ridiculous, instead of being undercut by each other, serve each other. He finds ways to be a social novelist while still submerging himself in the world view of his heroes, since the maddening social disconnectedness of these men, lost in their self-doubt and solipsism, becomes his social theme. In *The Good Soldier* Ford finally managed to make a living connection between his habitual surface elaboration and his profoundest observations.

« »

To understand the tone of *The Good Soldier*, we must remember the world into which it came in 1914. Ford described Ashburnham's milieu: "Edward was sunk in his chair; there were in the room two candles, hidden by green glass shades. The green shades were reflected in the glasses of the bookcases that contained not books but guns with gleaming brown barrels and fishing-rods in green baize over-covers. There was dimly to be seen, above a mantlepiece encumbered with spurs, hooves and bronze models of horses, a dark-brown picture of a white horse."[1] Edward Ashburnham, his walls lined with guns and rods instead of books, was one very important element in this world. *Blast*, Wyndam Lewis' revolutionary little magazine where the first installment of *The Good Soldier* appeared, was another.

In his Preface of 1919 to *Heartbreak House*, Shaw looked back on two prewar worlds that loosely correspond to that of Edward on the one hand and that of *Blast* on the other. He called Edward's world Horseback Hall, "consisting of a prison for horses with an annex for the ladies and gentlemen who rode them, hunted them, talked about them, bought them and sold them, and gave nine-tenths of their lives to them, dividing the other tenth between charity, churchgoing (as a substitute for religion), and conservative electioneering (as a substitute for politics)."[2] Shaw called his second world, Heartbreak House. Heartbreak House is too bourgeois and intellectually lax to be the world of *Blast*, but there is, nevertheless, some affinity between the hotheaded innovators of *Blast* and the cultural illness Shaw diagnoses in the residents of Heartbreak House.

Heartbreak House is "cultured, leisured Europe before the war." By

1. Ford, *The Good Soldier*, 184, hereinafter cited in the text by page number only.
2. George Bernard Shaw, "Heartbreak House and Horseback Hall," Preface to *Heartbreak House* (1919; rpr. New York, 1964), 9.

1914, however, this culture had become entirely cut off from the political life of the country: "Power and culture were in separate compartments."[3] The good soldier, Edward Ashburnham, the man with lands, the man who can lead other men, is a man with no ideas, no sense of what is happening in the world now that the feudal heritage he values has been completely undermined. And his story appears in Blast, a periodical that could never have appeared on the tables of Edward's own particular Horseback Hall, Branshaw Teleragh. The purposelessness, the blindness that are the themes of The Good Soldier come in part from this split in Edward Ashburnham's culture between power and meaning.

Blast was the voice of the new world Edward could never imagine, but Blast, too, had its own failures of imagination. Like the characters at the end of Heartbreak House who are ecstatic at the sounds of bombs bursting in air, the young moderns of Blast, the vorticists, worshiped an iconoclasm, an order, and a modernity that they could but half imagine. "Heartbreak House was far too lazy and shallow to extricate itself from [the] palace of evil enchantment. It rhapsodized about love; but it believed in cruelty. It was afraid of the cruel people; and it saw that cruelty was at least effective."[4] In spite of the affinity some of them later developed for fascism, is it unfair to the vorticists to bracket them with Shaw's decadent heartbreakers? The vorticists were serious about culture as the heartbreakers of Shaw's cultural nightmare are not. But the iconoclasm of vorticism was shallow. It did not and could not survive the real cataclysm, the war. Blast proclaimed: "Our Vortex is fed up with your dispersals, reasonable chicken-men." (This to the impressionists, who, like Ford, saw a mixed reality.) "Our Vortex is proud of its polished sides. Our Vortex is white and abstract with its red-hot swiftness."[5] After the war this voice could only sound fatuous. Edward Ashburnham did not read things like Blast not only because his world had lost all touch with cultural vitality but also because Blast could not conceivably have helped him to understand his condition. The vorticists were too wrapped up in their own romance, the romance of new worlds for old. Blast praised the machine-age sensibility, the industrial state—"this bareness and hardness"—and said that

3. Ibid., 7, 10.
4. Ibid., 15.
5. Unsigned editorial matter, Blast, 149.

the English, as the inventors of this hardness, "should be the great enemies of Romance."[6]

The sections of *The Good Soldier* that appear in *Blast* are indeed as ele-
gantly machined as any vorticist could desire. They are also layered with
an irony that lives comfortably with the chic paradoxes of *Blast*: "We only
want humour if it has fought like Tragedy. We only want Tragedy if it can
clench its side-muscles like hands on it's [sic] belly, and bring to the surface
a laugh like a bomb. . . . Humor is a phenomenon caused by sudden pour-
ing of culture into barbary. Tragic humour is the birthright of the North.
Any great Northern Art will partake of this insidious and volcanic chaos."[7]
These are, indeed, fitting epigraphs for *The Good Soldier*, but they leave
out one very important side of the book's sensibility—its pathos, its soft-
edged identification with its absurd sufferers. Ford's gradual abandonment
of anomic, bottomless, tragicomic irony at the end of his novel (which,
because of the intrusion of the war, *Blast* did not survive to print) is an
expression not only of his romanticism but also of his quest for genuine
feeling in modern circumstances.

The Good Soldier is about a society whose internal order and meaning
has dried up leaving nothing but a shell, an empty structure of social forms
by which its people can live. Ford uses irony as the most sensitive probe to
feel out this distance between passional life and empty forms. The novel is
a profound exploration of the ironic turn of mind, and its themes are particularly suited to the kind of irony Ford always used, a vacillating, uncertain, but probing voice tinged with something of the hysterical, a hysteria
either pathetic or absurd. For example, *The Good Soldier* is about people
who lie. Some lie to protect society while others lie to undermine it, but
they are all so confused about what is true that every perception is bifur-
cated and can only be expressed by irony. Hence Dowell speaks ironically,
but in a world of liars irony goes wild and rival meanings undercut each
other infinitely.

If irony is a fitting voice with which to describe a world of liars, it is also
fitting for describing a world in which few people experience things directly. The characters in the novel who feel strongly are defeated by this
world of exhausted repression. Their pain comes to us filtered through the

6. *Ibid.*, 41.
7. *Ibid.*, 31, 37.

sensibility of that most passive of voyeurs, John Dowell. He is an ironist because irony is an effective way to record contradictions without resolving them. Dowell and the other characters fear resolution; from their advanced condition of passivity or doubt or fear, irony is a small refuge.

Irony, and particularly comic irony, serves Ford well, too, when he comes to measure a collapse in the scale of his society's sense of life. Grandeur made mechanical or unsupported by real authority is ridiculous; the Ashburnhams' pretension that theirs is an orderly and gracious way of life is absurd. Dowell is overcome by a combination of hilarity and pathos as he compares the apparent solidity of the Ashburnham ménage with the truth that both husband and wife are desperate, lost, out of control. As an assured scale of meaning, of human stature, collapses, irony is the voice that yokes the large with the small. Dowell nominates small things for vast importance and speaks of things traditionally important, like fidelity, as finally, beside the point. He fixes on details that seem comically to be the wrong details, but who is finally to say that he is absurd or arbitrary? Ford is the great chronicler of humiliation, and humiliation is an amalgam of pain and absurdity; it comes from the scale of self-regard collapsed, from the contrast between hope and mortifying disappointment. The novel's brilliant tonal mixture, in which comic elements are consistently made to support serious ones, is central to Ford's hard-won triumph of technique in *The Good Soldier*.

Ford's use of the figure of Dowell as his narrator is the key device in this triumph over the entropy that usually disorganized the presentation of his themes. By choosing to use this first person point of view he solved several of his former narrative problems in a single stroke. He placed his vacillations, his uncertainty about the meaning of his observations, inside one of the novel's characters. Placing doubt inside Dowell and making him the narrator is a technique that lets doubt, confusion and irresolution proliferate into every corner of the narrative while still keeping these mixed emotions as a clear expression of one man's search for meaning.

In 1906 Ford had worked with Conrad, master of first person narration, on the fragment *The Nature of a Crime*, which employs a narrator who prefigures Dowell. The technical possibilities of such a narrator no doubt impressed Ford then and germinated in his mind. During the years between 1906 and 1913, though he used no first person narrator, Ford extensively explored the possibilities of the subjective point of view. His impressionism was always a dive into a particular consciousness. By 1913 when he sat down to write *The Good Soldier*, he was ready to face the implications of a severely limited point of view. Here no God Apollo comes down to relieve Dowell of the burden of daily life. Impressionism, which in some of the earlier novels seemed to entrap the characters in a blank, undifferentiated subjectivity, now becomes an expression of a fully known, unique narrator.

Since it is through Dowell's voice that we learn the story and through his variations in tone that we experience all these nuances of feeling, the first task in a close analysis of the comic irony in *The Good Soldier* must be to decide what our attitude towards him is as we read.[8] The difficulty in discussing Dowell is that to take a final view of him obscures the effect Ford has labored to produce. Though it is certainly true that Dowell is morally passive and at times seems inhumanly deficient in passion, it is also true that he has been deceived monstrously by people of an equal degree of moral deficiency. If we place too much of the fault in the eye of the beholder, an important part of the moral fable is lost. Understanding becomes a mere matter of reversing Dowell's judgments. If Dowell is totally unreliable as the novel's moral center, who in the novel replaces him? Ford keeps forcing us to ask this question by deliberately presenting us with a moral vacuum which begs to be filled, first by one character, then by another. The passive Dowell has trouble choosing a standard by which to judge, and Ford makes us identify with his unsureness by refusing us an overt hint of his own point of view. In other words, the problem the style of the novel poses to us is analogous to the problem the narrator faces

8. *The Good Soldier* has the aspect of a conundrum; it has attracted many subtle critical readings. Nevertheless, critics of the novel fall—to use D. A. Traversi's wonderful categorization of the critics of *Antony and Cleopatra*—into two groups, the Roman and the Egyptian. The Roman critics judge Antony and Cleopatra harshly, while the Egyptians think order in the state well lost for love. In the case of *The Good Soldier*, the Romans think Dowell is a weak, passionless fool, while the Egyptians see him as an Everyman, an existential hero who looks for the truth which can never be known. The first influential Roman was Mark Schorer, "An Interpretation," in *The Good Soldier* (New York: Vintage, 1957), v–xv. There he argued that Dowell was a completely unreliable narrator whose judgments were to be reversed by the reader. He was answered by Samuel Hynes who wrote the classic on the Egyptian side: "The Epistemology of *The Good Soldier*," *Sewanee Review*, LXIX (Spring, 1961), 225–35. More recently, the Egyptians have prevailed but the two groups continue to disagree about how much sympathy Dowell deserves.

within the novel itself. We must assess his qualities as observer without a clear standard by which to measure him. The author may be present, but it is not clear what his presence means.

In this way, Ford raised moral ambivalence to a structural principle. Because Dowell's position in the novel is intentionally ambiguous, as one is reading the novel and, if possible, even in remembering, it is best to think of him in the way the gestalt psychologists think of a simple design on a solid background. If one concentrates on the ground, it becomes the design and the design recedes in the mind and becomes the ground. One reverses this process again and again, figure-ground, figure-ground, until something the psychologists call flipping takes place. Perception of the design as first the background and then as the design again alternates very quickly so that one *almost* sees both qualities at once.

That is exactly what happens in looking at Dowell as narrator: first he is reliable judge, then execrable fool, then properly self-deprecating ironist, then condescending failure. All these partially true images of him must constantly be vying with each other in the reader's mind, a different one coming uppermost with each twist of the narrative. Only then can the many perspectives that interested Ford emerge from the mouth of a single narrator.

For example, to a new reader of the novel Dowell's description of the night Florence dies may look like a clear illustration of his inadequacy to separate the meaningful from the insignificant. He seems submerged beneath details. Indeed, he describes his entire experience of the suicide night as a collage of bobbing heads. All he can remember are the faces, "like floating globes," of the grand duke, the head of the police, and the hotelkeeper. First he would see "the bearded, monarchical, benevolent head of the Grand Duke; then the sharp featured brown cavalry-moustached features of the chief of police; then the globular, polished, and high-collared vacuousness that represented Monsieur Schontz, the proprietor of the hotel. At times one head would be there alone, at another the spiked helmet of the official would be close to the healthy baldness of the prince; then M. Schontz's oiled locks would push between the two" (100). This can indeed seem like the word painting of a child who cannot understand the meaning of what it sees. (Ford once compared Dowell to Maisie in James's *What Maisie Knew*.) But Dowell says of his impressionistic accumulation of details, "That was how it presented itself to me." He

has no pretension to an overview of events. Later, he ends his description
of the muddled observations he made on that momentous night by saying,
"Well, those are my impressions" (101). If we are tempted to say that they
are rather meager ones, Ford gradually undermines our confidence in this
judgment by insisting on the use of the small but telling detail as the most
real representation of what events feel like. In the midst of confusion such
as there was on the night of Florence's death, Dowell reminds us of Ford's
impressionist credo that "it is some little material object, always, that
catches the eye and that appeals to the imagination" (99). One must not
mistake Ford's impressionism for a moral judgment on Dowell's clarity, nor
mistake Dowell's acknowledgment of difficulty as a mere admission of
weakness. Ford always had his own reasons for identifying both with
Dowell's way of seeing events from a worm's-eye view and with his difficulties in retelling these events in a controlled order.

The Good Soldier begins, "This is the saddest story I have ever heard"
(15) and proceeds with a barrage of Dowell's facts, hints, personal opinions, and abstract formulations relating to this story. By the end of this
short first section Dowell's problems as narrator have become dramatically
clear. The "story" is linear, a clear plot line of events in an important sequence, but Dowell's real interest is not in the line itself but in the motives
that have given this extraordinary series its impetus. His real desire is to
put forward all the events at once and to keep them there constantly, so he
can juxtapose them, first one way and then another, until he has wrung
from them some understanding of life, an understanding which he increasingly feels has hitherto eluded him. At one point the narrator complains, "I have been casting back again, but I cannot help it. It is so difficult to keep all these people going. I tell you about Leonora and bring her
up to date; and then about Edward, who has fallen behind. And then the
girl gets hopelessly left behind. I wish I could put it down in diary form"
(192). This desire to show each event in the context of all the others is the
kind of technical and emotional preoccupation we have come to expect
from Ford.

Ford uses Dowell to give his carefully planned assaults on the body of
his material the appearance of ramblings. "Is this digression or isn't it digression?" the narrator asks (24). In each digression, new layers of facts
and impressions are added and the significance and density of what Ford
always called the "coil" increases exponentially. The narrator explains,

"When one discusses an affair—a long, sad affair—one goes back, one goes forward. One remembers points that one has forgotten and one explains them all the more minutely since one recognizes that one had forgotten to mention them in their proper places and that one may have given, by omitting them, a false impression" (161). Wearing this narrative mask of meticulous casualness, Ford builds up a delicate structure of repetitions. There can be no simple description of the plot; the story's shape derives from all the layers of associations that Ford has heaped upon the narrative line.

Dowell is both an author's trick, a rambling voice that is not rambling at all, and a self-conscious ironist, a manipulator of meaning in his own right. At the same time, however, he is the bearer of Ford's unresolvable ambivalence about his own material. That is why it is important to see how many are Dowell's functions in the novel, and how many in kind. We flip from one view of him to another. He himself keeps changing his mind about his story, so that we are forced to flip from one view of his material to another. And while these changes are happening still others are going on as well. Ford keeps changing the way in which Dowell mediates between us and his material. Ford himself is telling us something essential he feels about all linear story telling: it involves making moral and social judgments which Dowell tells us he finds it impossible to make and which the close reader of Ford's canon feels Ford also always found difficult.

If there is any constant in Dowell as either character or narrative device, that constant is irony. Meaning is always double meaning, meaning inferred from counter statements, meaning gleaned from the painful clash of contraries. This circuitous path to experience happens inside Dowell's consciousness as a part of the fiction Ford presents, and it happens inside the structure of the novel as Ford himself struggles with ambivalence, doubt, and weakness.

« »

One need only look at specific passages in The Good Soldier to see the problems which arise if one takes too strict a view of Dowell. Take, for example, Dowell's tantalizing description of his courtship of Florence. One becomes increasingly interested in knowing about Florence as more and more grotesque hints are given about her. Florence's aunts mysteriously beg Dowell not to marry her: "Don't do it, John. Don't do it. You're a good young man" (79). Ford contrives that our knowledge of Florence and her first lover Jimmy's extraordinary plan for continuing their liaison under Dowell's roof comes as slowly as possible. Ford justifies this elaborate withholding of vital information about Florence by establishing a dual nature in his narrator. At the same time that Dowell is telling us about his odd courtship in the light of what he has learned since, he is also intent on reexperiencing events as they were to him when they occurred. Critics who have found Dowell exasperating and idiotically limited are ignoring his often-stated desire to reenter events like a *halluciné*, miraculously shorn of hindsight and able to recapture the very shape and taste of his original mistakes.

This double perspective is further complicated by the reader's degree of initiation. For example, one who reads *The Good Soldier* for the first time can only take the following passage about Florence's early travels in Europe at face value as an unironic description of unexceptionable events:

> They [Florence and her Uncle Hurlbird] were to have spent two months more in that tranquil bosom, but inopportune events, apparently in her uncle's business, had caused their rather hurried return to Stamford. The young man called Jimmy remained in Europe to perfect his knowledge of that continent. He certainly did: he was most useful to us afterwards. (77)

But one who has read *The Good Soldier* before knows that this "tranquil bosom" is the home of a blackguard and the "inopportune events" that force Florence and her uncle to depart are that she has been discovered coming out of that "most useful" Jimmy's bedroom at five o'clock in the morning. Jimmy's knowledge of the continent, we later learn, has been gained at Uncle Hurlbird's expense: he has paid Jimmy to remain behind, away from his all too corruptible niece. Finally, during those years when Jimmy was "most useful" to Dowell and Florence in their travels, he was actually Florence's lover, the one who first helped her lay the ground rules of her elaborate and lifelong deception of Dowell. All this perfidy, melodrama and surprise is decorously hidden behind what must appear to the uninitiated first reader as a straightforward piece of narration.

If these are the facts, how are we to take Dowell's way of alluding to them? The new reader of the novel takes Dowell's flat description at face value and is only slowly, deliciously undeceived. No novel of Ford's offers so many kinds of excitement at the level of plot surprise. But if one has read the novel before, Dowell's voice is perceived as more complex. Is he being dry? ("He was most useful to us afterwards.") Is he being bitter, al-most sarcastic? (The "tranquil bosom.") Or is he merely so preoccupied by the demands of re-creating the past that for the moment he has become inattentive to what he now knows and is instead concentrating on the act of narration itself?

There is evidence for all these and for many other attitudes in Dowell's tone in the book as a whole. Sometimes, for example, the man who is, to a first reader, apparently unironic about Jimmy's sabotage of his marriage breaks away from his role as patient recorder or dry ironist to reveal more raw emotions. Florence's "room door was locked because she was nervous about thieves," one passage begins chastely. This is a misstatement, of course. Even first readers already know Florence has other reasons for keeping a locked door. But Dowell is not lying; he is merely re-creating an earlier state of mind, the state of mind of a trusting husband who believes his wife's plausible excuses. And Ford is using this supposed state of mind to slow the material down, to shape the incident. Then Dowell continues, "but an electric contrivance on a cord was understood to be attached to her little wrist." Now the tone is beginning to acquire some overtly ironic spin. "Contrivance" is not a friendly word for Florence's emergency ar-rangements, and "little wrist" begs a silent comparison with the monstrous enormity of Florence's deception. The passage continues:

> She had only to press a bulb to raise the house. And I was provided
> with an axe—an axe!—great Gods, with which to break down her
> door in case she ever failed to answer my knock, after I knocked really
> loud several times. It was pretty well thought out, you see. (84–85)

In this case then, if not in every one, Dowell recognizes an absurdity when he tells it. The axe is too much for him. Remembrance of his own credu-lity makes him burst out from his staid efforts at objectivity. He is over-come by the irony of his own story. But, typically, he feels a bit ashamed of this outburst of personal feeling only a moment afterwards. He retreats into the dry understatement, "It was pretty well thought out, you see." This is the canonical shape for a Dowell paragraph: a tone of innocence, swelling to some fuller emotional or intellectual expression and then col-lapsing into a self-deprecating understatement. (Note that this is not only a typical construction of Dowell's. It appears everywhere in Ford's novels.)

The ironic collapse into understatement that ends so many of Dowell's attempts at a deeper emotional expression has several effects. Deflationary codas announce Dowell's distance from events and from a full existence. Often he is quite conscious that this is the impression he is creating. Sometimes he offers an excuse for himself, sometimes not. Whether or not we accept his excuses is a function of many variables. When Ford shows Dowell to have been obtuse, he also gives Dowell a persuasive reason for his obtuseness, which we may call rationalization or we may call extenuating circumstance, depending on who we are. We may dislike Dowell for playing the part of "a woman or a solicitor,", but at the same time we may feel a sympathy for the man who knows this about himself and has suffered the particular indignities reserved for the passive and the weak. He is constantly observing the presence of intention and power in the people around him and recognizing that their response to him is, as he describes it himself, "as if I were an invalid, . . . a poor chap in a bath chair" (35, 39). Who are we? Are we, the audience, people who are impatient with fools or people who empathize with ignorance?

《 》

How successfully Ford has drawn his readers into a labyrinth: even a description of Dowell twists, turns, and folds back on itself. But it will not do for analysis of Ford's technique to mimic his art too far. Is it only a circle Ford describes, or must not the reader come at last to some conclusions about Dowell, to some resting point beyond flux and confusion?

Three-quarters of the way through *The Good Soldier*, Dowell mentions how it feels to be in the process of writing: "I have been writing away at this story now for six months and reflecting longer and longer upon these affairs" (162). At the end of the novel he gives a more discouraged description of the process. After a writing break of eighteen months, during which he brought the insane Nancy back from Ceylon, he calls his description of their journey "just a record of fatigue" (202). The short last section of the novel written after his return is characterized by this fatigue joined with a new determination to choose among the moral alternatives that have been vying in his mind throughout the novel. This last section is the culmination of a subtle realignment of sympathies Dowell and the reader share as the book progresses. By degrees, as more and more layers are added to our impressions, Dowell makes certain distinctions and choices. His irony loses its satiric bite and gradually becomes the medium for a more melancholy and intimate expression.

Locating these changes in attitude is complicated, first, by Dowell's shifting role in the novel and, second, by the homogeneity of style with which Ford concealed these shifts. The unity of Dowell's surface tone belies any generalization one seeks to make about his increased knowledge and sensitivity. Even Dowell's variation in feeling and awareness is part of this unity. He vacillates, but it is his nature to vacillate. So, paradoxically, his vacillations become constants. We come to expect him to be slippery. It is for this reason that it is difficult to pin down his growing sensitivity or disillusion. For example, compare this description of Florence's corpse:

> Oh, extremely charming and clear-cut—looking with a puzzled expression at the electric-light bulb that hung from the ceiling, or perhaps through it, to the stars above. Who knows? Anyhow, there was an end of Florence. (110)

and this description of how Colonel Powys married his daughter off to Edward:

> The Colonel . . . pointed out that [Edward's] visit would have cost them sixty pounds, what with the hire of an extra servant, of a horse and car, and with the purchase of beds and bedding and extra tablecloths. There was nothing else for it but the marriage. In that way Edward and Leonora became man and wife. (126)

In tone, there is no difference at all. The demeaning details of the electric light bulb and the beds and bedding give way to the crisp and devastatingly understated conclusions: "Anyhow, there was an end of Florence" and "In that way Edward and Leonora became man and wife." These passages work in much the same way and have a similar ring. Yet there is a difference which must be explained and located between Dowell as he describes Florence and the others in the first sections of the book and Dowell as he gives, in the second half of the book, "a very minute study of [Edward and Leonora's] progress towards complete disunion" (126).

The sentence "Anyhow, there was an end of Florence" is one of the last in Dowell's re-creation of how it felt to be Florence's husband. The change in narrative emphasis that comes in the second half of the novel reflects Dowell's changed idea of what is important. Gradually but unmistakably, his need for a compulsive repetition of Florence's acts wanes and his interest in the second "coil" of the novel, the triangle of Leonora, Edward, and Nancy, grows. He describes his dramatic discovery at her death that Florence "wasn't real; she was just a mass of talk out of guide books, of drawings out of fashion-plates" (111). The earlier part of Dowell's narrative re-creates for us his feeling for Florence as "an unattained mistress" (52). In the later sections this image is superseded by another human embroilment, one which is both more psychologically creditable than that of Dowell and Florence and more closely examined. This second preoccupation has more spiritual meat to offer the narrator than the first. His feeling for people is extended by contact with the Ashburnhams' sad and profound antagonism in a way that Florence was incapable of extending it.

If, indeed, the novel's characteristic ironies are gradually modified until their meaning and feeling finally become something else, the proof must lie in reading passage by passage, making comparisons. In a first example, an early passage, Dowell is a consciously ironic narrator; as always, he is relatively unambivalent about his own feelings when speaking of his wife. His judgment of *her*, at least, is clear, and he spears her with a relentless comedy: "Poor dear thing," Dowell ironically calls this poisonous pontificator, "I have heard her lecture Teddy Ashburnham by the hour on the difference between a Franz Hals and a Wouvermans and why the Pre-Mycenaean statues were cubical with knobs on the top" (25). In Florence we see civilization so far decayed that we cannot even remember any more what might once have been important about it. She is the tourist who looks on each thing only once, then talks. She berates Leonora Ashburnham for not educating her husband:

> She used to exclaim: "Well, if you knew it, why haven't you told it all already to Captain Ashburnham? I'm sure he finds it interesting!" And Leonora would look reflectively at her husband and say: "I have an idea that it might injure his hand—the hand, you know, used in connection with horses' mouths . . ." And poor Ashburnham would blush and mutter and would say: "That's all right. Don't you bother about me."
>
> I fancy his wife's irony did quite alarm poor Teddy; because one evening he asked me seriously in the smoking-room if I thought that having too much in one's head would really interfere with one's quickness in polo. It struck him, he said, that Brainy Johnnies generally were rather muffs when they got on to four legs. I reassured him as best I could. I told him that he wasn't likely to take in

enough to upset his balance. At that time the Captain was quite evidently enjoying being educated by Florence. She used to do it about three or four times a week under the approving eyes of Leonora and myself. It wasn't, you understand, systematic. It came in bursts. It was Florence clearing up one of the dark places of the earth, leaving the world a little lighter than she had found it. She would tell him the story of Hamlet; explain the form of a symphony, humming the first and second subjects to him, and so on; she would explain to him the difference between Arminians and Erastians; or she would give him a short lecture on the early history of the United States. And it was done in a way well calculated to arrest a young attention. Did you ever read Mrs Markham? Well, it was like that. . . . (44–45)

Dowell recognizes Leonora's ironic jab at Edward's expense and he takes it up and adds his own lampoon: "I told him that he wasn't likely to take in enough to upset his balance." The comic delicacy of this remark to Edward is aimed finally not at him but at Florence. As always, Florence is shown as utterly bankrupt while Edward's absurdity is viewed with less dislike. There is a warmth in the comedy of calling Edward "one of the dark places of the earth" while in the list of subjects that Florence's clean-up operation comprises there is a darkness more dense. Edward's fears that culture will ruin his hold on a bridle are childish ("calculated to arrest a young attention") while Florence's misapprehensions about the uses for culture are more ugly as they are more sophisticated. Together they are very dangerous, indeed, and Dowell senses this and is afraid of them. He probes at them, twisting and turning to get a jab at both of them from every side, with the stiletto of his irony. Nevertheless, when Dowell's comic ironies are turned on Edward, they become more complex, less stable, than they are in his harsh lampooning of that "piece of paper," Florence. Look, for example, at this description of Edward as Dowell sees him for the first time, entering the dining room at Nauheim:

His face hitherto had, in the wonderful English fashion, expressed nothing whatever. Nothing. There was in it neither joy nor despair; neither hope nor fear; neither boredom nor satisfaction. He seemed to perceive no soul in that crowded room; he might have been walking in a jungle. I never came across such a perfect expres-

sion before and I never shall again. It was insolence and not insolence; it was modesty and not modesty. His hair was fair, extraordinarily ordered in a wave, running from the left temple to the
right; his face was a light brick-red, perfectly uniform in tint up to
the roots of the hair itself; his yellow moustache was as stiff as a
toothbrush and I verily believe that he had his black smoking jacket
thickened a little over the shoulder-blades so as to give himself the
air of the slightest possible stoop. It would be like him to do that;
that was the sort of thing he thought about. Martingales, Chiffney
bits, boots; where you got the best soap, the best brandy, the name
of the chap who rode a plater down the Khyber cliffs; the spreading
power of number three shot before a charge of number four powder
. . . by heavens, I hardly ever heard him talk of anything else. Not
in all the years that I knew him did I hear him talk of anything but
these subjects. . . .

And that was absolutely all that I knew of him until a month
ago—that and the profusion of his cases, all of pigskin and stamped
with his initials, E. F. A. There were gun-cases, and collar cases,
and shirt cases, and letter cases and cases each containing four
bottles of medicine; and hat cases and helmet cases. It must have
needed a whole herd of the Gadarene swine to make up his outfit.
And, if I ever penetrated into his private room it would be to see
him standing, with his coat and waistcoat off and the immensely
long line of his perfectly elegant trousers from waist to boot heel.
And he would have a slightly reflective air and he would be just
opening one kind of case and just closing another.

Good God, what did they all see in him? for I swear there was all
there was of him, inside and out; though they said he was a good
soldier. Yet, Leonora adored him with a passion that was like an
agony, and hated him with an agony that was as bitter as the sea.
How could he arouse anything like a sentiment, in anybody?
(32–34)

The pigskin cases, the whole herd of Gadarene swine, are images as funny
and as biting as anything in Dowell's descriptions of Florence. But the
irony is modified by its surroundings. Or perhaps it would be more exact to
say that irony spilled on Edward has more functions than irony spilled on

Florence. She is desired but finally hated. Dowell's irony about her expresses his resolution of this double feeling into contempt. When he calls her a "poor dear thing," he finally means she is not poor, except perhaps in spirit, and she is not dear to him. She does not deserve the pity the use of such a phrase might sometimes imply, and she more than deserves the condescension and the reification that is another of its potential meanings. But about Edward, Dowell develops increasingly complex feelings that are less easily resolved. Ironies about Edward must express much more than Dowell's desire to undercut Edward's smooth surface image. Those pigskin cases of Edward's are typical of the sort of comic detail that builds up only to collapse into sadness when we later learn how Edward actually came to have those absurd cases: Leonora kept giving them to him as a consolation for the deprivations she forced upon him. Thus what begins as parody becomes something far more suggestive with a tap of the tonal kaleidoscope. The spectrum of voices Dowell uses about Edward is shot through with flashing rays of emotion—sympathy, horror, surprise, love, distaste, envy, contempt. These rays join in odd combinations, give rise to strange auras.

Here we meet irony as Ford's most developed and expressive tool: he uses it to delineate delicate shadings in emotional color. He uses the simple basis of any irony—a contradiction between what is said and what is truly meant—to give us the most complex of mental states in which what is said is only a stab at a whole world of shifting feeling, constantly in motion beneath the surface of seemingly stable words.

What, for example, can Dowell possibly mean the reader to take away from his sentence, "He seemed to perceive no soul in that crowded room; he might have been walking in a jungle"? Is this merely a joke, a play on contrasting images to make Edward look absurd? Or, more seriously, is this a joke on the fate of any extreme, that it borders on its opposite? Are we being told that Edward's fixity, his abstract and perfect English manner, ironically remove him from civilization? Certainly one central irony here is that Edward's perfection achieves the nullity of any social convention when it is seamlessly, unconsciously embodied. The pukka sahib is an absurdity in the elegant dining room. He may have been a good soldier, but he is an immobile human being, dead to the contradictions of his world and of his empire, dead to these contradictions which destroy him.

The sentence certainly has all these ironies within it. But there are others. Is Dowell aware that it is funny to locate Edward's perfect manner in a jungle? Is he being satirical when he follows the jungle image with the words "I never came across such a perfect expression before and I never shall again"? Are we not invited to burst out laughing and say, "I should hope not"? Certainly, in the context of the passage as a whole, we can credit Dowell with conscious comic ironic intent. Dowell is appalled by the memory of Edward's extraordinary appearance of blandness since he now knows that there were jungle passions in Edward which were perfectly concealed by his manner. But this conscious irony does not stop at such a simple reversal of meaning as can be contained in the perception that there is something mightily imperfect in a perfect expression that hides so much or in the perception that no doubt the jungle rather than the draw-ing room would have been a better place for the rutting animal Dowell sometimes sees Edward to be. There is a deeper irony in the jungle image that strips away some of its comedy, for Edward is in a jungle indeed, a jungle of pain. His civilization is a jungle in polite disguise. He is hunted by its laws. He is confused by its overgrown, decadent traditions. His "per-fections" have been set going by a culture that has no use for his real pas-sions and talents.

Dowell confronts Edward's absurdity, his duplicity, and his suffering. He struggles to recapture the strange contradictions in the incident. He tells us with a hindsight that increases both his irony and his empathy what Edward was really thinking behind his impassive mask which showed "neither joy nor despair; neither hope nor fear; neither boredom nor satis-faction." He looks to the door as Leonora and Florence appear, and in ac-knowledgment of Leonora his perfectly blank face registers the message "There you are, my dear," as one might say, "All this is my land," and in acknowledgment of the new woman, Florence, this same perfect expres-sion registers "Might just be done!" as one might say of a hard shot in polo. And Dowell, who saw these two women at the door and witnessed the two expressions with which Edward greeted them in turn is now in his own jungle: "How the deuce did they do it, those unflinching blue eyes with the direct gaze? For the eyes themselves never moved, gazing over my shoulder towards the screen. And the gaze was perfectly level and perfectly direct and perfectly unchanging" (35–36). There is that irony in "per-fectly" again, but the irony cuts deep into Dowell's whole sense of life. How can it be, he asks himself, that this perfect manner can be combined with such morally chaotic thoughts? The dining room was indeed a jungle in which Edward stalked Dowell's wife, but it seemed so unlikely and so entirely contrary to convention that this should be so. How was Dowell to believe his own perceptions at the time? He saw perfection; he saw a perfection too perfect to be real, a perfection that could only be that of a madman or an automaton. And now this contradiction has thrown him into a permanently ironic state of mind. He undercuts everything he says. Doubt becomes a means of self-protection against surprise.

Irony is not an effective way to clear up contradictions. It records them, rather. And at this stage Dowell is not ready to resolve his own crisis in judgment. He says, "Good God, what did they all see in him? . . . though they said he was a good soldier." Dowell's bewilderment is genuine and his irony is part of its expression. He admires the "perfect expression" at the same time that he is rather horrified by what it hides. He laughs at this impassive jungle cat but he is also impressed. The "light brick-red" face and the moustache "as stiff as a toothbrush" are slightly comic, but the assumed stoop Dowell sees as bordering on the pathetic. Edward's outer image, so perfect even in its imperfections, is frightening in its very banality. "How could he arouse anything like a sentiment, in anybody?" Dowell asks, but he has already answered his own question. Dowell is himself drawn into Edward's painful psychodrama.

Dowell sees that the ironies of history have forced Edward's perfect surface into a lie. He is not the good landlord and father of his people; he is not the constant husband; he is not the honorable caretaker of his ward, Nancy. The destruction of these roles is so monstrous that Edward has become a ghost painfully haunting old ideals, a simulacrum. His perfect, controlled, dignified surface is the most elaborate and nightmarish sort of bad faith.

As anti-Dowell critics have always seen, it is ironic that Dowell identifies with Edward. He lacks Edward's physical attraction and passion. But it is really with Edward's failures that Dowell identifies. Both men are torn apart by a cultural transition they can't understand. When Dowell undercuts each of his conscious ironies at Edward's expense with either admiration or sympathy, he has found a perfect vehicle for his ambivalence: he hates Edward who has cuckolded him, who has had the sexuality Dowell has denied himself, but he loves Edward's inability to cash in on his own passions and talents. Like Dowell, Edward fails to have what he wants and can find no place for himself in the world as it is.

Dowell's defense of Edward's failure (and hence of his own) may be self-serving and unpleasant as the anti-Dowellists have always felt it to be. But when Dowell shows us the absurdly calm Edward, entering that elegant dining room, his understanding of Edward's underlying pain is a genuine insight, the kind of knowledge granted only to those who truly love and empathize, for whatever reason. The irony is that sometimes, from the worst motives, we find the best friends; the irony is that by pretending to be Edward, Dowell takes on a sense of life he formerly lacked: understanding Edward's deadness has given him whatever life he is to have.

Though Dowell keeps digging, reinterpreting his love and his hate, his laughter and his sympathy, the reader, trying to understand Dowell better and better can only go so far. Finally, Dowell's irony is an expression of a confusion the novel, *The Good Soldier*, is incapable of resolving at the level of Dowell's personality. To understand more we must instead broaden our focus and look for that notoriously elusive figure in all first person narrations, the primary author, Ford himself.

« »

Ford has structured the novel as he has structured the typical Dowell utterance: first description, then a swelling of emotional expression, then a collapse into either despair or absurd understatement.

> I suppose you will retort that I was in love with Nancy Rufford and that my indifference [to Florence's death] was therefore discreditable. Well, I am not seeking to avoid discredit. I was in love with Nancy Rufford as I am in love with the poor child's memory, quietly and quite tenderly in my American sort of way. I had never thought about it until I heard Leonora state that I might now marry her. But, from that moment until her worse than death, I do not suppose that I much thought about anything else. I don't mean to say that I sighed about her or groaned; I just wanted to marry her as some people want to go to Carcassonne. (111–12)

Dowell cannot sigh or groan, just as Ford's earlier heroes cannot; they all tell us that in modern circumstances such carryings-on are merely ridiculous. But the romantic element, the desire for elevated passion, is nevertheless preserved in the passage in the image of Carcassonne, historical cradle of romance. Dowell wishes his story could be bathed in a romantic light as bright as the moon of Provence and he suffers when instead he finds his situation "all a darkness" (146). The comic inappropriateness of "I just wanted to marry her as some people want to go to Carcassonne" becomes something more, something else. Dowell cannot sigh; he cannot groan; he cannot marry Nancy Rufford; and he cannot live in the ideal of romance, his dream of Carcassonne. The deflation of the final sentence has a comic structure but a sad meaning: all hope is lost.

This collapse of the comic into nightmare, pathos, or grief is an increasing tendency as the novel proceeds. With the reverberations of Florence's death cleared away (at the end of the first section of Part 3) the second section of Part 3 turns its attention to a complete description of Nancy, Leonora, and Edward in their own terms. This changed, more distant focus is maintained until the last, short section of the novel, after Dowell's return from Ceylon with Nancy, when he allows his own feeling for the material to surface once again, this time with significant differences. The long descriptions of the Ashburnhams' history, extrapolated painstakingly and from a distance, are a kind of gestation period for Dowell.

In these Ashburnham sections of the book the reader's idea of Edward and Leonora is forced to fluctuate causing the same ambiguous gestalt I have described as Ford's technique in his creation of Dowell. Is Edward "the good landlord and father of his people" or is he an absurd sentimentalist who expresses his disaffection with decaying traditions through a series of irresponsible sexual affairs? Of course the double image is intended. Edward up close is sympathetic, a ruined man of principle. But when Dowell suddenly gives us a glimpse of him from a critical distance, his "Byronic gloom" seems quite preposterous (148, 145). Dowell vacillates between seeing Edward as comic (and therefore contemptible) and as sad (and therefore sympathetic). But the very complexity of Edward, who, like all men, is doomed to play both parts, extends Dowell beyond the rarefied atmosphere of his life with Florence into a more complex and humane idea of experience.

This extension of Dowell's imagination creates easily as many problems for him as it solves: "That question of first impressions has always bothered me a good deal—but quite academically. I mean that, from time to time I have wondered whether it were or were not best to trust to one's first impressions in dealing with people" (136). But then he goes on to say that during his excursion to America after Florence's death, he came to some kind of tentative working conclusion to this problem: "I found that to rely on first impressions was the best thing I could do" (137). As Dowell plumbs deeper into the Ashburnhams' history, we can see him trying to find in himself a response "to rely upon," a path through the maze of the Ashburnhams' complex affairs. It becomes increasingly clear that he is going to have to make a choice without any final justification for it. After all, Edward, "the collectivist," and Leonora, "the individualist" (132), are both committed to demanding, repressive codes—hers Catholic, his aris-tocratic. That in the end Dowell prefers Edward's restraints to Leonora's is an emotional preference, and the sympathy with which this choice emerges from the tortuous possibilities is the sympathy we would expect Ford to show to one who has chosen to romanticize the aristocratic ideal.

These developing choices of Dowell's surface slowly and are never given the ring of finality. However, Leonora, whom we know in earlier sections of the novel as the injured wife, is much less sympathetic in later sections as the keeper of Edward's accounts. Also in these later sections, Edward's often foolish dedication to romance increasingly strikes a chord of sympathy in Dowell, while Leonora's strength of character increasingly seems to him like an iron vise that destroys what it seeks to hold in place. Even while Dowell gives a convincing defense of Leonora's position, his rhetoric is increasingly slanted against her. His efforts to do everyone jus-tice have begun to seem to him like academic exercises. The law of impar-tiality gives way to feeling. The brittle ironic surface begins to show cracks. After a long description of Edward and Leonora's early married years, in which Leonora, even when most justified, is forever cold in her rectitude, Dowell says, "And now, I suppose, I must give you Leonora's side of the case . . ." (156). Only three pages follow in which we learn, among other things, that she cannot stand novels.

Beneath the convention of Dowell's ruminative style, Ford is changing his emphasis. The Ashburnhams' ignorance about sex is quite a different thing from Florence's sexual exploits. Her divagations are ultimately banal while Leonora and Edward's problems lead Dowell much closer to the mys-teries of romance, sexual feeling, and the relation of these things to social life. Then again, within this second situation, Leonora's suffering is quite a different thing from Edward's. She will manage quite well in a world with-out moral point; Edward will not.

Gradually satire, comedy of manners, witty asides drop away. Steadily an emotionalism, a tone of pathos, builds up in Dowell's voice. If one had to mark a place where this change is inescapable it would probably be at the beginning of the fourth and last part of the novel, although the shift in tone becomes even more marked in Part 5, which begins, "It is this part of the story that makes me saddest of all" (201). Though Dowell continues to collapse into understatement in this part, there is no more wit. Comic absurdity has been almost entirely replaced by pathetic absurdity. And a new voice is added, or rather, a voice formerly muted becomes augmented—the Conradian voice, which is histrionic. "Is there then any terrestrial paradise where, amidst the whispering of the olive-leaves, people can be with whom they like and have what they like and take their ease in shadows and in coolness? Or are all men's lives like the lives of us good people—like the lives of the Ashburnhams, of the Dowells, of the Ruffords—broken, tumultuous, agonized, and unromantic lives, periods punctuated by screams, by imbecilities, by deaths, by agonies? Who the devil knows?" (204–205).

At the ends of his romances and satires, Ford tended to draw back from mordant irony into a more romantic view of his material. Similarly, Dowell's story is, finally, a heroic reach for romance, for ideal meaning, for stasis. But at the same time, and as always in Ford, deflationary irony brings Dowell down from these symbolic heights. He cannot finally provide the book with a stable moral center. Though he does grapple with the eternal questions, he is doomed not primarily by the general fate of mankind but by the specific nature of his culture to finding nothing but tentative and ambiguous answers. His struggle to know, Edward's to find "an ultimately satisfying woman" (53), and Leonora's to preserve the status quo, are all made grotesque by the confusions on which the world presented in *The Good Soldier* is based. Sad rather than tragic, ridiculous rather than magnificent, the characters lack stature. They are robbed of flexibility and completeness by the debilitating madness of their time.

Any change in Dowell is circumscribed by this general madness. Neither Edward's death nor Dowell's understanding of it can redeem the permanent loss of rectitude symbolized by Leonora's final social ascendency. Even the fact that Dowell understands this "falling to pieces of a people" (17) fails to redeem the end. Dowell is part of this decay. "The falling to pieces of a people" is an event that overshadows the fact that Dowell has realized an obligation, felt love, and made a choice. When, at the end, Dowell retreats into private pathos, his retreat symbolizes a collapse in the entire social structure.

In one sense, then, *The Good Soldier* remains a social novel to its end. But in spite of Ford's claim that he was interested above all in anatomizing his times, the conclusion of the novel is a social novelist's swan song. The novel begins with social analysis, as a comedy of manners, but finds the tools of this analysis inadequate to express modern experience. The stable ironies of traditional social comedy fall apart under the pressure of modern circumstances. They become circular, disturbing, irresolvable. Finally, the social theme itself is eclipsed by a new emphasis on private desperation, and that wandering probe, irony, is laid aside in exhaustion. Dowell's subjective experience, earlier put through so many forms of scrutiny, dissection, reevaluation, is finally accepted for the limited but irreducible thing it is. At least no external social observation is offered to ironically undercut it.

Ford thought he should be a social novelist, and yet he felt an estrangement from what was happening in England during the Edwardian years that sometimes bordered on the pathological and that probably contributed to his nervous breakdowns, retreats, and private, asocial nightmares like those he described in *The Young Lovell* written in the same year as *The Good Soldier*.

Perhaps this collapse of specifically social comedy is one of the things Ford had in mind when he called *The Good Soldier* his "great auk's egg," "something of a race that will have no successors."[9] Indeed, the end of *The Good Soldier* is in some respects a dead end. "So life peters out" (218), says Dowell and so ends a number of his trains of thought. Dowell and Ford are together in recognizing that an old way of life has become impossible; they are together, too, in remaining emotionally committed to a culture that has lost its vitality.

‹‹ ››

In Part 4, Ford and Dowell come closer to being the same person than anywhere else in the book. Like Dowell, Ford is both a good and a bad anthropologist, an outsider who laughs ironically at the natives but who

9. Ford, Preface, *The Good Soldier* (American ed.; New York: Albert and Charles Boni, 1927), vii.

also feels jealous of their passionate engagement. He identifies patterns, tries for objectivity, observes accurately and minutely. But, like all Ford characters, Dowell misses key words, contradicts himself, is hopelessly passive. And the pain of this passivity is, as we have observed in novel after novel, Ford's as well as Dowell's. At the point at which Ford wants to draw his novel into some kind of concluding knot, the distance he was earlier able to place between himself and his narrator tends to narrow. Tone is a good clue to this narrowing. By the end of the novel ambivalence has become intolerable to Ford; what was brittle in the tone has finally broken. The characters, the narrator, and the novelist all suffer together beneath the same humiliating cloud of ignorance.

Endings are, as Ford knew, the critical moments when meaning must somehow be focused. He always spoke of Maupassant's last sentences with wondering praise. He admired these *coups de canon*. But such endings are the very antithesis of Ford's temperament. Vacillation always seduces him; the need to decide always terrifies him. The genius of *The Good Soldier* lies in its doubleness, its irresolvable ambiguities, its utterly recalcitrant ironies. The novel's weaknesses lie in the pretense of resolution wherever it occurs. Its meanings postulate a circular structure, one in which people keep moving but never change. By making Dowell change and allowing him a personal if limited set of preferences for one sort of dead end over another, Ford undermines some of the power the book accrues in its earlier sections. Any ending is bound to collapse some of this novel's sublime ambiguity.

It is difficult to understand what is happening in both style and meaning at the end of *The Good Soldier* because two contradictory things are going on at once. First, Ford is showing the breakdown of social morality, the retreat into personal, subjective solutions in an unsatisfactory social order. In this avatar he is the social ironist who recognizes the dead end down which all his characters, including Dowell, are helplessly rushing. Second, Ford is the romanticist, the writer who always chose the Edwards of this world over the Leonoras. In this guise, though he sees that the Edwards are on a collision course with history, he doesn't care.

For most of *The Good Soldier*'s length these two aspects of Ford's understanding are kept in tension with one another by means of a carefully balanced ambiguity: irony and social comedy undercut romance and romance redeems human absurdity. As the social observer, Dowell understands just how culture is changing; as the romanticist, he dislikes most of these changes and looks for patterns of feeling and meaning that are timeless. At the end of the novel Ford is still juggling with these two sides of his nature but the irony and controlled ambiguity that kept everything circling nicely earlier in the novel have been modified by Dowell's developing empathy with Edward. As feeling more and more replaces critical distance, some of the subtlety of the novel's themes is sacrificed to Ford's love for the man destroyed by history. He retreats from some of the implications of his ending. Critical distance dissolves. Ford joins his characters in their quest for romance, for absolute ideals, for escape. Dowell tells us there is nothing romantic left but he clings to the romantic image of Edward now, at the end of the novel, no longer the gurgling sentimentalist, but instead Him who died for our sins. It is presumably Ford himself who provides the novel's epigraph: "Beati immaculati in via qui ambulant in lege Domini" (Happy are they whose way is blameless who walk in the law of the Lord). If this is irony, it is a cruel one that looks beyond human life towards the first and last things that make social confusion seem small. In the world, Edward can be blamed; in the light of divine judgment, he is a victim and blameless. By the end of the novel, Ford has ceased to see the conflict between public and private life ironically; he lets the tension between these go slack because he has found irony to be inadequate to express the loss of any good life for Edward.

« »

These then are the weaknesses inherent in Ford's retreat from irony into romance at the end of *The Good Soldier*: the tension slackens; the wild and exciting proliferation of possible meanings slows down; irony stabilizes and sentiment becomes the cover for what was earlier naked, painful bewilderment. The emotional hysteria of the novel's last part dulls some of its fine, ironic edges. The coda of the novel is overweighted in relation to the more delicately balanced design of the earlier sections. Edward, whose fascination can never be more than that of a comically exaggerated type, begins, in Part 4, to seem instead to be a rather unique madman. As social referents are rejected, part of the fable is lost.

But one can look at this loss in another light. The novel's collapse at its close into histrionics, obsession, despair, absurdly inadequate private solutions can be seen as a stylistic correlative for what many people felt were the prospects for a socially ordered, satisfying private and public life in the year 1914. The end of the novel overinflates and is as full of hot air as was the end of the Edwardian era. Things speed up but don't seem to be going anywhere. Though concluding was always Ford's nemesis, there is nevertheless a great deal to be said for the shattering effect of the last part of *The Good Soldier*. The sexual theme and the question of the value of the romantic view of life, both subjects explored earlier in a number of keys— rational, ironic, pathetic—here become obsessive, demonic. The melodrama is no longer relieved by wit. The emotions described seem to burst all social bounds. Dowell's twopence worth of hard-won knowledge at the end is nothing to the flood of general loss. No one in the novel has what is needed to build a rich life or even to continue living. "The falling apart of a people" is no more than "the death of a mouse by cancer" (17). Edward, like Joyce's Bloom, is an absurd nominee for hero, but Joyce's joy in this deflation, his power to counter this collapse with new myths, is entirely absent in *The Good Soldier*. Or rather, since Ford does search for myths— the romantic world of Provence, the Christian absolute hidden in Nancy's mad assertion "*Credo in unum Deum omnipotentem*"—these myths don't sustain any of his characters. Fine sentiment and mythic belief can find no public expression. Instead, ordinary, debased, and empty lives flourish. The good lack all conviction—Yeats's line comes from the same cultural moment as *The Good Soldier*. Sexual obsession, suicide, and madness, the extreme states which are the subjects of the novel's last sections, make good sense in a world whose values are so utterly undermined that no one can imagine a future.

The Good Soldier was an early statement in art of what people did in fact come to feel about their hold on social reality and social power in the years around 1914. The war was a coda. After it, people had to find a new form of optimism or go under. But before it, what was to be the new optimism was still unimaginable and the old was so moribund that there was a spiritual vacuum. The description of this moment of emptiness is part of *The Good Soldier*'s subject.

Appearing in 1914, the novel was also a precocious exploration of themes endemic to much of the modernist writing that was to follow. Dowell ends by feeling that in the social sphere all that is fine is doomed to being burnt out, desecrated, made to appear mean and ridiculous. The personal life is romanticized here and society is the villain that ruins the purity of the self. These are among the great themes of modernism, the war between the individual life and social anomie, the war between different systems of meaning in a world where the center cannot hold, where no system has hegemony.

Ford's changes in tone at the end of *The Good Soldier* appear in part because he could not finally tolerate the novel's painful level of uncertainty, but this limitation is, in its own way, deeply expressive. Ford's search for a resolution fails, and this tells us, as much as anything else, that we are in a world without loopholes, without air or hope. No one in it has a future. Normality is death. Meaning is never more than subjective meaning. Life pretends to go on as usual but everything feels wrong. The action speeds up but towards a dead end. When Dowell finally decides that the only way to make judgments in this world is to rely on first impressions, he has stepped into a little lifeboat that is drifting out to sea. This describes a prevalent mental condition in the prewar months of 1914. Ford is critical of it while at the same time he falls in love with the man in the boat, seeing him as a hero, or like Peire Vidal and Don Quixote, ridiculous but magnificent, better than all those realists who stay at home on shore and pretend to a solid overview of what is going on.

Though Ford abandons comic irony and, finding doubt intolerable, decides for Edward, for romance, and for the private life over the public, it would still be misleading to end this description of *The Good Soldier* on such a conclusive note. Ford is never best served by conclusions. However nervous dialectical tension made him, he was at his best when able to maintain it. Irony changes in the course of the novel, but it does not entirely disappear; certainly the rich possibilities inherent in ambiguity are there to the end. In conclusion, then, here is one last close examination of *The Good Soldier*'s tonal mix. The novel ends thus:

> A stable-boy brought [Edward] a telegram and went away. He opened it negligently, regarded it without emotion, and, in complete silence, handed it to me. On the pinkish paper in a sprawled handwriting I read: "Safe Brindisi. Having rattling good time. Nancy."
>
> Well, Edward was the English gentleman; but he was also, to the last, a sentimentalist, whose mind was compounded of indifferent poems and novels. He just looked up to the roof of the stable, as if

he were looking to Heaven, and whispered something that I did not catch.

Then he put two fingers into the waistcoat pocket of his grey, freize suit; they came out with a little neat pen-knife—quite a small pen-knife. He said to me:

"You might just take that wire to Leonora." And he looked at me with a direct, challenging, brow-beating glare. I guess he could see in my eyes that I didn't intend to hinder him. Why should I hinder him?

I didn't think he was wanted in the world, let his confounded tenants, his rifle-associations, his drunkards, reclaimed and unreclaimed, get on as they liked. Not all the hundreds and hundreds of them deserved that that poor devil should go on suffering for their sakes.

When he saw that I did not intend to interfere with him his eyes became soft and almost affectionate. He remarked:

"So long, old man, I must have a bit of a rest, you know."

I didn't know what to say. I wanted to say, "God bless you," for I also am a sentimentalist. But I thought that perhaps that would not be quite English good form, so I trotted off with the telegram to Leonora. She was quite pleased with it. (219–20)

Dowell's inability to hinder Edward or even to give him a blessing can be seen as monstrous, while Edward's suicide can be seen as histrionic and absurd. There are plenty of tonal pointers in these directions. Edward's restraint goes so ridiculously far that he uses the smallest of penknives to kill himself. Both men are too sentimental to express any sentiments at all. Dowell has no hopes that can make death any different from life, and so he is unable to answer the question, "Why should I hinder him?" Nor has he strong beliefs, and so he cannot bless Edward. He explains his limbo of inaction and silence by saying that any expression "would not be quite English good form," but this is an absurdly inadequate excuse under the circumstances. In any case, the ideal of English reserve that keeps him silent only just barely applies to him. Finally, Dowell's description of himself as "trotting" off to Leonora is so abject and deflationary that we cannot take his claim to high-minded restraint seriously even in his own terms. His self-deprecation only underlines his moral flaccidity.

But there is another side. Why, after all, *should* Edward remain alive? In the terms the novel has established, he is indeed finished, as landlord, magistrate, and provider. He is already dead, a simulacrum of qualities that are likewise dead. His sentimentality is easily as pathetic as it is absurd since it demonstrates what a misfit he is. Dowell and Edward have a real moment of communication here for which words are entirely unnecessary. They agree about Edward's prospects. They agree about how far an Englishman should go before he may be allowed "a bit of a rest." Dowell's decision to follow "English good form" is a gesture towards Edward whose absurd restraints and hidden suffering he has come to understand, identify with, and love. It is Leonora, not Dowell or Edward, who seems morally monstrous by being "quite pleased" with Nancy's grotesque pretense at normalcy in her telegram. Edward has responded to the true ugliness of Nancy's playing up. Dowell, too, has recognized how the old tradition of restraint has gone horribly sour. Only Leonora is pleased, only she will continue to play the game as if everything is normal.

Which of these two readings of the ending corresponds to Ford's intention? Should a man speak or keep silent? Ford doesn't know. He never has known. In *Parade's End* he asks the same question with the same ambiguous results. The life of the novel must reside in the question itself. Once again, the only conclusion that deals adequately with the novel's complexity is no conclusion at all. "You may well ask why I write," says Dowell near the beginning of the novel, "And yet my reasons are quite many. For it is not unusual in human beings who have witnessed the sack of a city or the falling to pieces of a people to desire to set down what they have witnessed for the benefit of unknown heirs or of generations infinitely remote; or, if you please, just to get the sight out of their heads" (17). Ford's reasons for writing are "quite many" and his contradictory meanings are "quite many." Dowell is the witness to "the falling to pieces of a people." He is also the man who sees nothing, who tells his story in order to escape vision, "to get the sight out" of his head. A serious reader of *The Good Soldier* must perforce live with both Dowells since neither can ever, by any refinement of critical attention, be finally and absolutely expunged from the experience of reading the text.

If there must be an ending, perhaps biography can provide it. In his long essay of 1907 on English manners, *The Spirit of the People*, Ford's vacillations on the subject of English reserve end on the swing of the pendulum that affirms the success of this cultural tradition: "Good conduct means that there is in the world a place to which to return."[10] After writing *The Good Soldier*, Ford left England to go to war. "Good conduct" had failed to make the world safe or fine. After the war, Ford never felt comfortable in England again. *The Good Soldier* is an exploration, in many keys, of this terrible, debilitating ending to a valued and venerable way of life.

« »

Ford wrote in 1927 that when *The Good Soldier* appeared in *Blast* in 1914 he already knew it was a swan song for the old themes and techniques. "I prepared to stand aside in favour of our good friends—. . . Ezra, Eliot, Wyndham Lewis, H. D. and the rest of the clamourous young writers who were then knocking at the door. But greater clamours beset London and the world which till then had seemed to lie at the proud feet of those con-querors; Cubism, Vorticism, Imagism and the rest never had their fair chance amid the voices of the cannon and so I have come out of my hole again and . . . have taken heart to [do] some work of my own."[11]

"Taking heart" (or at least the struggle to do so) certainly describes the tone of Ford's writing in the ten years after the war. The cold despair of *The Good Soldier* is gone. In the war, Ford had seen worse things than the social hypocrisy, unrequited passion, and adultery that he had described in *The Good Soldier* with such an air of desperation. "The voices of the can-non" had enlarged his vision. In *Parade's End*, his postwar masterpiece, he was to continue to write his own kind of prewar impressionism, that deli-cate web of doubtful lights and shadows he always threw over everything, but he was to take the romanticism and the fragile moral conclusions of *The Good Soldier* much further.

10. Ford, *The Spirit of the People*, 153.
11. Ford, Preface, *The Good Soldier* (American ed.), vi–vii.

It is commonly remarked that 'there is no romance in modern war'. That is absurd, I am sorry to say.

It has frequently been contended that Agincourt, or even Waterloo with its 'thin red line' and its Old Guard of Napoleonic veterans, was 'spectacular': whereas modern war is 'drab and unromantic'. Alas! that is nonsense. To say that is entirely to misunderstand the nature of romance. . . .

The truth is, of course, that it is not what you *see*, at all, that makes an event romantic to you, but what you *feel*. And in war, as you might expect, you feel with considerable intensity.

WYNDHAM LEWIS, *Blasting and Bombardiering*, 1937

Coda

THE WAR AND AFTER: THE MAKING OF *PARADE'S END*

No intelligent brain that passed through the experience of the Great War emerged without being profoundly changed. . . . This, said I, in shrill jets of journalism, is the logical outcome of your parades and uniforms!

—H. G. WELLS, *Experiment in Autobiography*, 1934

«8»

EVERYBODY'S WAR AND FORD'S
A BREEDING GROUND FOR ROMANCE

T HAT the war was a great divide, giving people a permanent sense of "before" and "after" even while it was going on, is a fact so palpable that no one who lived through it or has since described it can be found in any camp or of any temperament to contradict its claim to mark the end of an entire way of life, economic and social.

So destructive of old certainties, the Great War nevertheless gave rise to its own set of universals. How many men were prompted to say, with Wells, "This . . . is the logical outcome of your parades and uniforms" and this is that parade's end?

Along with parades, innocence was another casualty of war. It lost all its charm as an ideal. As Shaw wrote in the Preface to *Heartbreak House* in 1919, "To British centenarians who died in their beds in 1914, any dread of having to hide underground in London from the shells of an enemy seemed more remote and fantastic than a dread of the appearance of a colony of cobras and rattlesnakes in Kensington Gardens." Shaw's centenarians dying peacefully in 1914, with no prescience, no sense of foreboding, became sinister to those who lived to see the transition. With the shock came rage at those former generations. Why had they not grasped that England was mortal? Why had they failed to imagine and hence to prevent the coming of cobras and rattlesnakes even to such a place as Kensington Gardens? (Model trenches were dug in Kensington Gardens during the war to help civilians imagine what remained, to them, largely unimaginable.) For such innocence, those who came after must pay a high price. In a ceremonial past, words like victory had a sentimental meaning. Now victory became an obscene irony, for as Shaw wrote in horror, "The earth is still bursting with the dead bodies of the victors."[1] The ceremony of innocence is drowned.

Those who went to the front were the ones to experience the first shock of the change. A central motif of all trench literature is a sort of Cassandra syndrome: men at the front are trying to tell everyone else that a disaster of unimaginable proportions is going on while it is business as usual in London.

This sensation of crying in the wilderness was to become a common element in much postwar writing. Knowledge cannot be communicated; the man who knows is a pariah. Nobody wants his unpleasant information. Insight loses its social reference points and becomes passive, incommunicable. Irony, instead of being a way of playing on shared values becomes instead an expression only of shared doubts, while comic irony becomes a private joke which may or may not be clear to anyone else.

The war attacked people's sense of having an overview of their situation; it undermined the assumption of permanence. Since it was impossible to overlook the war as a whole, soldiers' landscape fantasies were often of heights. (Ford's war hero, Tietjens, wishes he could levitate to a spot he sees high on a wall, and one of his recurring projections of postwar bliss while on active service is an image of a man standing high on a hill. When the war is done, a man will once again be able to stand up on the hills without instantly becoming a target.) The Edwardian upper classes still thought of themselves as landed gentry, people with ancestral landscapes, but the war struck a death blow to this country sensibility. In a quasi memoir, quasi fiction Ford wrote just after the war, No Enemy, his hero, Gringoire, remembers this specific deprivation of war. "There were no nooks, no little, sweet corners; there were no assured homes, countries, provinces, kingdoms, or races. All the earth held its breath and waited."[2]

How interesting it is, then to see in what landscape Ford situates his Gringoire after the war. He puts him in "a gingerbread house" in a "little nook of the earth" in a world to which color has returned, "pink and purple campions" and "the occasional gold of buttercups." "The plants in the garden wave in stiffness like a battalion on parade—the platoons of

1. Shaw, Heartbreak House, 4.
2. Ford, No Enemy: A Tale of Reconstruction (New York, 1929), 22.

lettuce, the headquarters' staff, all sweet peas, and the color company, which is of scarlet runners. . . . a nightingale is running in and out of the beanstalks. Yes, a nightingale of midsummer that has abandoned the deep woodland and runs through the garden, a princess turned housekeeper, because it has young to feed. Think of noticing that!"[3] Swords into plough-shares! Innocence regained, in a rural paradise. If this is sentimental, it is also a part of what was, during and after the war, a great groundswell of pastoral longing, of deeply emotional romantic feeling. If one of the by-products of the war was a sense of irresolvable irony, of an unfitness in the scale of things that constantly rendered experience absurd, another of its by-products was the fervent desire to escape from this irony, to find unity and transcendence in the midst of disorder and wholesale death. Forced to crouch beneath ground level, the soldier-writer of World War I dreamed of the hills, noticed with Wyndham Lewis the romance to be found in all extremes of experience, noticed the little things that remained from a past more human in scale when soldiers had names like Roland or Oliver and were not merely ciphers, too easily, too quickly dead. As Wyndham Lewis says, far from putting an end to romance, the war, with its very coldness and drabness, its meaningless horror and inflated, ungraspable scale, created a great thirst for romance.

Ford craved the transcendent moment, the romantic heightening of otherwise squalid events, as much as any writer who went to fight. His old preference for feudalism was sharpened by the war, this most grotesque of all manifestations of the modern state. If he had ever decried the bombast of the late Victorians, the war made him feel his cultural debt, if not to them, to the past that had formed them and made them stable. "It is obvious that these years which are years of the revision of all values: these years should witness a revision of literary estimates. Everything else has gone into the melting pot: political economy; theories of honour, theories of history, of civilisation, of government. We used before 1914 to have the simple old view: 'Que toutes joies et tous honneurs / Viennent d'armes et d'amour!' But upon those lines one could scarcely nowadays run a life with much expectation of success."[4] This is coy and comical, of course, as well as sorrowful and ironic. And yet how much he wishes that one could run a life according to "the simple old view." *Parade's End* is a salvage expedi-

3. *Ibid.*, 22–23.
4. Ford, "Towards a History of English Literature," n.p.

tion. What is left, it asks, of the joy of love, of the honor of war? A self-deprecating laugh answers this question. There is an irony in the very asking of it. Love and honor are ironic words in the context of the Battle of the Somme. But Ford's hero Tietjens does not accept the answer of a hollow laugh, nor the bottomless irony that attacks men's values and makes a mockery of them. Instead, idealized memories of a past felicity inform every minute of Tietjens' consciousness. The victory he takes away from the defeat and horror of the war is that he remains, if in a modified way, a romantic.

« »

World War I had an immense, transforming effect on literary tone. It began a chain reaction of culture shocks which has not yet stopped. It undermined an earlier sense of the fitness of things. It tore apart faith in social contracts to such an extent that people became stranded in personal systems of belief. Culture often became a private invention randomly constructed out of the sort of tidbits of intellectual history that Florence Dowell enjoyed teaching Edward Ashburnham. All this could not but affect profoundly all literary voice.

What makes Ford so interesting in this context is the way in which, during the Edwardian years, he had already fallen under the advance shadow of some of these changes and had groped for a tone to express how they made him feel. Even in the midst of his great confusion about just what these imminent changes in the scale and the feel of human community were actually to be, he wrote on, trying to put an increasingly atomized situation into his fictions. His very weaknesses were precocious, coming as they so often did from his effort to synthesize beliefs and experiences which, he kept finding to his chagrin, would no longer fit comfortably together.

The war gave the world what Ford and other pained souls had already—a sense that the old world was gone, while the new was perhaps unpleasant and most certainly strange and recalcitrant to the Edwardian mind. At first, the war made irony more blatant, less subtle: the ironies of the war—the man killed on Armistice Day, the man saved because he bent down at just the right moment to tie his shoe—are gross ironies when we compare them with the ironies of the tea table, or of The Good Soldier.

They are not tonal ironies at all but, rather, the grand gestures of fate. But in another sense, the war led to a wild expansion in the range of ironic tone. Before it, ironies were usually contained; social usages guided one to how to recognize them. After the war, confidence in absolute meanings was so drastically undercut that all meanings jockeyed each other promiscuously.

Another change in literary tone due largely to the cataclysm of the war was the deflation of grand language. We have already seen Ford's complex relationship to the big bowwow of the Victorians, and this struggle with language became common. The old voice was constantly being undercut, often with comic or ironic effect, by the new idea of reality. But there was still a great allure and still a stable source of meaning in the old voice. To anyone who has spent much time browsing in the literature of just before and during the war, one of the most startling effects of the work in general is the complex interpenetration of earlier modes of thinking and writing with new ideas and tones of voice. The war was not romantic in a simple way for anyone, as it pleased Wyndham Lewis to say, but it was not drab and unromantic either. It was always and miraculously both things. This doubleness is inherent in the particular kind of irony always typical of Ford's work. A kinetic mixture, on the one hand, of elevated, ideal values and, on the other, of doubt is at the very source of his use of the ironic. At the moment before the war when the old modes of expression were still alive and the new still in the making, irony was at its fullest flower as a subtle expression of the profoundest truths of social experience. During and after the war this remained true, but with a difference.

Paul Fussell has written the classic study of the war's impact on consciousness and hence on all literary tone, *The Great War and Modern Memory*. As he says, "There seems to be one dominating form of modern understanding; . . . it is essentially ironic, and . . . originates largely in the application of mind and memory to the events of the Great War." Though he hardly mentions Ford, he describes how the war created a sometimes strangely mixed mode of romance and realism, comedy and pathos, elevated and then instantly deflated language—indeed the very picture of the variety of mental furnishings in the Edwardian mind of Ford Madox Ford. Fussell describes the demise of this pleasant if muddled eclecticism during the war; he names the new pattern of thinking he sees emerging "the ver-

sus habit" and argues that people increasingly fell into the "imaginative habit" of "gross dichotomizing."[5]

This "*versus* habit" took many forms during the war. Take, for example, the dividing line of "before" and "after." Before the war there were innocence, heroism, unstrafed nature. After the war, there were disillusionment, the antihero, nature pathetically invaded by human destructiveness. Another such dichotomy lies between "us" and "them."

> "We" are all here on this side; "the enemy" is over there. "We" are individuals with names and personal identities; "he" is a mere collective entity. We are visible; he is invisible.
>
> . . . .
>
> "He's got a fixed rifle on the road," warns a sergeant guide in [David] Jones's *In Parenthesis*, and Jones notes: "He, him, his—used by us of the enemy at all times."
>
> . . . .
>
> Prolonged trench warfare, whether enacted or remembered, fosters paranoid melodrama. . . . The most indispensable concept underlying the energies of modern writing is that of "the enemy."[6]

Once one starts to play Fussell's game of finding paradigms from the war that informed the tone of art, one begins to see them everywhere. Take, for example, the fact that the armies of World War I were unmechanized and too cumbersome to advance. Put this fact next to the nineteenth-century military belief that only by advancing can an army win. The result of this old idea was that men were sent streaming over the top with bayoneted rifles in their hands only to be cut down by machine guns in fixed, defensive positions. Movement forward, instead of victory, was in this war always loss. But the generals never learned. They kept trying to win the old way. This lag in strategic thinking, like so many others in the war, shows how slowly the human mind moved to accept the need for new structures. Recognizably modern ways of doing things (Fussell gives the example of the form letter) came into being during the war, slowly, painfully and always against resistance, a strong rearguard action. The pain of giving up the old concept of battle seems to have been psychologically

5. Paul Fussell, *The Great War and Modern Memory* (New York, 1975), 35, 75.
6. *Ibid.*, 75–76.

worse, at least for the leaders, than the pain of sending millions to death. Reconceptualizing basic ideas, such as offense and defense, victory and defeat, was at the heart of the intellectual trauma of the war.

Ford was always interested in the crushing ironies inherent in conflicts among people living mentally in very different moments in history. At the end of *Parade's End* Tietjens digs in just like the army. He has slowly learned that defense and not assault is the only way to win. Against his will, he has become, in some sense, modern. Indeed, Tietjens relinquishes the idea of victory more gracefully, and with a more conscious sense of irony, than did many of those of his class who actually wielded power during the war. By the end of hostilities, he has accommodated to the idea of enemies everywhere. He cannot go back to London, to his wife, to his former government department. Peace and unity are no longer socially possible since to go beyond one's own hedgerow is to encounter "them."

Ford's sense of being an anachronism from a better time, an artist-stranger in the midst of philistines, was already well developed before the war. In *Parade's End*, however, this idea of the heroic misfit, the man too good for his times, whose motives must always be ironically misunderstood in a deformed world, has acquired grander proportions than anywhere else in his work. Much of the petty snobbery or self-doubt that invaded Ford's earlier paranoia is elevated into myth in *Parade's End*. The war gave universality to personal doubt. Ford's enforced subjectivity, which before the war had been so pained and often so vague, became after the war, in *Parade's End*, a more symbolically clear and resonant expression of his belief in man's isolation. Tietjens is in a state of absolute opposition to his surroundings. He lives among "enemies," in other words, among inferiors who can never understand his moral universe.

In Ford's case, "gross dichotomizing" had some interesting and surprising results. His wartime ironies are—just as Fussell's "either/or" paradigm would seem to predict—more clear in their moral reference points than his prewar ones, making *Parade's End* his most schematized work. This new clarity of theme and fixity of purpose gave to these postwar novels what were, in Ford, new strengths and new weaknesses: his intentions and his form acquired resonance; at the same time, the fatuity of some of these intentions also became more obvious.

How, one may well ask, can *Parade's End*, so much more far-flung, rich, and varied than *The Good Soldier*, be seen as more tonally and thematically simple than the earlier, smaller novel? What can be more grossly dichotomous, more either/or, than the tension between appearance and reality as Dowell experiences it?

> I can't believe that that long, tranquil life, which was just stepping a minuet, vanished in four crashing days at the end of nine years and six weeks. Upon my word, yes, our intimacy was like a minuet. . . .
>
> No, by God, it is false! It wasn't a minuet that we stepped; it was a prison—a prison full of screaming hysterics, tied down so that they might not outsound the rolling of our carriage wheels as we went along the shaded avenues of the Taunus Wald.
>
> And yet I swear by the sacred name of my creator that it was true.[7]

And yet the very tightness of this dichotomous world set the stage for small distinctions, delicate shadings in tone, excursions into carefully camouflaged mysteries. The war broke through these careful, delicate antitheses of polite culture. The rot was no longer hidden beneath the surface but now came streaming out in running sores. Nothing could tie down or outsound the screaming hysterics of the war. Small adjustments of feeling like those Dowell makes at the end of The Good Soldier are flooded out by the grosser ironies of Tietjens' final position, the once landed aristocrat now run to simpler, humbler earth, the lover of the past, now merchant of old furniture.

In Parade's End complexity comes not from an endless anatomy of doubt such as Dowell's but rather from the effort to describe new experiences and to build around these experiences new but still familiar and satisfying meanings. This meant a new kind of novel. The pained, groping ironies of Edwardian culture, say in Dubliners or The Good Soldier, become the mythic, celebratory ironies of Ulysses and Parade's End. The war was disillusioning and out of the dying ideals of the nineteenth century was born the very different mythmaking apparatus of the twentieth: ironic, eclectic, subjective.

《 》

Ten painful years lie between the publication of The Good Soldier and of Some Do Not, the first novel of Ford's great war tetralogy, Parade's End.

7. Ford, The Good Soldier, 17–18.

The enormous difference between these novels is not only a contrast between two books but between two quite separate eras in Ford's life and in
the cultural life of all Europe. In 1915 Conrad congratulated Ford in his
usual backhanded way on the publication of *The Good Soldier*, praising its
"tone of fretful melancholy."[8] In 1924 when *Some Do Not* appeared, Conrad was dead, the literary world that had supported him was gone, and
"fretful melancholy" was a tone of voice no one wanted to hear. Ford,
however, wanted to continue to use it and had done so in a number of
fragments and mostly unpublished novels written during and after the war.
Some Do Not represented his first wholehearted departure from the neurasthenic unevenness that characterized his writing of that terrible decade
during which he went to war and returned, shocked and exhausted, to find
that the London literary world had moved on. In 1918 Ford was in no
condition to reclaim whatever contacts or reputation had been his before.
It was not until 1923 that he could write to H. G. Wells from the safe
haven of Paris that "after many years of great anxiety and strain things
have rather suddenly gone all right together. . . . I've got over the nerve
tangle of the war and feel able at last really to write again—which I never
thought I should do."[9]

In the interim, Ford had written "tales of reconstruction" as he subtitled one of his half-fictionalized, hysterically static war memoirs.[10] Being
under fire in France had ruined his lungs and his memory, had depleted his
physical and mental resilience, and yet he wrote and wrote, trying to get
some kind of hold on the slippery war material. Ford's half tries at novels
from this period are hard to date. There are two long typescripts, complete
novels in various versions that were never to be published: "The Wheels of
the Plough" (known in other versions as "Mr. Croyd" and "That Same
Poor Man") and "True Love and a General Court Martial."[11] Both typescripts are interesting "tales of reconstruction" in themselves, and both are
harbingers of *Parade's End*. The most interesting and the only fully fictional piece Ford wrote between *The Good Soldier* and *Parade's End* is *The
Marsden Case*, a study of the mind not facing the war itself—which was

8. Conrad to Ford, n.d. [1903], in Henry W. and Albert A. Berg Collection, New York
Public Library, Astor, Lenox and Tilden Foundations.

9. Richard Ludwig (ed.), *Letters of Ford Madox Ford* (Princeton, 1965), 154.

10. Ford, *No Enemy: A Tale of Reconstruction*.

11. Typescripts and holographs, *ca.* 1920–21, Olin Library, Cornell University, Ithaca, N.Y.

the obsessive subject of much of Ford's fragmentary writing of this time—
but facing the equally taxing madness of the home front. Part 1 is particularly fine, a complexly structured and detailed description of one long summer day just weeks before the war. The narrator, an interesting figure who
recalls this summer of 1914 after having fought the war and with its grief
still, as it were, on his tongue, is in a perfect position to squeeze elegiac
irony out of this material. Each scene is another glimpse of a world the
narrator never allows us to forget has now gone forever, doomed in all its
fineness, loveliness, idiocy.

But these fine individual scenes fail to add up to an effective whole; if
one goes to *The Marsden Case* for people or for story one is even more
wearied than usual with Ford's handling of these aspects of fiction. With
the exception of the narrator, these characters are the Fordian types we've
met elsewhere and there is little new illumination cast here on the young
man who is helpless, neurasthenic, and absurdly honorable or on the
young woman who is rapacious, unscrupulous, and as active in her malig-
nancy as the young man is passive in his goodness. Nor does the plot move
away from Ford's old weaknesses as a storyteller. The story is, as the title
says, a "case," and Ford smothers the real interest of the action beneath
layers of tiresome "justification," exploring both legal details and psychological symptoms that never develop any thematic resonance for the
reader. Imagine yourself in chancery and doomed to have the case explained to you by a lawyer employing the verbal meanderings of Ford
Madox Ford.

The Marsden Case is a rehash of the prewar Fordian formula. It begins
delicately, complexly, and with wit. It is a comedy of manners with interesting satiric intent which, after a strong opening, begins a long slide towards the static, the subjective, and finally, the ironically but hopefully
romantic. Ford certainly had not yet found a way to link these old and still
treasured mental patterns with the new materials of the war. When he
wrote *The Marsden Case* he was still something of a "case" himself, exhausted, disillusioned, and as yet unable to fictionalize these important
emotions without at the same time sinking under them. In some ways, *The
Marsden Case* stands in the same relation to *Parade's End* that *A Call*
stands to *The Good Soldier*. Many of the materials and the techniques used
in the two great novels are to be found in only partially assembled form in
the earlier, weaker books.

The tone of *The Marsden Case* goes through the unstable fluctuations we have come to expect from Ford's rehearsal novels. In its voice, Ford is tuning up, trying to find the pitch uniquely suited for his spiritual distillation of the war. *The Marsden Case* is ambitious, and its overall failure must have indicated to Ford that if he wanted to describe the pressure the war placed on the sensitive mind, he would have to work on a canvas large enough to encompass his rival tones of irony, vagueness, pathos, absurdity, and passionate idealism without turning this mixture into the parody which, in the too compressed scope of *The Marsden Case*, it sometimes becomes.

As in *Parade's End*, Ford is very interested here to give his suffering hero a happy ending. He wants to reconstruct the shattered war mind. But he has not yet found a way to reconcile the romantic happiness he wishes his hero with the pain and loss that is shown to surround him. Ford breaks away from his story to complain: "It is impossible, though there are non-participants who demand it, to write the lives of people today aged thirty or so, and leave out all mention of the fact that whilst those young people were aged, say, twenty-two to twenty-eight, there existed—Armageddon. For the matter of that, it would be wicked to attempt it, since the eyes, the ears, the brain and the fibres of every soul today adult have been profoundly seared by those dreadful wickednesses of embattled humanity."[12] Because Ford has been unable to balance the claims of describing his characters' sufferings with his interest in writing satiric vignettes and romantic melodrama, the end of *The Marsden Case* is pleasant but silly. The neurasthenic hero has tried to hang himself from too low a beech tree and his true love, Clarice, and a constable arrive in time to cut the rope and lower him into a car "amidst the beechen shadows. . . . Clarice whispered in his ear that it was all right; that he was an Earl; she to be his countess; there would be no more fusses; just little bits of fun."[13] This, of course, is writing from a different universe from that of *Some Do Not*, begun only a year later. Perhaps Arthur Mizener had a key to the interesting difference between Ford's books made of wonderful pieces and his books that function as successful wholes. He said that the thing that distinguishes Ford neurasthenic from Ford healthy is that the healthy Ford had a sense of the absurdity in both his fictional world and his moral views. This recognition

12. Ford, *The Marsden Case: A Romance* (London, 1923), 143–44.
13. *Ibid.*, 320.

of his own absurdity would go when he was sick.[14] Certainly, in *The Marsden Case* Ford weaves between knowing irony and hopelessly un-self-conscious obsessiveness. The Christopher Tietjens of *Parade's End* is similarly portrayed in a mixture of tones. The difference lies in Ford's control of his tonal paradoxes. In *Parade's End* he juggles the two ideas, that Tietjens is magnificent and that he is absurd, without letting either one knock the other out of the air.

« »

In 1918, Ford had retreated to the country with the young Australian painter Stella Bowen to live a pastoral idyll punctured by the not so idyllic problems of indigence—a situation rather like Tietjens and Valentine's in *The Last Post*. This was Ford's second try at the simple life with the same dyspeptic results. But he felt he could not return to London, now so changed. "I don't know that the large words Courage, Loyalty, God and the rest had, before the war been of frequent occurrence in London conversations. But one had had the conviction they were somewhere in the city's subconsciousness. . . . Now they were gone. . . . I don't, again, know that large words in conversations are indispensable to make me happy. I knew that, at that moment, all was over between me and London."[15]

In 1922 Ford and Stella and their new baby moved to France where the postwar reaction was towards joy and away from gloom and where the big romantic words *Faith, Loyalty, Courage*, and the rest could, Ford hoped, still be uttered without satirical derision. These were words that he himself had sometimes derided, but usually with an irony that did not finally demolish them. And after the great numbness of the war, the big words were precious to Ford, like trophies salvaged from an earlier, better life.

But, though Paris was gay, it was not as Ford hoped. Those big words which, as that other exile in Paris wrote in *Ulysses*, make us so unhappy, were being called into doubt everywhere. Ford's romantic allegiance to them often made him seem pompous and ridiculous to the young generation of expatriate writers among whom he found himself in the Paris of the twenties.

In the second of his great ventures as an editor, the Paris-based *Transatlantic Review*, Ford published Hemingway, Robert McAlmon, Nathan

14. Arthur Mizener, in conversation, Spring, 1969.
15. Ford, *It Was the Nightingale*, 70.

Asch, John Dos Passos, Djuna Barnes, William Carlos Williams, Ethel Colburne Mayne, A. E. Coppard, Jean Rhys, Mary Butts, and many more of the gifted young, but for the most part, they knew not him. Ford admired them; he often sympathized with what they were doing, but the divide is total. Hemingway was particularly brutal in his way of underlining it, but they all felt it.

Ford dealt with this problem by playing the part of the older man of letters, the patron, but this role was bound to be forced. At some level he must have felt the strain that always accompanies an effort to join an alien crowd, particularly over a gap of generations. When, upset by Conrad's sudden death in 1924, Ford began to plan a memorial issue of the *Review*, he had trouble finding anyone for whom Conrad was not an old fossil.[16]

With Ford's usual gift for being in the right place at the right time, he was in Paris at a great moment of cultural excitement. But the London of 1909–1910 which greeted the *English Review* as one of the first popular breakthroughs of modernism had been Ford's world. After the war, for all his canniness as an editor and his instinct for quality and important cultural ferment, Ford was a man caught between generations. In London, Bloomsbury's conscientious objectors had inherited the earth and only Wells and Bennett, also noncombatants, still managed to flourish in a self-consciously post-Edwardian milieu. In Paris the new men embraced the new anomie that Ford decried. It was their birthright and they mined it without nostalgia or apology for whatever human values it might surprisingly contain. For these writers, whom Ford sometimes lumped together as *les jeunes*, romanticism in its nineteenth-century voice was not, anymore, in the available range of cultural choices. As Ford himself understood, postwar life was in violent reaction to things as they were before or during the war. Indeed, it was not until 1928 that war memoirs and novels came into fashion. During the years that Ford was patiently grinding out his great war story, no one wanted to hear about that epic clash between idealism, innocence, and peace on the one hand and utter devastation on the other. The real accomplishment of his years in France was not that he joined *la generation perdue*, which he never truly did,[17] but that

16. Bernard J. Poli has written a complete description of Ford's editorship of the *Transatlantic*: Poli, *Ford Madox Ford and the "Transatlantic Review"* (Syracuse: Syracuse University Press, 1967).

17. Ford wrote one work that showed how easily he could have adopted the style and the tone of *les jeunes* had he chosen to waste a few further years in imitation, his long narrative

in spite of financial worries, social overextension, nervous exhaustion, and the upsets, insults, and frenzies that came to him while working on the *Transatlantic Review*, Ford managed to sequester himself and to find in himself the emotional energy to call up that great, romantic vision of the past which is *Parade's End*.

---

poem, Mr. *Bosphorus and the Muses; or, A Short History of Poetry in Britain, a Variety Entertainment in Four Acts, with Harlequinade, Transformation Scene, Cinematograph Effects, and Many Other Novelties, as well as Old and Tried Favourites* (London: Duckworth, 1923), with cubist illustrations by Paul Nash, a book that looks and reads like a standard production of the international avant garde.

"God's England!" Tietjens exclaimed to himself in high good humour. "'Land of Hope and Glory!'—F natural descending to tonic, C major: chord of 6-4, suspension over dominant seventh to common chord of C major. . . . All absolutely correct! Double basses, 'cellos, all violins, all woodwind, all brass. Full grand organ, all stops, special *vox humana* and key-bugle effect. . . . Across the counties came the sound of bugles that his father knew. . . ."

FORD, *Some Do Not*

«9»

PARADE'S END

PARADE'S END IS A ROMANCE

I RONICALLY enough, Ford's most socially panoramic novel is more unequivocally a romance than any other he wrote. Its brilliantly realistic observations about prewar culture, wartime stress, postwar exhaustion and reconstruction in no way undermine this essential fact: *Parade's End* is a romance. It is all there, behind the trappings of a painstaking, subjective impressionism—the quests, the spiritual battles that are far more important than the physical ones, the ideal hero who suffers all, learns all, but never changes, he of the pure heart, whose end is true love and pastoral peace. Ambiguity is still the main way Ford has for facing conflict, but this time he takes sides without leaving himself many ironic loopholes. He shows social chaos from the gropingly subjective viewpoint of his characters, but he himself has an overview he almost never abandons. He has, and insists on having, his own romantic view of events; he staves off the old insecurities and uncertainties. He always craved an honorable fixity that could replace the more painful immobility of doubt, and in *Parade's End* he achieved it. Though his tone modulates, as it does in *The Good Soldier*, expressing many shades of idea and feeling, here it modulates between fixed poles. Certain ideas have hardened in him and escalating social change has only confirmed him further in his belief that one cannot

do better than stick to the old social codes in whatever odd and absurd way
one can find to do so in the ever new world.

« »

The figure of Tietjens embodies Ford's newly solidified defenses against
confusion. Tietjens is all the contradictory things Ford has always longed
for: he is the practical man. (As his friend Macmaster says: "Confound
you, Chrissie. You know everything.")[1] And he is the impractical man
who lives for gallantry, for the ideal. He knows how to farm, how to run a
regiment, how to find out the truth about England's farthest imperial
reaches by doing some statistical figuring in his head. He is the lover. He is
the visionary. He is capable of generating and keeping alive inside himself
values that have otherwise disappeared from the earth.

While Tietjens' friend Macmaster is "a smallish man," Tietjens himself
is an immense figure, epical, a sort of upper-class buddha, "on each knee
an immense white hand" (SDN, 4). Tietjens is, as his wife Sylvia says derisively, "a fabulous monster" (SDN, 167). If he is grotesque, this is because he is honorable, virtuous, and doomed, a most familiar person in
Ford Madox Ford's wax museum of character types. He is the seventeenth-
century man homeless in the twentieth. He is the last soldier to be a gentleman, the only one left who believes in "the gallant enemy" (SDN,
174). His blood and land and absolute rectitude all entitle him to look
down on everybody he encounters. Indeed his snobbery about niggers,
Jews, bounders, foreigners, other ranks, decadent gentlemen, aspiring
Scots, and society beauties is his birthright. He is the last Tory. He never
complains and never explains, until his wife drives herself first into sadistic
madness then into spiritual exhaustion in her effort to unsettle his moral
fixity, his monolithic certainty. He remains silent, long-suffering. He will
say nothing to Sylvia beyond asserting his immovable belief that a gentleman should treat all adversaries, even hysterically sadistic wives, as gallant
enemies.

1. Ford, Some Do Not, 19, in Ford, Parade's End (New York, 1961). All references are to
this edition, hereinafter cited in the text with the abbreviations SDN (Some Do Not), TLP
(The Last Post—in other editions called Last Post), NMP (No More Parades), AMCSU (A
Man Could Stand Up) and the page number. Arthur Mizener has pointed out that there are
several small errors in this edition, but the inconvenience of these is easily offset by having
all four novels of the tetralogy together in one volume, unified, as I believe them properly to
be, under the collective title Parade's End.

Ford piles it on. Tietjens is George Herbert, both country parson and poet; he is Hamlet; he's Admetus and Apollo. Tietjens is the feudal landlord, heir apparent to Groby, and in his final medieval-modern idyll, he is "Milord Chantecler" living with "Madame Partlet" and protecting her and her young from the murderous sparrow hawk always waiting at a distance to threaten their peace. "There are those who reprove [Milord Chantecler] because his eyes are always on the sky, because he has a proud head. But that is his function—that and gallantry" (*TLP*, 700–701).

Ford—who elsewhere has so often doubled and trebled his characters, dividing up the traits he is interested in, giving us a Dowell to comment on an Ashburnham—here gives Tietjens all the qualities of the Ford hero rolled up into one. Though the point of view in *Parade's End* is constantly shifting and the narrative is full of Tietjens' doppelgängers and foils, important figures who enrich and complicate our idea of the hero, nevertheless, few of these characters permanently undermine him as the novel's essential ideal. Often, indeed, these other points of view serve to second Tietjens in all his acts.

Ford has his hero say things like "I stand for monogamy and chastity" (*SDN*, 18), and he makes him an infallible prophet of his society's fate: "Tietjens had said that about the time grouse-shooting began, in 1914, a European conflagration would take place which would shut up half the houses in Mayfair and beggar their inhabitants. He had patiently supported his prophecy with financial statistics as to the approaching bankruptcy of various European powers and the growingly acquisitive skill and rapacity of the inhabitants of Great Britain" (*SDN*, 155). In addition, the clairvoyant Tietjens knows that this war, which will start about the time grouse-shooting begins, will transform social life, particularly sexual relations. "War," he tells his foolishly complacent friend Macmaster, "is as inevitable as divorce" (*SDN*, 21). Though war and divorce try Tietjens, he has a Christ-like aloofness from the moral turpitude of the modern Pharisees and Sadducees who surround him and who bring the war down on all their heads by being untrustworthy polygamists. Indeed Ford often compares Tietjens to Christ. Like Christ, he is innocent, but his very perfection singles him out as the appropriate bearer of others' sins. "He saved others, himself he could not save." Not only must he suffer for the sins of decadent fools; the sins of the fathers are visited upon him, too. "There's not been a Tietjens since the first Lord Justice cheated the Papist Loundeses out of Groby, but died of a broken neck or of a broken heart" (*SDN*, 177). There is a curse on the ancient house of Tietjens which only a man of perfect purity can cleanse away.

By now the sympathetic reader of *Parade's End* is probably sputtering with irritation. "No, no," he is thinking, "all this is only an aspect of the Tietjens I know." Indeed, this epical figure is modified by all kinds of deflationary devices. But Tietjens, shade him subtly as you will, is nevertheless a monolithic symbol of all that Ford values. No amount of deflationary irony brings him down from these symbolic heights, as Dowell and Ashburnham are brought down, or as George Moffat and Don Kelleg are brought down. Though Ford does indeed flirt dangerously with absurd exaggeration, making Tietjens impossibly knowing, irritatingly immovable, pompously perfect, Ford does not, finally, laugh at these traits in Tietjens or mean us merely to laugh at them. On the contrary, Ford loves Tietjens and all his ideals, all his pretensions. He has always loved this figure but never before with such confidence or with so focused an emotional fervor.

By the time Ford began writing *Parade's End* he had certainly read his James Joyce. A segment of *Finnegans Wake* appeared in Ford's *Transatlantic Review* in 1924 under Ford's temporary title "Work in Progress." Joyce is not the only reason why *Parade's End* is so steeped in myth—myths in modern landscapes appear frequently among Ford's contemporaries—but Joyce almost certainly provided Ford with a clue as to how he could make his hero both ideal and absurd at the same time without these qualities canceling each other out. In *Ulysses* Joyce loves Bloom and Stephen while he lampoons them mercilessly. They never lose their grandeur as richly suggestive, brave human figures because as soon as Joyce deflates his portrait of them as Ulysses or as Hamlet he immediately reinflates their mythic nature by insisting on a vital connection between beleaguered modern creatures (a Bloom or a Tietjens) and the cultural ideals of the past. Joyce allows his characters to carry the human story forward. He asserts its circular and continuous nature. Ironic deflation is only one phase in a cycle: in Joyce's prose, myths are serious and magnificent, then funny and pretentious, inflated and deflated, like the coming and going of the breath. *Parade's End* borrows this organic model for connecting the epical and the absurd aspects of human life.

Tietjens is not essentially different from earlier Ford heroes, but into all those earlier Tietjens incarnations—Count Macdonald, George Moffat,

Mr. Blood, and the rest—Ford placed contradictions he could not resolve, absurdities he could not face, fatuities he only half recognized. In these earlier novels, he is a juggler who throws up the holy grail, an old shoe, a school tie, a sentimental nosegay and tries to keep all these oddly shaped things from knocking each other out of the air. He had his success and his failures, though even the failures are impressive in their way when one stops to consider the variety of the materials he wished to combine in the same breathtakingly difficult trick. Nowhere, however, does Ford so skillfully manage to maintain contraries without undermining any of his meanings as he does in *Parade's End*.

The war changed the essential nature of Ford's predicament: the private and social upheavals he had always feared had finally happened once and for all. Instead of collapsing before the new order as the hero of *The Inheritors* does, or as Ashburnham and Dowell do, Tietjens is resilient. Prewar doubt was a passive luxury the postwar generation could not afford. Everything was new. One either embraced this newness and assigned it old meanings, like Ford, or one embraced this newness and decided to ignore the old meanings, like Hemingway, but one embraced it. It was everywhere and inescapable. This postwar atmosphere was insistently confident. (There was sometimes desperation beneath.) Ford could not hope to see feudalism in his lifetime, but he could assert that feudalism was his ideal, he could travel to the feudal castles of Provence, and as a middle-aged exile, he could ignore the present.

The more seriously Ford took his own myths of feudalism, of rectitude, of a once and future peace, the less ironic he became as a writer. Irony in him had always been an expression of self-doubt, of confusion, and of pain. Though those old ironies are still frequent in the texture of *Parade's End*, they are bounded by a romantic, mythic frame. Ford and his Tietjens must either believe in their power to re-create meaning in the wilderness or die; they choose to believe.

IRONY: THE SOURCE OF VITALITY IN FORD'S ROMANCE

The Tietjens ideal and romantic schematization of the work aside, what of the actual experience of reading *Parade's End*? What is its texture, the means it employs towards its romantic ends? As soon as we ask this kind of question, an interesting paradox emerges: in order to maintain the fixity of

Parade's End's moral and social values, Ford uses all his old techniques, his old voices, even his old confusions and incongruities. Ford saves his ideal by surrounding it with human fallibility, by mocking it, even by doubting it. The Tietjens character is a reed that bends that it may not be broken. Insofar as Tietjens is a sort of monolithic totem pole symbolizing all the English and Christian virtues, insofar as he is an immovable Groby Great Tree, he can only darken the windows of the modern Groby and be felled with relief to let in some air and light. If Tietjens were never more than an embodiment of the ideal, the ideal would be *only* pompous and ridiculous, and there would be no fictional vitality in *Parade's End*. But Ford humbles his hero that he may finally be exalted. He gives him so many heroic roles to play that they become, in conjunction, comic. If he is Christ, he is also "Milord Chantecler," a figure whose epical stature we know. And if Tietjens is "modelling himself on our Lord," he once again is too various and beleaguered to perfectly fit the part, for "our Lord was never married" (*NMP*, 41). If one wants to call Tietjens stiff and unreal, one finds that Sylvia has gotten there first and is busy criticizing him for that very failing. When he writes to her, she says, "It's like being addressed as if one were a monument and by a herald according to protocol" (*SDN*, 32). If one wants to call Tietjens a superior snob, one finds that Valentine has got there first and is telling Tietjens, "I'm sorry I was rude to you. But it *is* irritating to have to stand like a stuffed rabbit while a man is acting like a regular Admirable Crichton, and cool and collected, with the English country gentleman air and all" (*SDN*, 113). Just when it looks as though Ford's thematic schema will overwhelm the vitality of Tietjens and indeed of all his characters, making them stiff-lipped, almost allegorical, his life-long ironic attitude towards all ideological absolutes floods in and saves the book from its potentially confining motif. Nowhere else in his work does he so successfully combine a clear, overriding intention with local detours, with tonal undercutting, and with the exploration into unresolvable questions and irreducibly painful emotions. The old, muddled Ford is still at work, noticing that the parts do not quite fit together, that people are speaking to each other with no common language, that no matter what one's ideals, actuality keeps forcing one into a condition of isolation and doubt. As always in Ford, it is the mixture of elements, the cacophony of voices, that is wonderful and suggestive.

Ford's writing here is extraordinarily shapely; single, symbolically suggestive incidents activate huge grids of associative connections. Take the following passage, in which Tietjens gains three-dimensionality through changes in narrative tone; the ideal Ford postulates in him is modified and variegated by his actual experience of the war.

It gave him satisfaction to observe that he had got his men into their lines seventy-five per cent. quicker than the best of the N.C.O.s who had had charge of the other lines. . . . he drifted with regret across the plain towards his country street of huts. One of them had a coarse evergreen rose growing over it. He picked a leaf, pressed it to his lips and threw it up into the wind. . . . "That's for Valentine," he said meditatively. "Why did I do that? . . . Or perhaps it's for England. . . ." He said: "Damn it all, this is patriotism! . . . *This* is patriotism. . . ." It wasn't what you took patriotism as a rule to be. There were supposed to be more parades about that job! . . . But this was just a broke to the wide, wheezy, half-frozen Yorkshireman, who despised everyone in England not a Yorkshireman, or from more to the North, at two in the morning picking a leaf from a rose-tree and slobbering over it, without knowing what he was doing. And then discovering that it was half for a pug-nosed girl whom he presumed, but didn't know, to smell like a primrose; and half for . . . England! At two in the morning with the thermometer ten degrees below zero. . . . Damn, it was cold! . . .

And why these emotions? . . . Because England, not before it was time, had been allowed to decide not to do the dirty on her associates! . . . He said to himself: "It is probably because a hundred thousand sentimentalists like myself commit similar excesses of the subconscious that we persevere in this glorious but atrocious undertaking. All the same, I didn't know I had it in me!" A strong passion! . . . For his girl and his country! . . . Nevertheless, his girl was a pro-German. . . . It was a queer mix-up! . . . Not of course a pro-German, but disapproving of the preparation of men, like bullocks, with sleek healthy skins for the abattoirs in Smithfield. . . . Agreeing presumably with the squits who had been hitherto starving the B. E. F. of men. . . . A queer mix-up. . . . (*NMP*, 362–63)

Though it has been dragged through the mud, patriotism still means something to Tietjens. The sentimental subconscious of a hundred thousand individual men has saved England from dishonoring herself. For all its mass confusion, the war is still, for Tietjens, a personal matter, an expression, "glorious" as well as "atrocious," of his own will, honor, and love.

But if Ford had left it at that, giving us the evergreen rose, the fine Yorkshireman who loves "his girl and his country," we probably would not read *Parade's End* today. Tietjens' idealization of the war and of feudal honor left unmodified by some sense of what the true experience was—of how hard it was to maintain a sense of personal meaning during the war— becomes false like the optimistic voices of the home front. Ford saves honor and patriotism and love from having the ring of false optimism by putting all Tietjens' emotions and values through the wringer of the most painful experiences as seen through the most complex of styles.

The colloquial swing of Tietjens' thoughts (England "had been allowed to decide not to do the dirty on her associates") reminds us that his moments of sentimental fervor are real, are part of an alternating psychological current we can recognize and understand. Tietjens is traveling in his thoughts from insouciance, to irony, to romance on what is, in this novel, a well-traveled mental road. He makes this trip in both directions, first searching for personal sanity, then giving up in a cold, ironic fury, then remembering some treasured reason, like his love for Valentine, that gives the war point. In typical Ford fashion, the passage collapses by a deflation of Tietjens' sentiment. At the very moment of his connecting his feeling for Valentine with his patriotic emotions he remembers that Valentine disapproves of the abattoir of war. He has allowed himself to forget her view of the war and to forget the reality of slaughter around him in his rapture of sentimental associations, but the reality of her feeling, once he thinks of it, forces an end to his meditation—"A queer mix-up. . . ."

This is the process central to the construction of *Parade's End*: the posing of thoughts and meanings only to have them instantly modified, undermined. The most painful aspect of the war is the pressure it puts on the human mind's capacity to control and order experience. When General Campion orders Tietjens to the most dangerous part of the front line, he thinks: "There it was then: the natural catastrophe! As when, under thunder, a dam breaks. His mind was battling with the waters. What would it pick out as the main terror? The mud, the noise, dread always at the back of the mind? Or the worry! The worry! Your eyebrows always had a slight tension on them. . . . Like eye-strain!" (*NMP*, 477). When Tietjens' mind is fit, it knows. Now, in the war, Tietjens' mind is "battling with the waters." The passage begins with the epical disaster of the war, a mighty flood. But in modern circumstances, to the modern imagination, the flood is not only a flood, it is the flood-in-the-mind. Under stress, the mind becomes Tietjens' enemy. Can he trust it to continue knowing what it has always known? Will it find itself amid the flood? And finally, will there be anything left worth knowing? The worst threat to the mind is not the flood—epical, challenging, eternal, and impersonal—but "the worry! . . . Like eye-strain." It is, finally, the little irritations, the humiliations, the stupidities and wrangling that undermine heroic strength. Tietjens' worst enemy is not the Hun (whom in nineteenth-century style he still calls "gallant") but the modern world itself, which strips all gallantry and scale and clarity of purpose from men. Tietjen's claim to private whole-ness is hard won, wrested from a terrible and desolating wasteland: "His face was whitish in the pale light, but it was always whitish since he had come back from France and passed his day in a tin hut among dust heaps" (*SDN*, 157).

«»

We know from Ford's letters how interested he was in the extraordinary phenomenon that was the war. It brought unheard of things together; it offered experiences (all the glass in a church breaking at once) entirely new to the ear, eye, and mind. The impressionist who, in the London of the vorticists, had thought his skills old-fashioned found new use for them, to describe this new and unlikely concatenation of people and things, the western front:

> [Tietjens] reclined, on his right shoulder, feeling like some im-mense and absurd statue: a collection of meal-sacks done in mud, with grotesque shorts revealing his muddy knees. . . . The figure on one of Michael Angelo's Medici tombs. Or perhaps his *Adam* . . . He felt the earth move a little beneath him. The last projectile must have been pretty near. He would not have noticed the sound, it had become such a regular sequence. But he noticed the quiver in the earth. . . . We had begun a considerable artillery demonstration. It became overwhelming. There was some sort of Bloody Mary some-where a few yards off, or so it seemed. She pooped off. The planes had perhaps reported the position of the Austrian gun. Or we might be *strafing* their trenches to make them shut up that weapon. It was

like being a dwarf at a conversation, a conflict—of mastodons. There was so much noise it seemed to grow dark. It was a mental darkness. You could not think. A Dark Age! The earth moved.

He was looking at Aranjuez [one of Tietjens' men] from a considerable height. He was enjoying a considerable view. Aranjuez's face had a rapt expression—like that of a man composing poetry. Long dollops of liquid mud surrounded them in the air. Like black pancakes being tossed. He thought: "Thank God I did not write to her. We are being blown up!" The earth turned like a weary hippopotamus. It settled down slowly over the face of Lance-Corporal Duckett who lay on his side, and went on in a slow wave.

It was slow, slow, slow . . . like a slowed-down movie. The earth manoeuvred for an infinite time. He remained suspended in space. . . .

The earth sucked slowly and composedly at his feet.

It assimilated his calves, his thighs. It imprisoned him above the waist. His arms being free, he resembled a man in a life-buoy. The earth moved him slowly. It was solidish.

Below him, down a mound, the face of little Aranjuez, brown, with immense black eyes in bluish whites, looked at him. Out of viscous mud. A head on a charger! He could see the imploring lips form the words: "Save me, Captain!" He said:

"I've got to save myself first!" He could not hear his own words. The noise was incredible. (AMCSU, 636–37)

Here Ford is again, the literator, toilingly setting down this new experience, making a great effort to fuse his old literary skills and his new materials. The passage begins with Tietjens reclining like Michelangelo's Adam. He is, like all Ford's heroes, both "immense and absurd." This figure is not majestic like Adam but, like him, is made of dust, "a collection of meal-sacks done in mud." The war has supplied a new sculptural medium. But as we contemplate the hero, a phenomenon far greater than he shakes the image. The earth moves a little beneath him. Though he is Adam, Tietjens is reduced by this great heaving of the earth into a dwarf, "A dwarf at a conversation, a conflict—of mastodons." A darkness comes which, as usual, Ford immediately insists is "a mental darkness." There can be no thinking, no personal stature when the whole earth is heaving. "A Dark Age."

Carefully, using the old tools of his trade, Ford makes the new experience happen: Aranjuez's face is rapt like "a man composing poetry." The
earth moves slowly "like a slowed-down movie." Tietjens and his men end
buried in mud in positions that could have been designed by Dante. We
feel the distance between what is really happening to the little officer
Aranjuez and the metaphor used for the amazed expression on his face. He
is not in fact a man inspired; he is a man confronted with death. "Save
me, Captain," he says to the Christ-like hero, Tietjens, whom he idolizes.
"I've got to save myself first." All Sylvia's insults about Christopher as
Christ are gathered together here into an ironic, tragicomic moment. "He
saved others, himself he could not save" has become, in modern circumstances, "he can't save anyone else until he first finds himself." Then, in
fact, Tietjens does find himself, is helped from the mud, and acts heroically to save Aranjuez. For a moment it seems that, though it is a dark
age, the hero can still save. We see Tietjens carry the stunned Aranjuez in
his arms like a baby. But there is one more ironic twist to the incident.
Trying to save Aranjuez's life, Tietjens has carried him through sniper fire
so that his eye is shot out even as he is carried under his captain's protective arm. As the scene ends, Tietjens, unfairly blamed for the disarray of
his heavily strafed camp, learns that Aranjuez has lost his eye. Not only is
Tietjens to be falsely accused and condemned, but in the midst of the bitterness of his inability to save himself, he has also been unable to save
others. The war's ironies are gross ironies, and inside them men move un-
easily, caught in the subtler, private ironies of their doubts and confusions.
This is a dark age for Adam, for Christ, and for poetry. Tietjens remains
great in his pain. He does not move. But the earth moves beneath him,
changing his ultimate position in the scheme of things. Indeed, while
Ford's characters believe themselves to be stationary, or try to be so, he is
always shifting the ground beneath their feet.

PARADE'S END IS A COMEDY

The chaste and monogamous Tietjens is forced by history to conclude, in
the words of his mistress, that after "the long pull of the war . . . what
could an infidelity more or less matter" (*SDN*, 268). This incongruity is
the material of comedy, and *Parade's End*, for all the suffering and despair it
so fully presents, is essentially a comic work. Here, as elsewhere, Ford begins in the comic mode, introduces tragic elements, pathos, and despair,

then finally overwhelms his sadness and his nihilistic ironies with a great wash of, in this case, affirmative rather than tragic romance.

As always in Ford's writing, the comic elements of *Parade's End* are end-lessly varied and profuse. Here, then, is a sort of catalogue of Ford's comic effects in the tetralogy.

Breaks in Decorum

At the end of *Some Do Not*, Valentine and Tietjens say good-bye to each other. It is the night before Tietjens leaves for the front, and earlier in the afternoon he has asked Valentine to become his mistress and she has con-sented. Now that the moment has arrived, however, they both realize that they are not the sort to commit adultery. Tietjens suggests that they wash out the memory of his ever even having asked her such a thing:

> "You cut out from this afternoon, just before 4.58 it was when I said that to you and you consented . . . I heard the Horse Guards clock. . . . To now. . . . Cut it out; and join time up. . . . It *can* be done. . . . You know they do it surgically; for some illness; cut out a great length of the bowel and join the tube up. . . . For colitis, I think. . . ."
>
> She said:
>
> "But I *wouldn't* cut it out. . . . It was the first spoken sign."
>
> He said:
>
> "No it wasn't. . . . From the very beginning . . . with every word. . . ."
>
> She exclaimed:
>
> "You felt that too! . . . We've been pushed, as in a carpenter's vise. . . . We couldn't have got away. . . ."
>
> He said: "By God! That's it. . . ." (*SDN*, 285)

Two lovers are saying goodbye having only just acknowledged to each other that they are in love. Perhaps, since their scruples keep them apart, it would be easier for them to put their declaration aside, to cut it out of consciousness for the duration. Is this the moment to compare what has passed between them to colitis or to compare the act of mutual forgetting to cutting out a great length of the bowel and joining the tube up?

Ford is addicted to this kind of break in decorum. He saves his senti-mental love scenes by injecting them with bits of mental detritus. Colitis, the great length of bowel, the carpenter's vise which Tietjens and Valentine agree is the metaphor for how they have been brought together, these things distract us from what is woodenly sentimental in their parting. There is a psychological verisimilitude in the inappropriateness of these lovers' metaphors that convinces us that all the other things they say and do are also natural, human, recognizable.

Ford has always used colloquialisms, unlikely metaphors, breaks in tone and rhetorical level to disarm his readers so that they will not be too critical of either his thematic earnestness or his occasional lack of it. He has always been like the magician who misdirects our eye while the real trick goes on somewhere else. He is often insecure about his main intentions and eager to kick dust in the eyes of the critical spectator. Even in the confident shapeliness of *Parade's End*, Ford's old, disarming use of deflation and misdirection makes an appearance from time to time, but here it is the exception while more stable, clearly directed forms of irony and comedy are the rule.

Comedy of Manners

Many of Ford's novels before *Parade's End* contain scenes of pure social comedy, often beautifully done. Bits of *Mr. Apollo* and *Ladies Whose Bright Eyes* come to mind, as do long, hilarious patches of *The Simple Life Limited*. But nowhere does Ford place such comic set pieces with more grace and felicity than in *Parade's End*. And surely, of these jewel-like excursions into comedy of manners, none is a greater comic masterpiece than the scene at the Duchemins' breakfast.

Ford has assembled a group of people at a breakfast table. We know each one's reason for being there, each one's past history in relation to the others, and we see the beginning of new alliances, new enmities. As in similar scenes in the great tradition, like, for example, the meal at Lady de Burgh's in *Pride and Prejudice*, some of the characters are briefly sketched comic types while others are shown in greater depth. The scene is almost a play (and indeed, was once easily adapted as one and performed before delighted audiences at Hofstra University) in that even those characters we know well are seen as they must perforce present themselves in a social situation. As on all social occasions, everyone is playing a part and the differences between motive and appearance, inside and outside, differences that elsewhere moved Ford to pathos, here give rise to pure hilarity.

The scene is alive with various kinds of tension. Tietjens and Valentine size each other up in earnest, having met only once before in the skirmish

with the police on the golf links. Macmaster and Mrs. Duchemin also become a pair at this breakfast. Valentine's mother, Mrs. Wannop, like so
many characters in Ford's social comedies, acts in rhythm with her own
thoughts and is oblivious to all other social configurations in the room.
She begins by trying to annex Macmaster but stays to discover a former
connection and new friend in Tietjens. Indeed, many of the chief connections in the book are laid down on this quintessentially Edwardian social
occasion, Edwardian because its surface is unruffled while, beneath, all the
habits and conventions that should bind these people together have in
fact broken down. (Mrs. Duchemin to Tietjens: "Of course we should
be all gentle-folk here. One naturally arranges that." Tietjens to Mrs.
Duchemin: "Ah! But it isn't so easy to arrange nowadays. All sorts of
bounders get into all sorts of holies of holies!" [SDN, 94].) By the end of
the fourth volume of the tetralogy, Macmaster and Mrs. Duchemin will
have become corrupt, social-climbing bureaucrats, while Tietjens and Valentine will have become open adulterers with the reluctant blessing of the
nineteenth-century heart and mind of Mrs. Wannop. After the war, there
will be no more such breakfasts, just as there will be no more parades. Indeed, there cannot be any more such preposterously forced, precariously
balanced social occasions in the world. The code of manners, the ties of
marriage, the social security that seem so clear to everyone at the table
are, as everyone seated there half knows, at the point of combustion.

The deranged Mr. Duchemin is the comic symbol of this imminent loss
of control. The other tensions at the breakfast, both sexual and social, are
latent, but the fear of an untoward explosion from Mr. Duchemin is shared
by all. This, then, is a last, and comic, expression of Edwardian social
community, as everyone conspires to yell banalities in order to drown out
the Latin obscenities of the eccentric parson and don:

> "Chaste!" He shouted. "Chaste, you observe! What a world of
> suggestion in the word . . ." He surveyed the opulent broadness of
> his tablecloth; it spread out before his eyes as if it had been a great
> expanse of meadow in which he could gallop, relaxing his limbs
> after long captivity. He shouted three obscene words and went on in
> his Oxford Movement voice: "But chastity . . ."
> Mrs. Wannop suddenly said:
> "Oh!" and looked at her daughter, whose face grew slowly crim-

son as she continued to peel a peach. Mrs. Wannop turned to Mr. Horsley beside her and said:

"You write, too, I believe, Mr. Horsley. No doubt something more learned than my poor readers would care for . . ." Mr. Horsley had been preparing, according to his instructions from Mrs. Duchemin, to shout a description of an article he had been writing about the *Mosella* of Ausonius, but as he was slow in starting the lady got in first. She talked on serenely about the tastes of the large public. Tietjens leaned across to Miss Wannop and, holding in his right hand a half-peeled fig, said to her as loudly as he could:

"I've got a message for you from Mr. Waterhouse. He says if you'll . . ."

The completely deaf Miss Fox—who had had her training by writing—remarked diagonally to Mrs. Duchemin:

"I think we shall have thunder to-day. Have you remarked the number of minute insects. . . ."

"When my revered preceptor [Ruskin]," Mr. Duchemin thundered on, "drove away in the carriage on his wedding day he said to his bride: 'We will live like the blessed angels!' How sublime! I, too, after my nuptials . . ."

Mrs. Duchemin suddenly screamed:

"Oh . . . *no!*"

As if checked for a moment in their stride all the others paused —for a breath. Then they continued talking with polite animation and listening with minute attention. To Tietjens that seemed the highest achievement and justification of English manners! (*SDN*, 99–100)

Explosions from out of repression, eruptions of licentious anarchy in the midst of social decorum—these are classical comic devices and Ford is in complete control of the possibilities offered by a bad boy at a tea party. Though his most serious themes underlie the spontaneous combustion at work at the Duchemin breakfast, here he is gay, able to laugh lovingly at the complacent people who are, though they don't yet know it, living so close to the edge of change. The writing is beautiful, the control of each character's place in the symmetry of the occasion flawless. A conveniently deaf little old lady pours out the tea while a former prize fighter serves the sole to his potentially violent charge, Duchemin. It is a dance. Most people dance well and know which partner is which—they are an odd assortment—while Duchemin cuts across the pattern, changing tone continually. He mistakes Macmaster for the doctor, come to certify him as mad. ("He said: 'Good-morning doctor,' and then, drowning Macmaster's quiet protest: 'Yes! Yes! The stethoscope meticulously packed into the top-hat and the shining hat left in the hall'" [SDN, 95].) He has his strained Oxford voice, his sane conversational voice, his voice for shouting Latin obscenities, and his voice for the English translation. Because he is out of step, the artificial pattern of the social dance is highlighted, indeed, becomes grotesque in its own way.

Ford has another kind of comedy of manners that occasionally makes an appearance in *Parade's End*. It is a sort of Chekhovian narration—witty, understated, a bit melancholy. A good example is the little detour, really the little short story that begins, "Major Wilfrid Fosbrooke Eddicker Perowne of Perowne, the son of his mother, was one of those individuals who have no history, no strong proclivities, nothing" (NMP, 387). When Sylvia wants to goad Christopher, this Perowne is the man she chooses to run away with, though the combination of Sylvia and Perowne is incongruous. (Ford loves unlikely couplings.) Though Ford sees their absurdity, he is in perfect sympathy with the suffering of both lovers:

[Perowne's] affair with Sylvia Tietjens might have been something to boast about, but he was not boastful, and indeed he had been too hard hit when she had left him even to bear to account lyingly for the employment of the time he had spent with her in Brittany. Fortunately no one took sufficient interest in his movements to wait for his answer to their indifferent questions as to where he had spent the summer. When his mind reverted to her desertion of him moisture would come out of his eyes, undemonstratively, as water leaves the surface of a sponge. . . .

Sylvia had left him by the simple expedient of stepping without so much as a reticule on to the little French tramway that took you to the main railway line. From there she had written to him in pencil on a closed correspondence card that she had left him because she simply could not bear either his dullness or his craking voice. She said they would probably run up against each other in the

course of the autumn season in town and, after purchase of some
night things, had made straight for the German spa to which her
mother had retreated. (*NMP*, 388–89)

There are echoes of *The Good Soldier* in Sylvia and Perowne's exhausted
wandering from one place of pleasure to another, and Ford's tone here is
reminiscent of the funnier, earlier sections of that book, when Florence,
Dowell and the others are still precariously stepping their minuet, revolving from spa to spa.

Another aspect of Ford's talent for social comedy is his writing of social
cameos. For example, Edith Ethel Duchemin (later Macmaster), that
tender of the Pre-Raphaelite flame, is a great comic figure:

Mrs. Duchemin had sat down in a chair near one of the windows; she had her handkerchief hiding her face.

"Why women in your position don't take lovers . . ." the girl
[Valentine] said, hotly. "Or that women in your position *do* take
lovers . . ."

Mrs. Duchemin looked up; in spite of its tears her white face had
an air of serious dignity:

"Oh, *no*, Valentine," she said, using her deeper tones. "There's
something beautiful, there's something *thrilling* about chastity. I'm
not narrow-minded. Censorious! I don't *condemn*! But to preserve
in word, thought and action a lifelong fidelity. . . . It's no mean
achievement. . . ."

"You mean like an egg and spoon race," Miss Wannop said.

"It isn't," Mrs. Duchemin replied gently, "the way I should have
put it. Isn't the real symbol Atalanta, running fast and not turning
aside for the golden apple? That always seemed to me the real truth
hidden in the beautiful old legend. . . ."

"I don't know," Miss Wannop said, "when I read what Ruskin
says about it in the *Crown of Wild Olive*. Or no! It's the *Queen of the
Air*. That's his Greek rubbish, isn't it? I always think it seems like an
egg-race in which the young woman didn't keep her eyes in the
boat. But I suppose it comes to the same thing."

Mrs. Duchemin said:

"My *dear*! Not a word against John Ruskin in *this* house."
(*SDN*, 85)

John Ruskin remains enthroned for Mrs. Duchemin throughout the novel but chastity does not. One of the things that makes us like the otherwise unexciting Valentine, that "cockney school-girl" (AMCSU, 509), is the way her simplicity undercuts the absurd pretensions and hypocrisies of her friend, Edith Ethel. Ford contrasts the adultery of Christopher and Valentine with that of Edith and Macmaster. The latter is comically sentimental, veiled in hypocrisy, and condoned by the worst lines in poems by Rossetti. The former is a long-awaited, hard-won compromise with a world whose moral structure has so seriously changed that all honest men and women are forced to change with it in order to remain true to their former selves. Edith is on the way up a ladder that Valentine and Christopher disdain to climb. Edith and Macmaster will be successes in the modern circumstances Ford satirizes in which war profiteers become government ministers. Instead, Valentine and Christopher prefer the land, which cannot change, and old furniture.

We get our last glimpse of Edith Ethel in one of Ford's wonderful telephone scenes. He loved the telephone's potential for misleading communications, mistaken identities, and general fuzziness. Valentine misses the precise moment the war ends because she is in an underground tunnel going to answer the telephone. For a long time she cannot understand who is at the other end of the line. Can it be a patroness of the school some Lady "Blastus"? It is Edith Ethel who, in a canonical example of a hilarious, garbled, Fordian, nonconversation indirectly announces to Valentine the great news that Christopher Tietjens has returned from war.

In *The Good Soldier* the absurd posturing of Florence recedes leaving Dowell to feel deeper emotions, pathos and grief. In *Parade's End* the similarly crisp comic cameos of Edith Ethel and her Sir Vincent give way to quite a different concluding tone, affectionate sentimentality. *The Last Post* abounds in rustic types one might meet in the pastoral section of *A Winter's Tale*. There is also a Wife of Bath in Mark Tietjens' impeccable French bourgeois mistress Marie-Léonie, who pours out cider and a stream of gossip, platitudes, practical housewifery:

> She had views on virtue, pride, downfalls, human careers, the habits of cats, fish, the clergy, diplomats, soldiers, women of easy virtue, Saint Eustachius, President Grévy, the purveyors of comestibles, custom-house officers, pharmacists, Lyons silk weavers. . . .
> Her mind in fact was like a cupboard, stuffed, packed with the most

incongruous materials, tools, vessels, and débris. Once the door was opened you never knew what would tumble out or be followed by what. That was restful to Mark as foreign travel might have been. . . .

Her conversation had another quality that continually amused him: she always ended it with the topic with which she had chosen to begin. Thus, to-day having chosen to begin with *navets de Paris*, with Paris turnips she would end, and it amused him to observe how on each occasion she would bring the topic back. (*TLP*, 682–83)

Satire

In the Preface to *Heartbreak House*, Shaw commented:

War cannot bear the terrible castigation of comedy, the ruthless light of laughter that glares on the stage. When men are heroically dying for their country, it is not the time to show their lovers and wives and fathers and mothers how they are being sacrificed to the blunders of boobies, the cupidity of capitalists, the ambition of conquerors, the electioneering of demagogues, the Pharisaism of patriots, the lusts and lies and rancors and bloodthirsts that love war because it opens their prison doors, and sets them in the thrones of power and popularity. For unless these things are mercilessly exposed they will hide under the mantle of the ideals on the stage just as they do in real life.[2]

In one sense Shaw is right. The war could not be made a laughing matter in the satirical style that was his wont. Banter, however scathing, could be but a sign of detachment from the horror of the front. These things could only be discussed allegorically and after the fact. Hence we have *Heartbreak House*, published only after the war was over and still, perhaps, Shaw's most diffuse and symbolically indirect satire. *Parade's End*, too, could only have been written long after the fact, and it is, far more than *Heartbreak House*, an ambivalent, circuitous, and diffusely symbolical criticism of England at war. Nevertheless, *Parade's End*, by mingling different tonal attitudes to the war, manages to include in this mixture, along with much pathos and seriousness, quite a surprising amount of unambivalent, direct satire about how "men are heroically dying for their

2. Shaw, Preface, *Heartbreak House*, 47.

country . . . sacrificed to the blunders of boobies, the cupidity of capitalists, the ambition of conquerors, the electioneering of demagogues," and
the rest. In fact, Shaw's series of savage observations are among Ford's
main themes.

Tietjens criticizes Sylvia's home-front friends as "professional boodlers"
to which Sylvia answers "that the only people at home who kept social
matters going at all with any life were precisely the more successful political professionals. When you were with them you would not know there
was any war. And wasn't that what was wanted? Was the *whole* of life to be
given up to ignoble horseplay?" (*NMP*, 431). This is Ford's characteristic
tone for social satire. There is the light, colloquial surface—"boodlers,"
"ignoble horseplay"—and beneath this there is Sylvia's essential voice,
dripping with ironic disdain. She knows her words are anathema to Tietjens. "Keeping social matters going" is an obscene project in the face of
the war's miseries, and Sylvia's rhetorical questions are gibes at Tietjens,
more instances of his Christ-like sufferings. "When you were with them
you would not know there was any war." This fact is Tietjens' cross to bear,
and this sentence is an example of stable irony at its most direct.

Indeed, Ford's social satire in *Parade's End* is less ambivalent about the
issues then any other satiric writing in his entire canon. The essential social contradictions are clear in his mind when it comes to the war: there is
on the one side a "dust-coloured world," that is, the war; there is on the
other "the civilian population, tea-parties short of butter" (*NMP*, 341).
One is reminded of Fussell's theory that the war polarized thinking, making
ironies more blatant. Certainly Ford never undermines or complicates by
counter judgments his essential ironies at the expense of the home front,
the tea-party population.

Perhaps the funniest example of satire in *Parade's End* is the figure of
General Campion. An essentially sympathetic character, Campion's limitations are nevertheless symptomatic of the stupidity and recalcitrance of
a whole class. Here is Campion, yelling critically at his aide, Colonel
Levin: "'Damn it all, the fellow [Tietjens] ought to be in command of my
Intelligence instead of you. But he's unsound. That's what he is, unsound.
He's too brilliant. . . . And he'd talk both the hind legs off Sweedlepumpkins.' Sweedlepumpkins was the general's favourite charger. The
general was afraid of talk. He practically never talked with anyone except
about his job—certainly never with Tietjens—without being proved to be

in the wrong, and that undermined his belief in himself" (*NMP*, 352–53). This is a mind born to be driven mad by the scruples of a paradoxical enigma of a man like Tietjens.

Campion has a comic conversation with Sylvia in which he is scandalized to learn from her that Tietjens models himself "Upon our Lord Jesus Christ." "Good God!" exclaims Campion, "I always knew he had a screw loose" (*NMP*, 412). The irony is that Campion martyrs Tietjens; he is the Judas who sends him up the line. Like Christ, Tietjens foretells his own demise: "They'll never let me back," he tells Valentine. "They've got me out, with all sorts of bad marks against me. They'll pursue me, systematically. . . . You see in such a world as this, an idealist—or perhaps it's only a sentimentalist—must be stoned to death" (*SDN*, 237). The good man, Tietjens, is the magnet who draws forth a grotesque display of evils, stupidities, incompetence, base ambitions and motives, indeed, all Shaw's catalogue of human evils.

Imbedded in *Parade's End*, along with other voices, other intentions, is the voice of Ford the eighteenth-century satirist, the moral scourge, the angry and ironic man-who-knows. But Ford feels himself to be, in his satiric avatar, powerless. Like his hero Tietjens, his very knowing makes him a pariah. Satire, important as it is in *Parade's End*, can never be its principle note since Ford's expectations for a public return to feudal values are low. Satire is powerless to correct the present. Laugh at the social climbing Edith Ethel or at the corrupt politicians as Ford will, their star is on the ascendant. They are what he and Conrad called "the inheritors." Therefore, Ford's great hope in *Parade's End* lies elsewhere: first, in the individual human spirit; second, in the very long view of social evolution.

Comic Irony

Weary detachment and Olympian pretension appear in Ford's comic ironies after the war. He is no longer easily rattled by his own uncertainty. He is grand even in understatement, for example, in this description of carnage and noise at the front:

The pointing of the pistol downwards revealed that [the subaltern, Aranjuez] had practically coiled around his little feet, a collection of tubular, dead, khaki limbs. It didn't need any rift in the sound to make you understand that his loader had been killed on him. . . .

By signs and removing his pistol from his grasp Tietjens made the subaltern—he was only two days out from England—understand that he had better go and get a drink and some bearers for the man who might not be dead.

He was, however. When they removed him a little to make room for Tietjens' immensely larger boots his arms just flopped in the mud, the tin hat that covered the face, to the sky. Like a lay figure, but a little less stiff. Not yet cold.

Tietjens became like a solitary statue of the Bard of Avon, the shelf for his elbow being rather low. Noise increased. The orchestra was bringing in *all* the brass, *all* the strings, *all* the woodwind, all [*sic*] the percussion instruments. The performers threw about biscuit tins filled with horse-shoes; they emptied sacks of coal on cracked gongs, they threw down forty-storey iron houses. It was comic to the extent that an operatic orchestra's crescendo is comic. Crescendo! . . . Crescendo! CRRRRRESC. . . . The Hero *must* be coming! He didn't!

Still like Shakespeare contemplating the creation of, say, Cordelia, Tietjens leaned against his shelf. From time to time he pulled the trigger of the horse-pistol; from time to time he rested the butt on his ledge and rammed a charge home. When one jammed he took another. He found himself keeping up a fairly steady illumination.

The Hero arrived. Naturally, he was a Hun. He came over, all legs and arms going, like a catamount; struck the face of the parados, fell into the trench on the dead body, with his hands to his eyes, sprang up again and danced. With heavy deliberation Tietjens drew his great trench-knife rather than his revolver. Why? The butcher instinct? Or trying to think himself with the Exmoor staghounds. The man's shoulders had come heavily on him as he had rebounded from the parados-face. He felt outraged. Watching that performing Hun he held the knife pointed and tried to think of the German for *Hands Up*. He imagined it to be *Hoch die Haende!* He looked for a nice spot in the Hun's side.

His excursion into a foreign tongue proved supererogatory. The German threw his arm abroad, his—considerably mashed!—face to the sky.

Always dramatic, Cousin Fritz! Too dramatic, really.

He fell, crumbling, into his untidy boot. Nasty boots, all crumpled too, up the calves! But he didn't say *Hoch der Kaiser*, or *Deutschland uber alles*, or anything valedictory. (AMCSU, 558–559)

This is complex, ironically deflationary, as the weary Tietjens inappropriately assumes the meditative stance of the Bard of Avon. Name all the noises known to man, pile them on top of each other, top them off with biscuit tins filled with horseshoes, and still they cannot intimate what a noise is war. Surely such a musical fanfare must announce the arrival of a hero. But, of course, it doesn't. Or rather, the hero does arrive but he is a dead Hun, rather than a figure from Shakespeare or from opera. He is the last hero, "Cousin Fritz," too operatic really, considering the actual circumstances. And though he is the last hero, he has nothing "valedictory" to say.

This irony is wry, urbane, witty, literary. It is comic both in its understatement and in its outbursts of verbal brio. It is comic, too, in its mixture of rhetorical levels—from the elaborate "excursion into a foreign tongue" which proves "supererogatory" to the jovial, colloquial "Always dramatic, Cousin Fritz!" Nor does all this comic elegance trivialize the seriousness of Tietjens' situation. If anything, we understand his lilting train of thought as a mental anodyne which keeps him from fully reacting to the horror of Cousin Fritz's horrible arrival as a walking corpse who "hadn't . . . really got what you might call a head, though there was something in its place" (AMCSU, 560). This passage shows Ford as the consummate comic ironist, able to suggest in his tone many levels of feeling.

All these jostling ironies, this avuncular undercutting of serious thoughts, these dire meanings hidden beneath innocent gestures—do none of them undermine Tietjens' stature as hero, but they do suffuse his characterization and all of *Parade's End* with their modern music, mixed sounds that never simply resolve themselves into a single, tonic chord.

Comic Pastoral: *The Last Post*

In *Some Do Not*, Ford gives us the Edwardian world, which, with hindsight, he pictures as a world holding its breath or as an overripe fruit about to drop rotten to the ground. There are breakfasts and there are summer fields—the novel is a comedy of manners we can recognize—but at the same time Ford shows us that these outward signs of order and health are misleading. War and divorce are, as Tietjens knows, inevitably coming into this world.

In *No More Parades* and *A Man Could Stand Up* we see the fate of Edwardian culture. Constructed painfully out of a delicate matrix of impressions, these two volumes of *Parade's End* dramatize a series of elaborate readjustments in the social and private worlds of all the characters. Before the war a shared code kept Christopher and Valentine apart. After the war Valentine asks herself what now can separate them. "Middle Class Morality? A pretty gory carnival that had been for the last four years! . . . What on earth did she want, unknown to herself?" (AMCSU, 534).

After such enormous shocks and changes, Valentine's question is every man and woman's. They must each reconstruct. They must discover what the desires are that inform their actions "unknown to themselves." Tietjens, of course, that all-knowing seer, with his "blasted, complacent perfections" (AMCSU, 527), has been clear all along about what his desires and values are. His question must now be, "In such a 'disgustingly inefficient and venial world' (*TLP*, 740) as this, can any of my desires be realized?" "What he had been before, God alone knew. A Younger Son? A Perpetual Second-in-Command? Who knew. But to-day the world changed. Feudalism was finished; its last vestiges were gone. It held no place for him. He was going—he was damn well going!—to make a place in it for . . . A man could now stand up on a hill, so he and she could surely get into some hole together!" (AMCSU, 668). While feudalism still seemed alive in the world, in however attenuated a form, Tietjens had been content to put up with corruption in the system, with playing a thankless part—younger son or second-in-command—as long as the system itself remained to give his sacrifices meaning. But now that that world is gone, the public sphere can no longer exact from him his old, dutiful sacrifice. Instead, he will live out those passions and meanings that have always informed his life—privately. If English society is noxious to Tietjens, her fields and hedgerows and woods are not. ("The land remains. . . . It remains!" Tietjens choirs to himself as he dreams of the hills and quiet fields of Bemerton just before a big strafe on the very different fields of France.) In the last volume of *Parade's End*, *The Last Post*, Tietjens returns to the land. His hope is threefold: he will enjoy the present; he will reconstruct; and with the superhuman patience of the symbol that he is of the best in English society, he will wait for England to make good on her ancient birthright: "quiet fields, Anglican sainthood, accuracy of thought, heavy-leaved, timbered hedge-rows" (*AMCSU*, 566).

The question of whether or not rural values could survive was a common motif in the literature of the war and after. Robert Graves spent his leaves walking on the hills and Leonard Woolf, remembering those years from the hindsight of the 1960s, describes a walk he and Virginia made in 1914 from Asham to Peacehaven and explains this simple event "in some detail because when I look back to it, I see that part of the civilization which the war destroyed was the environment, the country and the country life, through which Virginia and I walked to the sea that day."[3] Had Ford lived to the 1960s, perhaps he too would have been in Leonard Woolf's elegiac, saddened, and resigned state of mind. But in the 1920s, Ford's voice had quite a different tone; it celebrated his survival into a new era, and it stated an unequivocal belief in peaceful, rural havens.

The Last Post is an idyll. Chaucerian chanteclers jostle country bumpkins from *As You Like It*. If anything Ford ever wrote can be said to have an overriding tone of voice then *The Last Post* is informed in its every line with a note of hope. The feudal system is not really dead at all but only sleeping. In the meantime, Tietjens, the feudal landlord, recuperates from the war; he hibernates in the peaceful countryside. Sylvia, when she arrives to spy on the new Tietjens ménage, is rather disappointed to find, not the secret home of the Sun King, but a very humdrum household: "It was as if a man should have jumped out of a frying pan into—a duckpond" (*TLP*, 792). Certainly, if this is the green world or the golden age, it is these things playfully, ironically. Tietjens may be in heaven with his Valentine, but their heaven is mockingly described as the heaven of one of Tietjens' wartime fantasies, where God is "a colossal duke" while Christ is "an almost too benevolent Land-Steward, son of the Owner" (*NMP*, 365). Sylvia, ironically surveying the scene, thinks to herself:

> It had been obvious to her for a long time that God would one day step in and intervene for the protection of Christopher. After all Christopher was a good man—a rather sickeningly good man. It

3. Leonard Woolf, *Beginning Again: An Autobiography of the Years 1911 to 1918* (New York, 1963), 147.

is, in the end, she reluctantly admitted, the function of God and the invisible Powers to see that a good man shall eventually be permitted to settle down to a stuffy domestic life . . . even to chaffering over old furniture. It was a comic affair—but it was the sort of affair that you had to admit. God is probably—and very rightly—on the side of the stuffy domesticities. (*TLP*, 795)

It is, at the last, just as Sylvia says, "a comic affair." And the comedy here is not just that of ironic deflation, nor that of comic set pieces about old feudal retainers or bustling housewives like Marie-Léonie. Though all these kinds of comedy are sprinkled throughout *The Last Post*, a larger, more central comic vision underlies and supports them. No other Ford hero has been allowed so unclouded a happy ending as Tietjens. Where there had been "air-raids not so long ago," now there are nightingales (*TLP*, 829). He is a man who has come through.

But as ever, no such summing up, no distillation, catches the true quality of Ford at his best. To understand him well is always to keep following him closely as he makes his rounds from comedy of manners to satire, from irony to pathos, from despair to romance. The Ford we sympathetically know after making this journey with him is above all an ironist. And typically, in *The Last Post* Ford takes his idyllic closing and skews it. As the novel ends, Tietjens' situation is potentially serene. Sylvia has decided to release her hold on him, and with the felling of Groby Great Tree, the curse is off the house of Tietjens. Valentine, too, is happy. Like Marie-Léonie, "Elle ne demandait pas mieux." As Mark Tietjens dies, Valentine is about to bring a new Tietjens into the world, and if he becomes what Christopher wishes, he will be "a contemplative parson farming his own tythe-fields and with a Greek testament in folio under his arm. . . . A sort of White of Selborne." Now let thou thy servant depart in peace (or as Ford puts it, "divorce in peace") (*TLP*, 814, 812, 834). But no. Christopher has forgotten an important set of prints in a jar he has left behind him at a sale. He and Valentine must sell such things to eat and feed the future White of Selborne. Absent, except in everyone's thoughts, throughout *The Last Post*, Tietjens appears on the last page of the novel, entering the idyllic scene pushing a bicycle. He is weary from his secret, purgative journey to Groby and his only greeting is to be told by his beloved, in the voice of a fishwife: "You left the prints for Lady Robinson in a jar you gave to Hudnut the dealer? How could you? Oh, how could you? How are we going to feed and clothe a child if you do such things?" (*TLP*, 835). Christopher, hardly a triumphant rooster or a peaceful parson, hardly even the most ironic Christ-figure, wearily turns his bicycle around and departs to get the antique prints, hence leaving the novel after a comically short stay. How like Ford to keep his people circling until the end, never quite meeting. Into this restless piece of choreography, Mark Tietjens drops his few, gnomic dying words: "Never thou let thy barnie weep for thy sharp tongue to thy goodman" (*TLP*, 835). Valentine needs these last words, and because she will follow them, Tietjens' pastoral happiness is assured. Yet the novel ends with this typically Fordian picture: the hero is on his way ignominiously out the door, and the heroine is crying—all so that Ford's sentiment, his gift to his characters of love and peace and hope, can convince, satisfy, and not cloy.

If Ford had been writing tragedy, as he sometimes tried to do but never really succeeded in doing, Tietjens, a man caught between contradictory imperatives, could only have died, have gone underground in earnest. If Ford had been writing a realistic novel about manners, as he sometimes tried to do but never really succeeded in doing, Tietjens could never convince. His postwar situation could only look unreal, a collage of impossible solutions. But Ford was writing romance. His hero can symbolize regeneration. He can escape an impossible situation by transcending it, not with the tragic transcendence of death, but with the comic transcendence of climbing into "some hole together" with his sweetheart and, wishfully, laughingly, calling it paradise.

《 》

A turning from comic irony, which deflates our sense of our own destiny, back towards romance, which inflates it, marks the stages of a common twentieth-century journey. Before 1945 many writers made this trip much as Ford made it, proposing paradigms for experience that they could not maintain in their own imaginations without the aid of laughter or self-deprecation or some tonal loophole through which doubt could pour. Postwar ironies and myths are in a somewhat different relation to each other, a difference which is radically shifting once more in our own *fin de siècle*, as postmodernists either eschew myth altogether or appropriate it without its romantic baggage. In spite of these shifts, an account of Ford's struggles with tone reveals a mental state still very much with us—a profound romanticism under an intense pressure. The story of Ford's strained effort at combining and recombining these elements is a representative narrative; it leads us forward, into a conception of the artist's, and everyone's, difficulties and hopes in our present moment.

LIST OF WORKS QUOTED

FORD'S WORKS

The Benefactor. London: George Bell and Sons, 1905.
A Call: The Tale of Two Passions. London: Chatto and Windus, 1910.
Christina's Fairy Book. London: Alston Rivers [1906].
Collected Poems. London: Max Goschen, 1914.
The Critical Attitude. London: Duckworth, 1911.
An English Girl: A Romance. London: Methuen, 1907.
The Good Soldier. Vol. I of *The Bodley Head Ford Madox Ford*. 1915; rpr. London: Bodley Head, 1962.
Henry James. 1913; rpr. New York: Octagon, 1969.
The Inheritors: An Extravagant Story. 1901; rpr. Garden City: Doubleday, Page, 1923.
It Was the Nightingale. Philadelphia: J. B. Lippincott, 1933.
Joseph Conrad: A Personal Remembrance. 1924; rpr. New York: Octagon, 1965.
Ludwig, Richard, ed. *Letters of Ford Madox Ford*. Princeton: Princeton University Press, 1965.
MacShane, Frank, ed. *Critical Writings of Ford Madox Ford*. Lincoln: University of Nebraska Press, 1964.
The Marsden Case: A Romance. London: Duckworth, 1923.
Memories and Impressions. New York: Harper and Brothers, 1911. (Published in London by Chapman and Hall in 1911 as *Ancient Lights*.)
Mr. Apollo: A Just Possible Story. London: Methuen, 1908.
Mr. Fleight. London: Howard Latimer, 1913.
The New Humpty-Dumpty. London: Bodley Head, 1912. (Published under the pseudonym Daniel Chaucer.)
No Enemy: A Tale of Reconstruction. New York: Macaulay, 1929.
Parade's End. New York: Alfred A. Knopf, 1961.
Poems for Pictures. London: John MacQueen, 1900.
Portraits from Life. Chicago: Henry Regnery, 1936.
The Pre-Raphaelite Brotherhood. London: Duckworth [1907].
The Queen who Flew. 1894; rpr. New York: George Braziller, 1965.
Return to Yesterday. New York: Horace Liveright, 1932.
Romance. 1903; rpr. New York: Signet, 1968.
"Seraphina." Unpublished tyepscript, *ca.* 1896–98. Olin Library, Cornell University, Ithaca, N.Y.

The Shifting of the Fire. London: T. Fisher Unwin, 1892.

The Simple Life Limited. London: Bodley Head, 1911.

The Soul of London. London: Alston Rivers, 1905.

The Spirit of the People: An Analysis of the English Mind. London: Alston Rivers, 1907.

Thus to Revisit: Some Reminiscences. 1921; rpr. New York: Octagon, 1966.

"Towards a History of English Literature." Unpublished typescript, *ca.* 1922. Olin Library, Cornell University, Ithaca, N.Y.

ALL OTHER WORKS

Auden, W. H. *The Dyer's Hand*. New York: Vintage, Random House, 1968.

Barker, Dudley. *The Man of Principle: A View of John Galsworthy*. New York: London House and Maxwell, 1963.

Belloc, Hilaire. *On Everything*. London: Methuen, 1909.

Bennett, Arnold. *Books and Persons: Being Comments on a Past Epoch, 1908–1911*. London: Chatto and Windus, 1917.

Bergson, Henri. *Laughter*. In *Comedy*, ed. Wylie Sypher. Garden City, N.Y.: Doubleday, 1956.

Blackburn, William, ed. *Joseph Conrad Letters to William Blackwood and David S. Meldrum*. Durham, N.C.: Duke University Press, 1958.

Chesterton, G. K. *The Club of Queer Trades*. London: Collins' Clear-type Press [1905].

———. *The Man Who Was Thursday: A Nightmare*. Harmondsworth, Middlesex: Penguin, 1908.

———. *The Napoleon of Notting Hill*. 1904; rpr. Harmondsworth, Middlesex: Penguin, 1946.

Conrad, Joseph. *Chance*. 1912; rpr. New York: Doubleday, 1924.

———. *Heart of Darkness*. 1899; rpr. New York: Signet, 1910.

——— to Ford Madox Ford, n.d. [1903]. Henry W. and Albert A. Berg Collection, New York Public Library, Astor, Lenox and Tilden Foundations.

——— to Ford Madox Ford, n.d. [1903]. Typed copy in Violet Hunt Papers, Olin Library, Cornell University, Ithaca, N.Y.

Edel, Leon, ed. *The Complete Tales of Henry James*. London: Rupert Hart-Davis, 1962.

Eliot, T. S., ed. *The Literary Essays of Ezra Pound*. Norfolk, Conn.: New Directions, 1954.

Forster, E. M. *Abinger Harvest*. London: Edward Arnold, 1965.

Fussell, Paul. *The Great War and Modern Memory*. New York: Oxford University Press, 1975.

Garnett, David. *The Golden Echo*. London: Chatto and Windus, 1953.

Harvey, David Dow. *Ford Madox Ford: A Bibliography of Works and Criticism*. Princeton: Princeton University Press, 1962.

Harvey, W. J. *Character and the Novel*. London: Chatto and Windus, 1970.

Hynes, Samuel. *Edwardian Occasions*. London: Routledge and Kegan Paul, 1972.

James, Henry. *The Art of the Novel*. Ed. R. P. Blackmur. New York: Charles Scribner's Sons, 1934.

Jean-Aubry, G. *Joseph Conrad: Life and Letters*. Vols. I and II. Garden City, N.Y.: Doubleday, 1927.

Kenner, Hugh. *Paradox in Chesterton*. London: Sheed and Ward, 1948.

Lewis, Wyndham, and Ezra Pound, eds. *Blast*. London: First number, June 20, 1914.

Lewis, Wyndham. *Blasting and Bombardiering*. 1937; rpr. Berkeley: University of California Press, 1967.

Lindberg-Seyersted, Brita. *Pound/Ford: The Story of a Literary Friendship* (New York: New Directions, 1982).

McDonald, Edward D., ed. *The Posthumous Papers of D. H. Lawrence*. New York: Viking, 1936.

Machen, Arthur. "The Terror." In *Tales of Horror and the Supernatural*. Vol. II 1948; rpr. New York: Pinnacle, 1973. pp. 179–284.

MacShane, Frank. *Ford Madox Ford*. New York: Horizon, 1965.

Mizener, Arthur. *The Saddest Story: A Biography of Ford Madox Ford*. New York: World, 1971.

Najder, Zdzasław, ed. *Conrad's Polish Background: Letters to and from Polish Friends*. Trans. Halina Carroll. London: Oxford University Press, 1964.

O'Brien, Justin, trans. *The Journals of André Gide*. Vol. IV: 1939–1949. New York: Knopf, 1951.

Ohmann, Carol. *Ford Madox Ford: From Apprentice to Craftsman*. Middletown, Conn.: Wesleyan University Press, 1964.

Pritchett, V. S. *George Meredith and English Comedy*. New York: Random House, 1969.

Shaw, George Bernard. "Heartbreak House and Horseback Hall." Preface to *Heartbreak House*. 1919; rpr. New York: Penguin, 1964.

Spender, Stephen. *The Struggle of the Modern*. Berkeley: University of California Press, 1963.

Wells, H. G. *Experiment in Autobiography*. 1934; rpr. London: Jonathan Cape, 1969.

———. *The Invisible Man: A Grotesque Romance*. London: Harper and Brothers, 1898.

———. *The New Machiavelli*. 1911; rpr. Harmondsworth, Middlesex: Penguin, 1946.

Woolf, Leonard. *Beginning Again: An Autobiography of the Years 1911 to 1918*. New York: Harcourt, Brace and World, 1963.

Wright, Walter, ed. *Joseph Conrad on Fiction*. Lincoln: University of Nebraska Press, 1964.

INDEX